TOWARD A THEOLOGY OF STRUGGLE

Eleazar S. Fernandez

ORBIS BOOKS

Maryknoll, New York 10545

The Catholic Foreign Mission Society of America (Maryknoll) recruits and trains people for overseas missionary service. Through Orbis Books, Maryknoll aims to foster the international dialogue that is essential to mission. The books published, however, reflect the opinions of their authors and are not meant to represent the official position of the society.

Queries regarding rights and permissions should be addressed to: Orbis Books, P.O. Box 308, Maryknoll, NY 10545-0308.

Renato Constantino's "The Parable of the Big Man and the Small Man" is taken from *Issues Without Tears: A Layman's Manual of Current Issues,* vol. 8, ed. Leticia R. Constantino (Quezon City, Philippines: Karrel, Inc., 1989). Reprinted with permission of the publisher.

Manufactured in the United States of America

ORBIS/ISBN 0-88344-982-X

Contents

iii

Acknowledgments

As the theme of this study is the struggle of a suffering people, so has the writing of this book been a struggle on my part and on that of my family: a struggle to put into conceptual categories and words what has been a matter of life and death to a people; an arduous and painful struggle for my family and me to go on with this project in spite of various pressures. One could not, however, go on with this theological *paglalakbay* (journey) upon which I have embarked without *mga kasama* (companions) along the way. To these companions who have contributed in various ways to make this study possible, my deep sense of *utang na loob* (debt of gratitude) belongs.

At the risk of not properly acknowledging everyone who has contributed along the way to this project, I would like to express my *utang na loob* to Professors Fernando Segovia, Peter Hodgson, Edward Farley, Sallie Mc-Fague, and John Compton, members of my dissertation committee at Vanderbilt University, who accepted the risk of being a part in the making of my dissertation which is the seed of this book. Each of them helped in a distinct way in the completion of my project and in the eventual publication of this book. My especial thanks goes to Professors Segovia and Hodgson, without whose encouragement I would not have dared to submit my manuscript for publication, and to Robert Ellsberg of Orbis Books for his enthusiastic response.

I would also like to make use of this opportunity to express my gratitude to friends and scholars—Lester Ruiz, Levi Oracion, Carolyn Pressler and Robert Bryant—who had given generously their time and wisdom in reading my manuscript and giving their invaluable critique, which helped me to see in a much better light the limitations of my project and the course that I should take, for which I am ultimately responsible.

Like other projects, this book would not have come to reality without the encouragement and the material and technical support of people and agencies. I am grateful to the Southern-Western Leyte Conference of the United Church of Christ in the Philippines for a long study leave; Vanderbilt University for a research grant relative to my dissertation; the Presbyterian Church (USA), through Haydn White and Richard Rodman, for its financial support throughout my studies; the United Church of Christ in the U.S.A., through Ching-fen Hsiao, for scholarship assistance;

Maxine Clark Beach of Scarritt-Bennett Center for her generosity, especially in offering a place for my family to stay while I was writing my project; and to a host of churches in the U.S.A. Likewise, my appreciation is due to Donald Carey, Helen Cummins, Dennis Lloyd, Larry George, Jean Bareis, Elizabeth Dominguez, Liberato Bautista, Nenita Bautista, and Ramon Abad of the Philippine Resource Center, Berkeley, California.

My deep appreciation also goes to my new community at United Theological Seminary of the Twin Cities for its encouraging enthusiasm upon knowing that my labor of love had been accepted for publication. Precious words from friends at United gave me the courage to pursue the publication of this work in the face of my initial hesitation.

More than words can truly convey, my sincere appreciation goes to my companion who has struggled along with me to the very end of this project—Jo. I owe to her a deep gratitude for shouldering an enormous amount of the family responsibility and for her critical insights and technical assistance in the making of this book. My appreciation also goes to my daughter Zarine Banagbanag, who even at an early age understood that Dad had to do his work to finish his project. To Jo, Zarine, and my youngest daughter—Joelle Malaya, whom I have watched grow almost every day along with the progress of this project—I dedicate this work. Along with them, I also dedicate this work to the suffering and struggling Filipino people who have committed their lives to the birthing of a new and better tomorrow for our bleeding land.

After a long reluctance on my part to have this experimental and fluid reflection published I finally decided to take the risk, not because I am certain at this early stage of my career that this will be my unchangeable position, but it is my hope that in so doing I may help to awaken those who suffer but do not struggle, inspire those who suffer and therefore struggle, strengthen those who struggle and therefore suffer, and open up a theological conversation among fellow companions in the struggle. If in having this work published a theological conversation is generated and in the end a better articulation of the theology of struggle is to emerge from it, then my efforts are not in vain.

Eleazar S. Fernandez
United Theological Seminary of
the Twin Cities
New Brighton, Minnesota
Fall 1993

Introduction

Sounds of laughter, songs of celebration, shouts of jubilation, and salvoes of pompous fiestas ring throughout the land that "sits on a pot of gold" — the Philippines. But all these sounds, songs, shouts, and salvoes of joyous occasions could, in a moment, turn into salvoes of bloody massacres, staccatos of gun fires directed at a mass rally, cries and wailings of those who survive the heinous crimes, and thunders of jeremiads. For this country that is "sitting on a pot of gold" is also "sitting on top of a social volcano."

This social volcano is not dormant. It has already erupted and has been erupting since its rapacious foreign invaders, in the name of the cross and the sword, first set foot and trampled on its sacred shores. Concocting an unholy alliance with the most vulnerable but powerful strata of the Philippine society — the native elite (*principalia*) — the invaders raped the lush and bountiful land, sea, and forest; plundered and despoiled its wealth; and created a country with subservient subjects. For years many Filipinos were cowed into submission, even to the extent of accepting their plight with resignation and fatalism — the will of God. The culture of violence has become, for many, a normal reality.

Yet, though subjected to the most sophisticated means of political machination and cultural genocide, the Filipino soul has never been totally crushed. After years of living under the culture of silence, the sons and daughters of the Filipino people have realized that their dehumanizing situation is not the will of God but a product of history — and, as a product of history, it can be changed. Realizing this dangerous truth, many have gained the courage to bring their long muted anguish into public expression, and they have gained further encouragement upon encountering others on the same journey. Soon each one has realized that she or he is not alone; that there are companions on the long and arduous journey in the struggle for a better society. To each other they could say, *"Hindi ka nag-iisa"* (You are not alone).[1]

Out of the experience of Christians who are involved in the struggle for

---

[1]This slogan became popular with the assassination of Senator Benigno Aquino, Jr. on August 21, 1983.

a better tomorrow, a certain way of doing theology has been born from the womb of history — the theology of struggle. Though expressive of the broad experience of those who suffer, even those who suffer but do not struggle, it is primarily an articulation coming from those who suffer and therefore struggle together with those who struggle and therefore suffer. The theology of struggle is a companion of Filipino Christians in their struggle for liberation.

If the theology of struggle is a theology that claims to view reality from the epistemological privilege of the poor and struggling people, it presupposes that there is also a kind of theology that is supportive of the reigning social arrangement. The theology of struggle then manifests a struggle in theology: that theology is one arena in which a struggle has to be waged. Not to storm the heavens would be to miss the crucial connection between what is projected to heaven and what happens on earth. Knowing that Christianity and theology have been instrumental in the subjugation of the Filipinos by the West and the native ruling elite, a theological revolution must accompany the nationalist democratic struggle. This means that Filipinos must attempt to theologize from their own experience; Filipino theologians must cease being mere theological *compradors* of the Western theological megamarkets. In Edicio de la Torre's powerful words: "Christ must be a Filipino if Filipinos are to be Christians."[2]

Given my vocation and training, I see that I could contribute to a larger cause by helping to articulate the theology of struggle. It is my claim in this study that: (1) theological struggle is important in the struggle of the Filipinos for national liberation; (2) the Filipino Christians must stop being mere theological *compradors*, but start articulating a theology that best expresses their identity, dreams, and struggles; (3) the emerging theology of struggle in the Philippines is expressive of the Filipino sentiments and aspirations, hence, a necessary companion in the struggle of the people; (4) it is more appropriate for the theology of struggle to see indigenization or the search for "Filipinoness" from the vantage point of contextualization-liberation; (5) the theology of struggle, although it belongs to the same genre of theological reflection as the theology of liberation, offers a "distinctive" contribution to theological reflection.

In light of these claims, this study attempts in the most general and modest way: first, to contribute to the continued growth of the theology of struggle; second, to critically assess its growth and present expression in relation to its stated claims, methodology, and content; third, to thematize its salient points; fourth, to sharpen its critical apparatus and perspective; and fifth, to engage in a constructive hermeneutical activity. This means pursuing the themes started by the theology of struggle, specifically

---

[2]Edicio de la Torre, *Touching Ground, Taking Root: Theological and Political Reflections on the Philippine Struggle* (Quezon City, Philippines: Socio-Pastoral Institute, 1986).

sharpening the blurred points; proposing some theological areas and possible interpretations as a response to the Filipino aspirations; attempting to put together what I consider to be the basic elements of the theology of struggle; and envisioning the directions that the theology of struggle should take. Finally (sixth), I would like to see the theology of struggle in the context of third-world theological reflection.

This study is divided into three phases: (1) Context, (2) Theological Construction, (3) and Method.

Phase I — The Context as the *Locus Theologicus*: An Interpretation of the Philippine Scenario — comprises Chapters I and II. Chapter I sets the context in which the theology of struggle arose, and Chapter II articulates the early beginnings, development, and main thrusts of the theology of struggle.

Chapter I — The Context: The Pathos and Hope of a Struggling People — opens with a critical analysis of the Philippine context, highlighting the important events that led to the enslavement of the Filipinos and to their struggle to forge a better tomorrow. Taking the perspective of the victims and the eyesores of society, this analysis views synchronically and diachronically the economic, political, and cultural developments of events. Root experiences are identified because they influence the shape and contents of the theology of struggle.

After having set the context, Chapter II — Christians in the Struggle and the Emergence of the Theology of Struggle: A Theological Reading of the Philippine Context — proceeds to situate the emergence of the theology of struggle. In connecting the emergence of the theology of struggle with Christians in the struggle, it is my intention to underscore that there is already a broad people's struggle in which many Christians have been actively participating. This struggle is the struggle of the whole Filipino people for self-determination and national liberation as well as the struggle for self-determination of various communities within the country: this is the struggle for peace, justice, and integrity of creation.

The active involvement of Christians in a wider struggle has generated a distinct form of conversion experience or spirituality and fresh reflections on basic Christian themes. I point out, as has been shown in the writings of some leading exponents of the theology of struggle, that this kind of conversion experience establishes a link between national consciousness and the Christian gospel, a conversion that is not anti-Filipino because it is a conversion to the struggle of the Filipino people.

Furthermore, I attempt to situate the theology of struggle within the canvas of third-world theological upheavals. Basically, the theology of struggle can be placed within this upheaval, but it is also distinctively expressive of the Philippine context and the Filipino experience.

Phase II — The Filipino Struggle: Towards a Theology of Struggle — covers my constructive work. This constructive work is shaped by the context. The concerns of the Filipino people—their root experiences, questions, and hopes—shape the outline and set the themes that are considered in this theological construction.

Chapter III—Cry for Deliverance: Suffering, Hope, and Politics of Struggle—commences my exposition of the contents of the theology of struggle with a particular focus on four themes: suffering, hope, struggle, and how God is to be understood in relation to the preceding themes. Starting from the Filipino people's experience of suffering, I approach the perennial problem of theodicy, not in the traditional sense, in which the question of suffering is linked to the proofs of God's existence, but rather in a way that links suffering (theodicy) to the people's hope (eschatology) through the way of struggle (political praxis). Through the way of struggle, I argue, suffering and hope are saved from being futuristic escapes: only by struggle can the oppressed forge a better tomorrow; only by struggle can the memory of the dead be resurrected; only by struggle can parents truly love their children and future generations.

The Filipinos are among the most colonized people in this world: they were colonized by the Spaniards, the North Americans, the Japanese, and then again by the North Americans. Perhaps, more than other Third World peoples, they despise their own selves, their culture, their heritage, and the products of their own hands. They like to think of themselves as little, brown North Americans. Is there a way in which theological anthropology can be supportive of the quest for identity, self-determination, and liberation of a people? Chapter IV—Struggle for Historical Selfhood and Humanity—explores this concern.

Chapter V—The Christo-Praxis of a People: The "Pasyon," Death, and Resurrection of the "Sambayanang Pilipino"[3] —is my attempt to construct a christology that links the Jesus of the gospels with the Jesus that has become a part of the Filipino Christians' popular religiosity. This link through the people's popular religiosity is, I believe, very appropriate, because popular religiosity is in actuality the religiosity that people live and a concrete expression of their interpretive and appropriative act. Something along this line happened when, out of their experience of oppression from the hands of the Spanish *conquistadores*, the Filipinos in the 19th century transformed what to them was a symbol (cross) of subjugation into an instrument that awakened the people to revolt. Through the genius of the Filipinos, Jesus' passion and crucifixion narratives were transformed into a Filipino *pasyon* (passion), which is often recited during the Holy Week.[4]

---

[3]*Pasyon* means passion or suffering. *Sambayanang Pilipino* means the Filipino people.

[4]Reynaldo C. Ileto's ground-breaking work has paved a new way of understanding the relevance of the *pasyon* (passion), especially in relation to the people's struggle. See his work, *Pasyon and Revolution: Popular Movements in the Philippines, 1840-1910* (Quezon City, Philippines: Ateneo de Manila University Press, 1979).

From the Filipino version of popular religiosity—which includes such practices as the *pasyon*, *salubong* (Tagalog) or *sugat* in Cebuano (which means a dawn meeting with Jesus),[5] fiesta spirit, and some values that Christian Filipinos attribute to Jesus like *pakikiisa* (solidarity), *pakikiramay* (empathy and vicarious suffering), *malasakit* (willingness to undergo pain because one truly cares), and many more—and my own hermeneutics of Jesus in the Gospels as a figure who exemplifies a life of struggle, I weave my christological construction.

Chapter VI—A Search for an Ecclesiology of Struggle, Peoplehood, and Human Dwelling—is the chapter that seeks to interpret ecclesiology as a space, sign, and seed, in which a new sense of "humanity" is affirmed and experienced, and liberative ways of thinking and dwelling are explored.

From a christology that identifies Jesus with the Filipino struggle for identity and subjecthood (Chapter V), I then make the connections of my anthropological interpretation (Filipino identity and humanity) and christology (passion, death, and resurrection of the Filipinos) with ecclesiology—interpreted as a pointer to a sense of "peoplehood" and "communal dwelling." In this chapter I also explore the various ways in which the church under the new ecclesial paradigm is to be construed.

Phase III—Theological Method—comprises one chapter that is devoted to my quest for the theology of struggle's theological method.

Chapter VII—In Search of a Theological Method—closes my constructive work with a proposal for a theological method and issues related to theological construction. Here, I deal with issues such as the nature of theological reflection and its tasks, sources, norms/criteria, the theology of struggle's view with regard to the Scripture and traditions, a community of accountability, and basic hermeneutical presuppositions and method.

The theological method that is operative in this book is discernible from Chapter I through Chapter VI. Throughout these chapters, the suffering and struggle of the Filipinos is fused with the horizon of Christian and other sources. This fusion does not only mean, as is often the case, interpreting the Filipino experience in light of the Christian tradition, but also interpreting the Christian tradition in light of the Filipino people's suffering and struggle. It is my hope that this fusion will enable the interpreter to project a new reality in which she or he may dwell poetically and construct politically.

---

[5]In this study I use words derived from various Philippine languages. *Tagalog* is one language in the Philippines and the basis of our national language (Manila and neighboring provinces). *Pasyon* is a *Tagalog* word. *Cebuano* is another language spoken by most people in the Visayan region (a group of islands in the central part of the Philippines) and also for many Filipinos in Mindanao (southern part of the Philippines).

1

The Context

The Pathos and Hope of a Struggling People

On March 16, 1521, the Philippines was "discovered" by Fernando Magallanes, so many noted historians say. Discovered? From whose perspective? From whose point of view? Is it not from the conquerors of the Filipino people? Is it not that history has often been written from the point of view of the conquerors and the winners, and hardly, if ever, from the point of view of the losers and the victims? That is why a colleague of mine at Union Theological Seminary in the Philippines inverted this so-called historical fact by saying, "On March 16, 1521, Magellan was discovered by the Philippines."

READING HISTORY FROM THE UNDERSIDE

This point of view has been treated by many so-called trained historians as if it were a "neutral-historical fact," and not a perspective that has put on the mask of universal validity; as if it were not a point of view that seeks to universalize and totalize, and hence, imperialize. Though in reality particular, this point of view has been transvalued to the level of universality through the alchemy of power and ideological blindness. Seizing the status of universal validity, it has continued to parade in an air of "scientific objectivity," concealing in effect that power is constitutive of this truth, or that this claim to truth is inextricably as much a contest of power.[1] This particular-turned-universal should not continue unquestioned, because what is involved here is not simply an off-tangent philosophical problem, but the actual life and death of a people: for this "discovering" and

---

[1]See Michel Foucault, *Power/Knowledge: Selected Interviews and Other Writings 1972–1977, ed. Colin Gordon* (New York: Pantheon Books, 1980); see also Sharon Welch's appropriation of the thoughts of Foucault in "The Battle for Truth: Foucault, Liberation Theology and the Insurrection of Subjugated Knowledges" (Ph.D. Diss., Vanderbilt University, Nashville, Tennessee, 1982).

totalizing perspective has incarnated in the face of the conqueror of my own race. It could only be total since it is conquest: for "conquest is totalitarian."[2] It could not be total without being concretely real, because this totalizing view is the theoretical manifestation, as Enrique Dussel says, of the practical oppression of the peripheries or of the dominated races.[3]

In this chapter I subvert the so-called neutral historical and analytical facts of the "objective" scholars by analyzing the Philippine context and its people's history from the experience of the losers and the victims. There is no claim for neutrality being made here, nor is it necessary to do so. Every reading of a societal text involves interpretation: "We don't simply see; we 'see as'."[4] This is certainly true of my reading of the Philippine social realities. More particularly, my reading claims to be a reading from below — from the experience of those whose history has long been muted. It is a reading derived from the experience of those who are daily threatened by another kind of trinity: the absence of breakfast, lunch, and dinner. This trinity, though not abstract, has baffled the mighty and the wise, for they cannot understand why these poor people still insist on living in places designated by the military as "no man's land." The answer is simple. They say, "If we stay, we have one enemy: the bullet. If we move, we have three: breakfast, lunch, and dinner."

I emphasize this reading of reality from below because not all Filipino citizens view reality from below, i.e., from the experience and interest of the suffering Filipino majority. In fact, the dominant interpretation of the Philippine social realities by Filipino social scientists has been antinationalist and antipeople. This is not surprising, considering that many of the so-called educated interpreters of the Philippine realities have been trained

---

[2]Virgil Elizondo, "Mestizaje as a Locus of Theological Reflection," in *The Future of Liberation Theology: Essays in Honor of Gustavo Gutiérrez,* ed. Marc C. Ellis and Otto Maduro (Maryknoll, NY.: Orbis Books, 1989), p. 359.

[3]Enrique Dussel, *Philosophy of Liberation,* trans. Aquilina Martinez and Christine Morkovsky (Maryknoll, NY.: Orbis Books, 1985), p. 5. Dussel speaks of classic philosophy or classic ontology as the ideology of ideologies. It is for him the theoretical consummation of the practical oppression of the peripheries, for this ontology (being), the *ego cogito* of Descartes, is also the *ego conquiro* (I conquer) — the practical foundation of the "I think, therefore I am." See also the work of Lester Ruiz, "Towards a Theology of Politics: Meditations on Religion, Politics, and Social Transformation," *Tugón,* vol. 6, no. 3 (1986): pp. 18–31. The philosophical hegemony of the West (classical ontology as theoretical consummation for Dussel) starting from the "I" in the *cogito* of Descartes, to the "I" as "I conquer," beginning with Pizarro, is further transvalued into the Hobbesian "possessive individual." Finally, it finds its practical consummation (from theoretical consummation to practical consummation) in Ronald Reagan's "Star Wars" program, which, for Ruiz, is the example *par excellence* of the "I conquer therefore I am," or "I am therefore I conquer." For further support of this argument, see the work of José Comblin, *The Church and the National Security State* (Maryknoll, NY.: Orbis Books, 1979).

[4]Ian G. Barbour, *Myths, Models, and Paradigms: A Comparative Study in Science and Religion* (New York: Harper & Row, 1974), p. 120. More on the interpretative nature of any reading will be discussed in Chapter VII.

in the educational institutions of the imperialist center (I for one), and thus have been trained to think like their conquerors and have benefited from the system over their fellow Filipinos. What can we expect, noted Dussel, from "castrated professors"—professors who have been intoxicated by the wisdom of the center—but to go on "castrating" their students, thus spreading an alienating education.[5]

Furthermore, my reading is not simply a reading from below, but from the struggling Filipinos, that is, from those who have come to realize the nonnecessity of their deplorable plight. So submerged in their dehumanization, the majority of the underdogs no longer question their plight, but instead view it as natural or as the will of God. Only from those Filipinos who have come to realize their dehumanization and have started to struggle is a different reading of the Philippine realities possible. It is from this perspective that I think an authentic Filipino history can be written. A reading of Philippine history and social realities could not be but an account of the oppressed and struggling Filipinos, for the emergence of the Filipino national consciousness is synonymous with the struggle of the Filipinos from colonial and neocolonial masters and their local conduits. "The only way," said nationalist historian Renato Constantino,

> a history of the Philippines can be Filipino is to write on the basis of the struggles of the people, for in these struggles the Filipino emerged. . . . Filipino resistance to colonial oppression is the unifying thread of Philippine history[6]

If the only way the history of the Filipinos can be written is through the history of their struggle, this is the only way too of a theology that claims to be of the Filipinos (this will come to light in the succeeding chapters). To make this account of struggle vivid, which is the main tenet of this chapter, I give a sketchy historical account of the Filipino people's struggle.

HISTORY OF RESISTANCE AND STRUGGLE

The history of the Filipino people is a history of struggle: a struggle to form a nation that truly embodies the sentiments and aspirations of the people, and a struggle against the negative forces, both within and without, that continue to abort the people's cherished dreams. Caught up in the vortex of the rise and fall of global empires, the Filipinos found their

---

[5]Dussel, *Philosophy of Liberation*, p. 12. *Castration*, though it is always associated with males (removal of testicles), can also be applied to women (removal of the ovary). See *The American Heritage College Dictionary* (Third Edition, 1993).

[6]Renato Constantino, *The Philippines: A Past Revisited*, vol. 1, in collaboration with Letizia R. Constantino (Quezon City, Philippines: Renato Constantino, 1975), p. 11.

dreams always nipped in the bud by their supposed liberators. This is an irony that Constantino has aptly expressed:

> The Filipino people had the misfortune of being "liberated" four times during their entire history.
> First came the Spaniards who "liberated" them from the "enslavement of the devil," next came the Americans who "liberated" them from Spanish oppression, then the Japanese who "liberated" them from American imperialism, then the Americans again who "liberated" them from the Japanese fascists. After every "liberation" they found their country occupied by foreign "benefactors."[7]

Though oppressed and despite the fact that many have accepted their plight with resignation, Filipinos have risen from the culture of silence to reclaim their rights as a people. The long history of oppression did not totally crush the spirit of the Filipinos. Filipino history is not only a history of exploitation, betrayal, cowardice, and subservience to both local and foreign powers, it is also a history of resistance and struggle. The resistance of Lapu-Lapu against the forces of Fernando Magallanes, in which the latter was killed, gave birth to an important tendency in Philippine history — resistance to foreign domination.[8] Time and time again, village chiefs and entire communities would rise against the *conquistadores*.

During the Spanish colonial era, the Filipinos engaged in several revolts against Spain. There were more than 200 rebellions and uprisings in various parts of the archipelago, which were rooted in one form or another of peasant exploitation and oppression.[9] The early revolts were regional, almost tribal, in scope and appeal as well as nativistic.[10] In the latter part of

---

[7]Ibid., p. 12.

[8]James B. Goodno, *The Philippines: Land of Broken Promises* (London and New Jersey: Zed Books Ltd., 1991), p. 18.

[9]See Commission on the Churches' Participation in Development of the World Council of Churches and the Philippine Ecumenical Writing Group, *Moving Heaven and Earth* (Manila: CCPD, 1982), p. 87. Constantino points out that the underlying cause of most of the early resistance was the tribute and its cruel method of collection. Forced labor was another cause of a number of uprisings. See *The Philippines: A Past Revisited*, p. 87. Another exploitative practice instituted in the first half of the 17th century was the *bandala*. *Bandala* was an annual quota imposed on each province for the compulsory sale of products to the government. It actually amounted to a virtual confiscation of the products because the government did not pay for these. Conscription was also another form of exploitation. The execution of conscription was intensified especially when Spain had to fight wars against Portugal and Holland. See *Makibaka: Join Us in the Struggle!* (Holland: Filipinengroep, 1980), p. 7; also Hernando J. Abaya, *The Untold Philippine Story* (Quezon City, Philippines: Malaya Books, 1967), p. 5.

[10]Constantino, *The Philippines: A Past Revisited*, p. 46. Also Mariano Apilado, "Revolution, Colonialism, and Mission: A Study of the Role of Protestant Churches in the United States' Rule of the Philippines, 1898–1928" (Ph.D. Diss., Vanderbilt University, Nashville, Tennessee, 1976), p. 38.

Spanish rule, the revolts, inspired by growing nationalist sentiments, also gradually became national in scope, and this time the nativistic expression slowly faded to the background. In fact, the revolutionaries made use of Christianity to support their cause, implying that Christianity had already permeated their lives. In this struggle for national liberation, the Filipino emerged — the Filipino was born. Filipino resistance to colonial expansion became the unifying thread of Philippine history.[11]

Though driven by some nationalist sentiments, the early struggles were not so clear in defining the Filipino national interest. For the *principalia* and later on the *ilustrados*, in which the nuclear form of nationhood first found expression, struggle was expressed in terms of agitation for reforms. In fact, they were not so much concerned with the separation of the Philippines from Spain as can be deciphered in their sacrosanct demands that were, as pointed out by historian Teodoro Agoncillo, "Philippine representation in the Cortes, the expulsion of the friars, freedom of speech and of the press."[12] Since most of the leaders belonged to the wealthy *clase ilustrada*, the *ilustrados'* aim was primarily to secure for their class participation in the political rule and a greater share in the economic benefits. If their acceptability was premised on their hispanization, it should not be surprising that their demands would be limited to that of giving the Filipinos the right to a Spanish culture.[13] Not surprising too was their reformist stance.

With the failure of the reformist demands, many were disillusioned with the reformist struggle. This experience gave way to the revolution of 1896, with the characteristic stamp of the masses, particularly under the leadership of the Katipunan. Under the aspirations of the masses, the struggle had finally become one of complete separation from Spain. "The stage was set", said Constantino, "for an anti-colonial, national revolution whose ebb and flow would depend on which of the two currents was temporarily dominant, the revolutionary decisiveness of the masses or the temporizing and reformist nature of their allies."[14]

The Filipinos had almost won their war of independence against Spain when another colonizer came. Determined to be truly a sovereign and independent nation, the Filipinos were again led into another bloody struggle for independence against the new colonial power — the United States. Again, the reformists expected that the United States would readily give independence to the Philippines. They were mistaken. On February 4, 1899, the Philippine-American war started when a U.S. patrol shot a Filipino soldier at San Juan bridge. In spite of the collaboration of the

---

[11]Constantino, *The Philippines: A Past Revisited,* pp. 11, 151.

[12]Teodoro Agoncillo, *The Revolt of the Masses: The Story of Bonifacio and the Katipunan* (Quezon City, Philippines: The University of the Philippines, 1956), p. 103.

[13]Constantino, *The Philippines: A Past Revisited,* pp. 152, 156.

[14]Ibid., pp. 159, 167.

native elite with the North Americans, the people's resistance continued on a wider scale. The tenacity with which the struggling Filipinos defended their right to freedom can be deduced from the growing size of the pacification forces and the barbarity with which they carried out their plans.[15]

When World War II made the Philippines a magnet for attack by the Japanese, again the Filipinos launched a massive resistance against the invaders. The Filipinos organized a guerilla movement throughout the country, even when the United States Armed Forces in the Far East (USAFFE) forces had already surrendered.[16]

After the Philippines was granted independence by the United States (July 4, 1946), the struggle continued, for U.S. interests continued to dominate the country, but with a new face (neocolonialism in a full-blown capitalist system). Filipino struggle, especially the progressive and radical groups, continued to attack the so-called three evils: feudalism, imperialism, and bureaucratic capitalism.[17] Nationalists and even moderate politicians began to perceive the maneuvering that the United States and its local cohorts had done to maintain control of the Philippines. The resistance continued and finally led to the imposition of Martial Law (September 21, 1972) under Ferdinand Marcos. In spite of severe repression, the people's movement blossomed until the deposition of Marcos and the installation of Corazon Aquino in office, the widow of an opposition leader, through the people's power. A festive mood pervaded the atmosphere, and the main streets of Manila and other cities rained with confetti. It was at that time when Filipinos could stand tall and proclaim to the world: "I am proud to be a Filipino."

The "people's power" achieved a "democratic space" that sent the people to the streets rejoicing, but this jubilant mood was short-lived when the people began to see with their very own eyes the evanescent democratic space. Yet, despite discouraging realities of growing poverty, exploitation, destructive insurgency and counterinsurgency warfare, and human rights violations, Thomas O'Brien has noted the resurgence of strong and united

---

[15]Makibaka, pp. 11, 12. The stubborn resistance of the masses is reflected also in the brutal torture employed by the American troops. Such torture could go on for a number of days until the victim confessed or died. The Filipinos waged a real war; they were by no means a bunch of insurgents. The United States, according to accounts, deployed forces four times more than the Spaniards ever had (120,000 soldiers in all), of whom 4,000 were killed. On the Philippine side, it was estimated that 7,000,000 were killed during military operations and 700,000 more died from war-related diseases. See *KSP Kilusan*, vol. 3, no. 1+2 (Utrecht, Netherlands: Publication of Komite ng Sambayang Pilipino), p. 8.

[16]For a brief account of the guerrilla groups and the place of Huks, see Eduardo Lachica, *Huk: Philippine Agrarian Society in Revolt* (Manila: Solidaridad Publishing House, 1971), pp. 110–117.

[17]See José Maria Sison, *Struggle for National Democracy* (Quezon City, Philippines: Progressive Publication, 1967). This book identifies the three evils as the main obstacles to national democracy and the liberation of the Filipino people.

people's organizations of various sectors as well as the emergence of new "cause-oriented" groups as encouraging developments.[18] Up to the present, various sectors of Philippine society have continued to carry on the dreams that their forefathers and foremothers had died for.

Among the most oppressed, the peasantry continues to be the backbone of the struggle for national democracy and independence. Under Spain, the peasants were forced to produce more, not for themselves, but for the absentee landlords and other consuming classes. During the U.S. colonial period, the country was all the more deeply integrated into the capitalist world market, and the percentage of tenanted farms rose even higher. Trained to produce the raw materials for the capitalist centers, the peasants were forced to produce export-oriented crops at the expense of their domestic consumption. Exploitation of the tenants and landless workers intensified with the capitalist crisis of the 1930s sparking several peasant uprisings in central and southern Luzon areas.[19] While the government continues to promote feudal practices in the countryside and lip-service land reform programs, many peasants have chosen the tradition that is oriented toward organizing and mobilizing their ranks in alliance with other exploited workers. The national peasant movement continues to see its struggle within the framework of the whole struggle for national democracy and emancipation.[20]

The workers have also continued the tradition of a nationalistic struggle. In the 19th century, the embryo of the Filipino working class was formed out of the impoverished peasantry when Spain needed shipbuilders, warehousemen, and printers to step up foreign and domestic trade. Thereby arose the first elements of the proletariat. The Filipino workers have since become a vital factor in the struggle for national independence.[21]

By the beginning of the century, Filipino workers had already organized into various cooperatives and unions. And as early as 1903, the workers were already able to stage a huge demonstration to demand an eight-hour working day and freedom from U.S. domination. An estimated 100,000 workers from greater Manila and several provinces of Luzon participated in the demonstration.[22] With the deepening crisis, many of the workers were able to see the structural basis of their oppression and so demanded more radical measures. Fearing the growing militancy of the workers, the ruling elite through the government machinery organized counter-labor unions and more punitive measures.[23] There was a period of enforced quietude, but

---

[18]Thomas O'Brien, *Crisis and Instability: The Philippines Enters the Nineties* (Davao City, Philippines: Philippine International Forum, 1990), pp. 66–67.

[19]*Moving Heaven and Earth,* pp. 88, 89.

[20]Steven Hick, *Land our Life* (Quezon City, Philippines: Claretian Publications and the United Church of Christ in the Philippines, 1987), p. 104.

[21]Makibaka, pp. 33–56.

[22]*Moving Heaven and Earth,* p. 69.

[23]As a counter-labor union to the Kilusang Mayo Uno (KMU), the ruling elite has put-up a "yellow" trade union — Trade Union Congress of the Philippines (TUCP). See Karin Aguilar-

the radical labor movement experienced a new lease on life when a resurgent militancy stirred at the end of the 1960s and the beginning of the 1970s.[24] In spite of the imposition of martial law by Marcos, workers staged strikes. The first "silent" strikes were held as early as 1973, but the first open strike (*Unang Putok*), by the La Tondeña workers, took place in 1975. Soon more strikes followed.[25]

Urban poor and slum dwellers have also played active roles in the national struggle. In Manila, the capital city, as of 1990, two-thirds of its 11 million inhabitants live below the poverty line, and 35% are slum dwellers.[26] Due to depressed conditions in the countryside, militarization, and the belief that the city is the place where they can find a better future, many Filipinos from the provinces move to the cities. However, because of the shortage of job opportunities in the cities, they end up in extreme poverty, forcing them to live in *barong-barongs* (temporary shanties) in the so-called "squatter areas."

Viewed as eyesores to society, squatter areas are frequently subjected to "whitewashing" operations by the government, especially during international conferences: this means eviction or relocation of the squatters to places far from their means of livelihood. Realizing their oppression and strength in unity, these squatters have struggled to resist eviction and relocation to another site designated for them by their own government.[27]

Likewise, the people's struggle cannot be narrated without mentioning the contributions of students. Knowing that they are heirs of the future, students have always been an important force in the Filipino struggle for self-determination and sustainable peace. Nationalist articulation among the Filipino youth reached a new peak in the 1960s.[28] In the First Quarter Storm of 1970, a new wave of demonstrations exploded in the streets of Manila and other urban centers. The government fought back, especially during the martial law period, sending many students to jail and executing several others.

The middle class and other sectors have shown that they can be counted on in the struggle too. Throughout the country, teachers, medical practitioners, and lawyers have organized themselves to advance the cause of the struggling people. As in the case of the execution of Dr. José Rizal toward the end of the last century, the cold-blooded murder in August 1983 of opposition leader Sen. Benigno Aquino, Jr. sparked a reawakening,

---

San Juan, "Labor Movement Sparks Philippine Resistance," *Resist Newsletter*, Somerville, MA, January 1986.

[24]*Moving Heaven and Earth*, pp. 69, 70, 74.

[25]Mary John Mañanzan, "Theological Perspectives of a Religious Woman Today," in *The Future of Liberation Theology: Essays in Honor of Gustavo Gutiérrez*, p. 421.

[26]Matthew Wesfall and David Weisman, *On Borrowed Land* (An Amphion Production, 1990). Videocassette.

[27]Makibaka, p. 86–98. For additional account of the plight of the urban poor, see *On Borrowed Land*.

[28]*Moving Heaven and Earth*, p. 121.

especially of the middle class. They were awakened to the fact that even one of their own kind is not free from the danger. The middle class' contribution became visible in the "people's power" uprising that finally toppled the dictator.

Another group that has continued the revolutionary tradition of the Filipino people are the mountain tribes. In fact, they are proud of being a people who has resisted various forms of domination since the early foreign invaders arrived.

Following the tradition of resistance, the tribal people have always made known in various ways their strong disapproval of a kind of development in which their very survival is sacrificed. They have made it known that the government has chosen the wrong path by sponsoring projects that only serve the interests of the powerful, both local and foreign; that there can only be true development if the national minorities are not sacrificed; that there can only be a true democracy if the national minorities can exercise genuine self-determination. The national minorities of the Cordillera mountain ranges, some scattered groups throughout Luzon and Visayas, and the huge concentration of "Lumads" in Mindanao, have all raised their voices for self-determination. William Claver, member of the Indigenous Peoples of the Cordillera Region, asserted:

> What is most important today is that hundreds of thousands, possibly millions, of the Philippine Indigenous Peoples are acutely aware of this juncture in their history where they can collectively give form and reality to the dream of their race — regaining the Ancestral Domain, as a prelude to the meaningful pursuit and practice of genuine Self-determination.[29]

In the tribal people's struggle to assert their rights for ancestral domain and self-determination, the powers that be have always tried to silence them. Yet the tribal communities have continued the struggle because their lives are inextricably bound with the land of their ancestors, which *Apo Kabunian*, the Lord of us all, has given. This thought is powerfully expressed in the verse of the *Salidumay*:

> The Problem of the Kalingas
> Is reason enough to die
> For the land of the Kalingas
> Is the source of life and survival.[30]

---

[29]William Claver [Representative: Kalinga-Apayao], "Our Struggle Endures, The Land of Our Ancestors Shall Yet Be Ours," in *Struggle Against Development Aggression: Tribal Filipinos and Ancestral Domain* (Quezon City, Philippines: TABAK, 1990), p. xvi.

[30]"Salidumay," cited in Rosario Battung, "The Cordillera Story," in *Signs of Hope: Stories of Hope in the Philippines,* ed. Ed Gerlock (Davao City, Philippines: Philippine International Forum; and Quezon City, Philippines: Claretian Publications, 1990), p. 68.

Hence, the tribal communities have remained steadfast in their struggle with this rallying cry: "Our lands are marked for destruction, and we with them. To defend our lives, we have to defend our lands!"

The Muslims in Southern Philippines have been noted too for their continued resistance and struggle for self-determination. For centuries the Moro people of the Philippines have fought bitter wars against the Spanish colonialists. The Spaniards failed to colonize them. When the new colonialists (U.S.) came, another resistance was put up by the Muslims of the South. Ferocious in their war against the Filipinos of the North, U.S. forces were as ferocious in their war of conquest and colonization against the Muslim Filipinos. North American forces "cut the Moro foot to fit the American shoe," to use Peter Gordon Gowing's paraphrase of a Chinese proverb in describing the terrible slaughter that the North American forces had done to the Muslims.[31] Unlike the Spaniards, the North Americans were partly successful. The North American colonial government of the Philippines soon encouraged Christians to resettle to Mindanao and persuaded foreign investors to acquire commercial lands. This contributed to the displacement of the Muslims and other national minorities.[32]

Experiencing the constant threat of their survival as a people, the Muslim people of the South staged protests, resistance, and uprisings. The elite-controlled government of the Philippines stepped up its suppression of the Muslim Filipinos, even supporting local politicians and their terrorist groups, like the "Ilagas" (or Rats).[33] Sensing the need to consolidate their forces, Nur Misuari, former professor of political science at the University of the Philippines, organized the Moro National Liberation Front.[34] The Muslim Filipinos of the South and the Philippine government soon found themselves in a full-scale war; a war that was often downplayed by the martial law-controlled press. The Muslim struggle was soon eclipsed by the Tripoli Agreement and by conflicts in leadership and direction,[35] but the fervent hope and struggle of the Muslim Filipinos for self-determination has continued to this day. Though armed resistance seems to have disappeared at the moment, a spark could easily reignite a fire.

Together with the other sectors of Philippine society, the church sector (comprising the clergy, seminarians, nuns, and all lay church workers) has been known to play an important role in the struggle of the people. It can be said that generally the church has sided with the power wielders. During the Spanish colonization, it had identified with the conquerors; the same is

---

[31]Peter Gowing, *Muslim Filipinos: Heritage and Horizon* (Quezon City, Philippines: New Day Publishers, 1979), p. 35.

[32]*Moving Heaven and Earth,* p. 177.

[33]T. J. S. George, *Revolt in Mindanao* (Kuala Lumpur: Oxford University Press, 1980), specifically pp. 143-161.

[34]*Moving Heaven and Earth,* p. 178.

[35]Aijaz Ahmad, "The War Against the Muslims," *Southeast Asia Chronicle,* Issue no. 82 (February 1982), pp. 20-21.

true during the U.S. occupation, both with regard to Roman Catholics and Protestants. This is not to say that the church has not done something to support the victims. Catholic and Protestant church involvement in human rights advocacy is well known. The withdrawal of support by the Catholic Bishops Conference of the Philippines to the Marcos dictatorship contributed to his downfall.[36] Protestant groups, like the United Church of Christ in the Philippines and the National Council of Churches in the Philippines, have made statements, especially from the moribund stage of the Marcos dictatorial regime to the present, that are critical of the prevailing system and in support of transformative politics.[37] Yet the church continues to be divided with regard to the position to be adopted in relation to the pressing sociopolitical problems.

In this history of abuse and polarization, the church has also produced people with courage. When Christianity had permeated the texture of the Filipino life, the early Christians appropriated the revolutionary elements of their newfound religion against their colonizers. The native Filipinos asserted that the politics of reform and revolt was not anti-Christian, but rather justifiable by Christianity.[38] In this revolutionary interpretation of Christianity, Filipino priests were always in the forefront, while at the same time demanding the Filipinization of the parishes. This helped to ignite the Philippine revolution against Spain.

When the country was a colony of the United States, members of the church sector were again actively involved in the struggle for independence. Documents record how the priests were kept under intense surveillance due to their support for the struggle.[39] During the neocolonial period, members of the church sector have continued to play a supportive role in advancing the people's struggle, many of whom have fallen without seeing the dawn of the new age.

---

[36]Catholic Bishops Conference of the Philippines Post Election Statement, February 13, 1986. In this statement the Bishops declared that "a government [which indirectly means the Marcos government] that assumes or retains power through fraudulent means has no moral basis."

[37]Aware of the structural character of the social malaise, the UCCP Council of Bishops made the call to seek peace through "active participation in building structures that promote human development and uphold human dignity." See Statement of the Council of Bishops, United Church of Christ in the Philippines, *Peacemaking: Our Ministry*. Likewise, the same council made a statement denouncing U.S. intervention in the Philippines; see *A Statement of Protest Against U.S. Interventionist Policy Towards the Philippines* (March 18, 1986). Due to its pro-people stance, the UCCP has been accused by the government of being a Communist front. For a comprehensive critique of the National Council of Churches in the Philippines' position in relation to the sociopolitical crisis in the Philippines, see the work of Oscar Suarez, "History, Politics and the Sacred: Philippine Protestantism and the Quest for Transformation" (Ph.D. Diss., Princeton Theological Seminary, Princeton, New Jersey, 1992).

[38]Leonardo Davis, *Revolutionary Struggle in the Philippines* (New York: St. Martin's Press, 1989), p. 158.

[39]*Kilusan,* p. 11.

In all these groups women have played a distinct role in the advancement of the people's cause, a role difficult to perform because, even as they participate in the struggle, they are expected to be mothers, "nursing the baby while stirring the pot" — a full-time job without a salary.[40] As early as the revolution of 1896 against the Spanish invaders, women have been known to play a significant role in the struggle for liberation.

Though the liberation of women has been considered a "distinct" concern, having dynamics of its own, Filipinas who have been involved in the building of a just society have not viewed the women's struggle as a "separate" concern; rather, they viewed their struggle as being within the whole thrust of the people's movement. Adul de Leon asserted that it is both "integral" and "vital" to the national democratic struggle.[41] A people's movement can only claim to be truly representative of the people if it is informed by the experience, oppression, struggle, and vision of women. The inseparability of the Filipina struggle for womanhood/humanhood with that of the struggle for national democracy is clear in the position taken by GABRIELA, a militant women's organization that stands for General Assembly Binding Women for Reforms, Integrity, Leadership, and Action.[42] It is my observation that communities committed to national liberation in the Philippines have also struggled to become avenues in which patriarchal ways of relationship are criticized and more humane ways of relating have been explored.

While on the one hand the history of the Filipinos has been a history of collaboration and betrayal of the people's interest, it would be unfaithful to its history not to take account of the people's resistance against enslaving forces, both from within and from without. Throughout the history of the Filipinos, the people's struggle and resistance has taken various forms: some have opted to engage in parliamentary struggle, community organizing, and protest actions, while others have seen the necessity for armed struggle.

---

[40]*Peasant Women Study for Critical Consciousness and Self-Organization* (Davao City, Philippines: Women Studies and Resource Center), n.d., p. 23.

[41]Adul de Leon, "Women's Rights Are Human Rights: A Perspective for the Philippine Women's Movements," in *And She Said No!: Human Rights, Women's Identities, and Struggles,* ed. Liberato Bautista and Elizabeth Rifareal (Quezon City, Philippines: Program Unit on Human Rights, National Council of Churches in the Philippines, 1990), pp. 19–33.

[42]Ana Mae B. Dolleton, "The Women's Place is Still in the Struggle," *Philippine Human Rights Update,* vol. 6, no. 7, International Edition (March 15–April 14, 1991), p. 14. Although the author has used the word *separate* in speaking of the women's struggle for humanhood, I prefer to use the word distinct to underscore the point that women's struggle for womanhood, though having its own dynamics apart from that of men, is part of the struggle for humanhood and, in particular, Filipino humanhood. While I do not want to suggest that the women's struggle has no dynamics of its own, I also do not want to convey the impression that there is no connection with which the words *separate* or *apart* may convey; though this is clearly not the intention of Dolleton. I see this instead as the interstructuration of domination. See also Aida Santos Maranan, "The Women's Movements: A Culture of Revolt Comes Full Cycle," *Kalinangan,* vol. 4, no. 4 (December 1984), p. 30.

There are those also who have seen the necessity for both; others see one as primary and the other as secondary;[43] while others view armed struggle as a last resort. It was a common political joke during the martial law period that medical doctors found it difficult to perform a tonsilectomy on Filipino patients because they would not open their mouth (meaning, they were afraid to speak up against martial law). Another joke also circulated that there is only one brave person in the Philippines — Marcos; the rest are cowards. This is not exactly true, for many Filipinos have given their lives so that a new tomorrow may dawn on their bleeding land.

Ever more determined to pursue their dream, the struggling people have raised their voices throughout the hills and plains, barrios and cities, of their bleeding land: *"Kung hindi tayo kikilos, sinong kikilus? Kung hindi ngayon, kailan pa?"* (If we do not act, who will act? If not now, when?).

---

[43]Bernabe Buscayno (Kumander Dante), former commander of the New People's Army, in an interview after his release from prison, interprets armed struggle as secondary in nature. See Nettie Wild, *A Rustling of Leaves: Inside the Philippine Revolution* (1989). Videocassette.

2

Christians in the Struggle and the Emergence of the Theology of Struggle

A Theological Reading of the Philippine Context

Suffering, extreme suffering, is a mother of both virtue and vice: It is a mother of hope and fatalism, of faith and unfaith, of struggle and passivity. Fatalism, unfaith, and passivity are characteristic marks of a people who has not come to the awareness of the nonnecessity of their suffering, a people who has not broken the clutches of suffering without hope to embrace the kind of suffering that is pregnant with hope. Caught up in what appears to be an inevitable cruel fate, they can only think of *kapalaran* (literally dictated by the lines on one's palm) or *gulong ng palad* (wheel of fortune), like the message of Rico Puno's popular song:

> Bakit kaya sa buhay ng tao
> Mayr'ong mayama't may api sa mundo?
> Kapalaran . . .
> Kung hanapi'y di matagpuan
> At kung minsa'y lumalapit
> Nang 'di mo alam.

> (Why in this life are there wealthy and poor? Fate . . . when you look for it you seem not to find it, but there are times when it just comes to you, even without your knowledge)

Sensing that *kapalaran* gives no rhyme or reason for their suffering existence and seeing how their present plight contradicts their cherished Christian beliefs, the suffering people could not help but sigh, cry, and raise their jeremiads to heaven, to use the lines of Karl Gaspar while he was in prison:

How long, Lord, before those in captivity are set free? How long before the night gives way to the new dawn so eagerly awaited but which seems to take forever to break out on the horizon? How many more bruised and dead bodies before the madness ends?[1]

This time their cry, however, is no longer a cry of resignation, but a cry of protest; no longer a cry of desperation, but a rallying cry of hope and struggle; no longer a cry of the inevitability of the *kapalaran,* but a cry of hope and challenge for the Filipinos to offer themselves in forging a better tomorrow. The Filipinos have declared that passivity is now over and crying is not enough. As the song of the rising people expresses it:

> Ngayon na ang panahon
> Ang pagkilos mo ay kailangan
> . . . .
> Huwag ka nang magsawalang kibo
> Pagluha ay 'di sapat
> Ang kailangan ay pagganap
> Ibahagi ang iyong panahon
> Sa pagtugis ng nilalayon.

> (Now is the time to act. . . . Passivity is over. Crying is not enough, one must act. One must share her or his time to realize the dream)

There is a time for crying, for crying is an expression that things are not right. But crying must give way to struggle if the sacrifices of those who have passed are not to be in vain and if the longings of the new generations are to be born. The people have resolved, after years of being silenced, that they will not keep silent forever. They have finally spoken in loud protest: *Tama na! Sobra Na!* (enough is enough).

Today, the anguish, pandemonium, and loud protestations of the victims can no longer be ignored. Gone are the days when they can just be brushed aside or met with deafening silence, especially by the institutional church. The church may pretend to be neutral, but from the critical eyes of many of its parishioners, it is only prolonging the life span of the ailing social body. It can choose to be silent in the face of suffering and injustice, only at the expense of abetting the repugnant situation. The struggle continues to pose a challenge to the church to be faithful to its calling, although in spite of the church the struggle of the people has to go on.

CHRISTIANS IN THE STRUGGLE

In the face of this challenge to the church, Christians from various walks of life have struggled to make sense of their faith and have responded to the call of the moment. They have heeded the voice of the people which, for

---

[1]Karl Gaspar, *How Long?: Prison Reflections from the Philippines,* eds. Helen Graham and Breda Noonan (Maryknoll, NY.: Orbis Books; and Melbourne: Dove Communications, 1986), p. 76.

them, is the voice of God, in spite of the equivocal support of the institutional church. In the broad national struggle they have immersed and put their lives at stake for a common dream, working hand in hand even with those who do not share their religious faith. From this crucible of struggle questions that they have never raised before emerged: questions about their role as Christians in the struggle and the relation of faith and politics. Bewildered, perplexed, and threatened as they grappled with the questions that confronted them, they have come to understand better their vital but supportive role — a role that the church and Christians must assume as a demand of the sociopolitical realities, and a role that must be assumed because a sound Christian faith demands it.

In speaking of Christians in the struggle, I would only like to emphasize that there is already a broad struggle that has been going on in spite of the church, although also with the church. Acknowledging this point is very important for the church and for Christians. This should remind us, first, that the church is itself caught up in the vortex of conflicting interests; that it is itself part of the problem; that it cannot be expected to be an *avant-garde* of change, let alone of radical change. In fact, although the church figured prominently during the famous "people's power" revolution that toppled the Philippine dictator, it was actually a Johnny-come-lately onto the scene.[2] The people, in spite of the church, are capable of discerning their own enslavement and of working for their liberation. Second, it should also remind us that the church should learn, with all humility, to accept a supportive role, without relinquishing its prophetic ministry.

Positing the broad struggle in which Christians have participated is vital for a sound understanding of the nature of the struggle itself, a point that Christians ought to learn. The thoughts of de la Torre, one of the early proponents of the theology of struggle, are helpful in clarifying the relation of the broad national struggle and the place of Christians in the struggle.[3] First, to place the Christian involvement vis-'a-vis the broad struggle is to admit the independent nature of the struggle itself. The struggle operates on its own principles that are not inherently Christian; it has a dynamic of its own. This means that Christians, like other participants in the struggle, have to learn these principles. As de la Torre has pointed out, whereas Christians tend to know more about the "power of principle," this may not be exactly true when we speak about the "principle of power."[4]

---

[2]See Kathleen Coyle, "Was There a Real Conversion?" in *Nagliliyab: The Burning Bush* (Quezon City, Philippines: Claretian Publications, 1986), p. 60. On the side of the National Council of Churches in the Philippines, see Oscar Suarez, "History, Politics and the Sacred: Philippine Protestantism and the Quest for Transformation" (Ph.D. Diss., Princeton Theological Seminary, Princeton, New Jersey, 1992).

[3]See de la Torre, *Touching Ground, Taking Root.* Also see his essay, "Social Action: Its Relation to Socio-Political Change," *Simbayan,* vol. 7, nos. 2 and 3 (1988), pp. 21–33.

[4]Edicio de la Torre, "The Philippines: Christians and Politics of Liberation," *Tugon,* vol. 6, no. 3 (1986), p. 64.

Second, being clear on the involvement of Christians in an already existing broader struggle should keep us from being misled into thinking that this is a Christian struggle. This struggle is the struggle of the whole people, some of whom may not profess a Christian belief, although they are very small in number. In this situation, Christians must learn to work with those with whom they do not agree on everything but agree on something that is vital.[5]

Finally, it is in relation to this broad struggle that Christianity is being put on trial. There is no secure place for Christians in this struggle, simply because they are Christians. Christians have to take account of their presence, and gone are the days when Filipinos in the struggle would automatically associate Christianity with liberation. Philippine history is replete with Christian pronouncements on the directions that Filipinos should take, but they often betray the people's cause.

THE EMERGENCE OF THE THEOLOGY OF STRUGGLE

Out of the involvement of Christians in the struggle of the whole Filipino people, the theology of struggle has struggled to be born. From this womb of struggle it came to see the first light of day, and from its cradle it has been nurtured. Born in and out of the struggle, it has no life apart from this struggle; it has taken shape in and out of the struggle; and it cannot be properly understood apart from this struggle. Its basic presuppositions, shape, and content all bear the indelible mark of this involvement in the wider struggle. From this panorama of struggle I believe that we are in a better position to understand why it has taken some presuppositions as essential and why it has taken shape the way it has. Before I expound on its basic orientation, I recall the events and reasons advanced by those who started to call this brand of theology in the Philippines the *theology of struggle*.

Filipino Christians have long theologized their involvement in the people's struggle. However, unlike most of their Western counterparts, Filipino theologians have been so active in the struggle that they have not had enough time to put in writing their rich faith-life reflections. Filipino theologians are not traditional professional theologians who spend most of their time lecturing and publishing their lectures. Furthermore, these theologians do not have the usual sabbatical leaves that some, if not most, of their Western counterparts enjoy with financial benefits.

The theology of struggle did not emerge into the scene in a quick fashion, nor were the proponents of the theology of struggle propelled to prove that there is a unique and distinct theological stirring that is going on in the

---

[5]de la Torre, *Touching Ground, Taking Root,* p. 184.

Philippines. In fact, the early articulators of the theology of struggle were somewhat comfortable to identify their theological reflections within the more well-known Latin American liberation theology, although also critical in appropriating the insights of this theology. One thing is certain, commented Louie Hechanova, in that whether one identifies the recent theological reflection in the Philippines with one version of liberation theology or another, some kind of liberation process is going on in which involved Christians have tried to reflect theologically. Hechanova is more inclined to describe this as a "struggle towards liberation." Hence, he proposed that this theology be named the "theology of struggle."[6]

Hechanova's modest claim for the possibility of the emergence of the theology of struggle in the Philippines finds a similar tone in Feliciano Cariño.[7] As a matter of fact, there are other theologies that have taken a similar name, and perhaps similar themes and methodology.[8] In spite of some similarities, Cariño still pursues the point that "it can nevertheless be said that among Christians who have been involved in the Philippine struggle, the theology of struggle has been a primary focus in their theological effort."[9]

Ed de la Torre, one of the early articulators of the theology of struggle, captures the appropriateness of the term *struggle* to name the emerging theology in the Philippines in speaking of it as a movement, a becoming, from *pakikisama* to *pakikibaka* (from smooth interpersonal relations to struggle).[10] For him it captures a spirituality and a new experience of conversion — a new attitude and lifestyle, one that is not marked by indifference and resignation but a commitment to struggle for the fundamentally new and better. Liberation, as I perceive it, is still the direction of the theology of struggle, but the focus of the theology of struggle is on the struggle. The struggle is still long and protracted before the dawn of the new day may fully come. What needs to be focused on and grappled with, according to the Filipino theologians involved in the struggle, is the struggle.[11]

The name *theology of struggle* befits the focus given to the struggle of the people for liberation. That it is indeed a theology "of" struggle is made manifest in the very risk involved by those engaged in articulating this kind of theology. A story by de la Torre makes this connection between theology

---

[6]Louie Hechanova, "The Christ of Liberation Theology," *With Raging Hope*, vol. 1, SPI Series (Quezon City, Philippines: Socio-Pastoral Institute and Claretian Publications, 1983), p. 13.

[7]Feliciano Cariño, "Editorial," *Tugón*, vol. 6, no. 3 (1986).

[8]Bishop Roy Sano, "A Theology of Struggle from an Asian American Perspective," *Branches* (Fall/Winter 1990), pp. 8-11.

[9]Cariño, "Editorial," *Tugón*, vol. 6, no. 3 (1986).

[10]de la Torre, *Touching Ground, Taking Root*, p. 199.

[11]Sharon Ruiz Duremdes, "A Theology of Struggle," *Praxis*, no. 3-4 (WSCF Asia/Pacific Region, 1989), p. 4.

and risk vivid.[12] Recalling a sharing of *talambuhay* (a life story where there is an exchange of accounts of one's political development) with fellow political detainees, he tells how each one gave an account of the reasons for being in jail. The leaders of mass rallies easily connected their being in jail with what they were doing. This was much more true of those suspected of involvement in the armed struggle. But when it was Ed's turn (as he is popularly called) to narrate the reason for his detention, there was laughter, for he used his search for a Filipino theology as the reason for his detention.

The theology of struggle thus acquired its name and is now moving to assert its identity. But the theology of struggle is still in its infancy; to fault it for what it has not yet articulated is, I believe, unfair. This infancy stage is expressed in Karl Gaspar's remark that if anyone wants to know more about the indigenous theology emerging in the Philippines, the theology of struggle, "do not look for a book. There isn't one; and none may be written soon."[13] There has not been a single systematic work written on the theology of struggle; a compilation or anthology—yes.

BASIC ORIENTATION OF THE EMERGING
THEOLOGY OF STRUGGLE

The theology of struggle is still in its infancy, yet its basic orientation and configuration is already discernible such as, like other liberation theologies, its clear stance that this theology is one coming from the perspective of the struggling victims; its emphasis on the contextual nature of theology, praxis, and the use of social analysis as a *theologia ancilla*; and its orientation toward making the theology of struggle a people's theology, that is, one that enables the common people to become theological subjects themselves, with the academically trained theologians maintaining an "organic" relationship to the struggling communities.

In the area of theological themes, theologians of struggle have started to articulate from their perspective some of the basic Christian themes (namely, spirituality, salvation, God and the oppressed communities, christology of struggle, and ecclesiology), although in a very minimal and nonsystematic way. Theological articulation from trained theologians on basic theological themes resonate very much with what has been going on in liberation theologies around the world, except for the more popular approach of some individuals (impressively by laypersons) and organizations (BCC-CO, Institute of Religion and Culture, ECD-People's Theology

---

[12]de la Torre, "The Philippines: Christians and Politics of Liberation," *Tugón*, pp. 63–64.

[13]Karl Gaspar, "Doing Theology (in a Situation) of Struggle," *BCC-CO Notes*, vol. 6, no. 1 (Quezon City, Philippines: BCC-CO Inter-Regional Secretariat), n. d., p. 1. Mimeographed.

Project). Much work is still waiting for anyone who would venture to put the people's experience into a comprehensive theological project.

The Theology of Struggle as Contextual Theology

Rooted in the suffering, aspirations, and struggle of the people, the theology of struggle claims to be a contextual theology. Contextualization, as I understand it from the major proponents of the theology of struggle, does not mean "application," "translation," or "adaptation" of some readymade theological goods from the European or North American supermarkets.[14] Contextualization even suggests something deeper and critical than "indigenization" or "inculturation."

Translation or adaptation implies that there is already a given theological product, and the problem of Filipino theologians is to communicate it into another context. Without totally rejecting the notion of context as important for communication, Cariño suggests that we should move further toward understanding the context, not simply as an instrument of communication, but as a "mode of apprehension."[15] This means that the context itself shapes the perception of reality, the way theology is to be done, and the themes that may emerge. The question, as posed by some Filipino theologians, is not "How can we adapt theology to our needs?" but rather, "How can our needs create a theology which is our own?" The intention is not to adapt or modify a theological product, but "to *produce* the product in a new way and for a new purpose."[16]

When the intention is not to translate nor to transplant the potted Christianity, but to produce, the traditional supremacy given to the Scripture and classical tradition is overturned. The scriptural text is no longer the "springboard" for reflection, nor the data of tradition, but becomes instead "what is going on in the world."[17] The "raw materials" that

---

[14]"A Filipino Theology for Liberation: A Working Paper," *Radical Religion*, vol. 2 (1976), p. 6; also Carlos Abesamis, "Doing Theological Reflection in a Philippine Context," in *The Emergent Gospel: Theology from the Underside of History*, eds. Sergio Torres & Virginia Fabella (Maryknoll, NY.: Orbis Books, 1978), p. 121; Feliciano Cariño, "The Theology of Struggle as Contextual Theology: Some Discordant Notes," *Tugón*, vol. 9, no. 3 (1989), p. 209.

[15]Cariño, "The Theology of Struggle as Contextual Theology: Some Discordant Notes," *Tugón*, p. 209; cf. Clodovis Boff, *Theology and Praxis: Epistemological Foundations* (Maryknoll, NY.: Orbis Books, 1987), p. 30. For Boff, the socioanalytic mediation is constitutive for liberation theology; it is not exterior (relationship of application) but interior (relationship of constitution) to it.

[16]Feliciano Cariño, "What About the Theology of Struggle?", in *Religion and Society: Towards a Theology of Struggle*, ed. Mary Rosario Battung et al. (Manila: Forum for Interdisciplinary Endeavors and Studies, 1988), p. xiv. Emphasis supplied.

[17]"A Filipino Theology of Liberation: A Working Paper," in *Radical Religion*, pp. 6–7, citing Catalino Arevalo, "On Theology of the Signs of the Times," *Philippine Priests' Forum*, vol. 4, no. 4 (December 1972), p. 18.

serve as a springboard for theological construction, as Carlos Abesamis pointed out, is,

> far from being doctrinal truths which one seeks to organize into a system, and far from being biblical texts or truths which one seeks to apply to a given human situation—is contemporary Philippine Third World history, and life itself.[18]

If the "needs" serve as the basic materials from which a contextual theology shall be shaped, this requires a different procedure and a different understanding of the Scripture and other Western theological sources. "The procedure," for Abesamis, "is not taking a Western tree and transplanting it on African or Asian soil; rather, it is *planting* our own African or Asian tree and grafting on whatever is needed for its life and health."[19] It is not even transplanting a potted plant, an idea suggested in the known lament: "Christianity is still largely a 'potted plant'. . . . It has been transported without being transplanted."[20] Planting, continues Abesamis, requires a "bracketing" of the Western traditions when one does theological reflection, which does not mean complete exclusion. But from now on they can be treated as attempts of other people to reflect theologically from a certain context or as models.[21]

Contextualization is an imperative if theology is to be responsive and relevant to the suffering and struggling people, that is, if it is to be liberating. This, I believe, is what the proponents of the theology of struggle are saying. The final thrust of contextualization is liberation, not for the sake of mere inculturating or indigenizing a theological given. Indigenization, which in the case of the theology of struggle is Filipinization, is not rejected but viewed within a liberating thrust. With indigenization viewed within the encompassing liberation thrust, the theology of struggle prevents itself from falling into "romantic Filipinization" while maintaining a critical appreciation of the Filipino culture, popular religiosity, and the people's

---

[18]Carlos Abesamis cited in Karl Gaspar's, *Pumipiglas: Teyolohiya ng Bayan: A Preliminary Sketch on the Theology of Struggle from a Cultural-Liturgical Perspective* (Quezon City, Philippines: Socio-Pastoral Institute, 1986), p. 5.

[19]Carlos H. Abesamis, "Doing Theological Reflection in a Philippine Context," in *Asian Christian Theology: Emerging Themes,* ed. Douglas Elwood (Philadelphia: The Westminster Press, 1980), pp. 89–90.

[20]Gerald Anderson, ed., *Christ and Crisis in Southeast Asia* (New York: Friendship Press, 1968), p. 11. See also Feliciano Cariño, "Some Recent Developments in Asian Theology," *Kalinangan,* vol. 3, no. 3a (September 1983), p. 8; also Rebecca Asedillo, *"From Potted Plant to Fertile Ground": Notes on the Theology of Struggle.* Mimeographed. I used to think of contextualization as transplanting the potted plant (Christianity) and had quoted many times that familiar verse, only to realize later how inadequate is the idea of transplanting.

[21]Abesamis, "Doing Theological Reflection in a Philippine Context," in *Asian Christian Theology: Emerging Themes,* p. 97; cf. Sallie McFague, *Models of God: Theology for an Ecological, Nuclear Age* (Philadelphia: Fortress Press, 1987), pp. 40–45.

idiom.[22] Without losing sight of the liberating thrust, there is an increasing interest and appreciation of the Filipino mode of thought or "popular idiom" in the theology of struggle.[23]

A Theology "In" and "Of" Struggle:
A Theology that Sets the Primacy of Praxis

Arising out of the experience of Christian partisanship in the broad struggle of the suffering Filipinos, I emphasize that the theology of struggle is an outcome of the struggle, that it is primarily a theology "in" and "of" struggle and not a theology "about" struggle, as Cariño put it, as if Christians have the blueprint on how the struggle should take shape.[24] To emphasize the "in" and "of" in the theology of struggle is to say that it is rooted in the struggle — it is an expression of the struggle; it sprouted out of the struggle; it has its wellspring in the struggle; and it is a faith reflection on the struggle. It is more of a fruit or a flower of the struggle than a grandiose theoretical treatise on the struggle, although it also contributes in shaping the struggle.

Emerging out of struggle, theological novelty is not on its agenda, nor is scholarly quest, nor the intention that it may soon be included in the expanding theological encyclopedia. Like its counterpart in Latin America, it is indeed a reflection on praxis, a "second moment" which, like Hegel's owl of Minerva, only rises at sundown.[25]

It must always be kept in mind that the theology of struggle was not born in the academic chamber, much less to satisfy intellectual curiosity. Although it does not escape the rigors of an intellectual discipline, its orientation is primarily to support the praxis of struggle. "Praxis is primary, both chronologically and epistemologically," as pointed out by de la Torre.[26] From the struggle it derives its life and motivation; it is struggle that it serves. Geared toward enhancing the people's struggle, it is only proper that its primary community of accountability is the struggling community, primarily to strengthen and equip it for the long and arduous struggle. What was foremost in the minds of those who tried to reflect theologically on the struggle, noted Cariño, "was the sharpening of the

---

[22]"A Filipino Theology for Liberation: A Working Paper," in *Radical Religion,* pp. 5-6; Theresa Dagdag, "Emerging Theology in the Philippines Today," *Kalinangan,* vol. 3, no. 3a (September 1983), p. 6.

[23]Cariño, "Some Recent Development in Asian Theology," *Kalinangan,* p. 10.

[24]Cariño, "What About the Theology of Struggle?", in *Religion and Society,* p. x.

[25]See Gustavo Gutiérrez, *A Theology of Liberation,* 15th Anniversary Edition, with a new introduction, trans. and eds. Sister Caridad Inda and John Eagleson (Maryknoll, NY.: Orbis Books, 1988), p. 9.

[26]de la Torre, *Touching Ground, Taking Root,* p. 190. The emphasis on praxis is common among various types of liberation theologies.

Philippine struggle itself and how Christians can participate and contribute fully in that struggle."[27]

A Theology from the Perspective of the Struggling Victims

Giving primacy to the praxis of struggle is actually to get into the experience of those out of which the theology of struggle has emerged, that is, the suffering people. Cariño has observed this connection of praxis and "people" when he noted that the ascendancy and the recognition of "people" coincided with the focus on praxis.[28] More particularly, the juxtaposition of "people" and praxis came out of the praxis of the struggling people. The much popularized people's power that helped topple a dictator in the Philippines is a testimony of this coinciding of praxis and people.[29]

Because we cannot expect those who are comfortable to engage in the praxis of struggle, the theology of struggle can only be a theological reflection of the struggling marginalized people, which the word *people* essentially means; therefore we can speak of the coinciding of praxis and *people*. Although the theology of struggle claims to view reality from the point of view of the suffering people as a whole, it is primarily a reflection of those who suffer and therefore struggle, together with those who struggle and therefore suffer (those who have opted to struggle with the poor).

The Grassroots People as Theologians in Relation to Professional Theologians and Other Technicians

If the people's experience is the privileged *locus theologicus* and the people set the theological agenda, it follows that we should also help pave the way for them to articulate their faith. If the theology of struggle is a theological voice of the struggling people and a companion in their liberation, there should be an increasing participation of the struggling people in the articulation of this theology. Enabling people to become active theological subjects is necessary for their empowerment and liberation. Abesamis, in particular, asserted the need "to affirm strongly that the formulation of the Asian theology which is really liberating to the masses of the poor and oppressed in Asia is the work of Asian poor with liberated consciousness."[30]

The theology of struggle claims that theological reflection is an activity of the whole struggling community and not an exclusive domain of the

[27]Cariño, "What About the Theology of Struggle?", in *Religion and Society*, p. x.

[28]Cariño, "Some Recent Development in Asian Theology," *Kalinangan*, p. 10.

[29]Cf. Pedro Ribeiro de Oliveira, "An Analytical Examination of the Term 'People'," *BCC-CO Notes*, vol. 4, no. 6 (Quezon City, Philippines: BCC-CO), n.d. Mimeographed.

[30]Abesamis, cited in Karl Gaspar's *Pumipiglas: Teyolohiya ng Bayan*, p. 37.

professional theologians.[31] Those who have immersed themselves in the lives of the struggling people have realized how the people themselves are capable of deep theological reflection, although they may express it in a mode quite different than what has been traditionally accepted by the academic community. A theology of the people that denies the people their right to theologize is really antipeople.

When the struggling people take an active role in the theological articulation of their faith and refuse to leave theology to the professional theologians, we need to redefine the relationship between the trained theologian and the people. In the theology of struggle this relationship has to be understood within the context of the professional theologian's membership in a faith community. The professional theologian is someone who is a member of the community, who shares the agony and hope of the community. Having special expertise by virtue of long training, the theologian must put her or his expertise at the service of the people, and this service is more authentic if he or she remains in solidarity with the common struggle.

Social Analysis as a *Theologia Ancilla*

A theology that gives due weight to context, praxis, and "people" should be a theology that makes the "socioanalytic mediation" a vital companion in the doing of theological reflection. This is what the proponents of the theology of struggle have perceived.[32] Social analytic tools are crucial for understanding the context, to guide praxis, and to equip the people for transformative praxis. If medical practitioners need diagnosis before they can give treatment and prognosis, the struggling people too should be equipped with tools of social analysis. They must acquire social-analytical tools in order to see not only the "issues," but also the structural and systemic basis of the problems, thus to work for a more comprehensive solution. Social-analytical tools must not only be at the hands of the intellectuals and the elite, but must also be available to the struggling people.

THE THEOLOGY OF STRUGGLE
AND ITS THEOLOGICAL PLACE

The theology of struggle, claim its leading proponents, is a theology within the genre of liberation theology. To say this invites an outright

---

[31]Gaspar, "Doing Theology (in a Situation) of Struggle," in *BCCO-Notes*, pp. 23–26; Abesamis, "Doing Theological Reflection in a Philippine Context," in *The Emergent Gospel: Theology from the Underside of History*, pp. 115–116.

[32]Gaspar, "Doing Theology (in a Situation) of Struggle," in *BCCO-Notes*, pp. 7–12; Abesamis, "Doing Theological Reflection in a Philippine Context," in *The Emergent Gospel: Theology from the Underside of History*, p. 116; Rebecca Asedillo, "Faith in Struggle," *Faith and Ideology Series*, C1-88 (Quezon City, Philippines: Socio-Pastoral Institute), pp. 5–8.

misconception to the effect that the theology of struggle is Latin American theology *applied* in the Philippines. Academic theologians are more prone to this misconception because the judgment of what-applies-to-whom is generally based on the criterion of who publishes first.

What has been overlooked is that long before Latin American liberation theology had come to press, the struggling Christians of the Philippines had appropriated the Christian message to guide and strengthen them in their struggle for liberation. This can be said too of other third-world peoples. The struggling Filipinos did not apply Latin American liberation theology, because they have been doing a form of theology that is liberating to them. That they have gained insights and been enriched by the publication of liberation theology, I can say, yes.

Similarities exist between liberation theologies—especially in its Latin American expression—and the theology of struggle, but this does not mean that the theology of struggle is not distinct. Christians in other parts of the world who have undergone a similar experience of struggle can claim the same name and emphasis. But, rather than being used to discredit the distinct emphasis of the Filipino theologians on struggle, it should be construed that the Filipinos have other companions in the struggle. There are similarities in experiences, especially given the common context of being at the margins of the global capitalist system, but the Filipinos cannot simply import revolution from Nicaragua, nor can Nicaragua export revolution to the Philippines. Mario Bolasco, in particular, has sounded a warning against easy borrowing. "To a great extent," noted Bolasco, "theologies of liberation imported from Latin America have filled this need for theological idiom. But inadvertence of their political frameworks could easily lead many to succumb to pitfalls of misappropriation."[33]

Written theological reflections on the theology of struggle are still fragmented. As a theology trying to break from the cocoon of captivity by the dominant theological reflections, it should not surprise us if, in many instances, it is still heavily influenced by the language and manner of the dominant theology. The theology of struggle is still struggling for its life and identity alongside the suffering and struggling people.

MOVING FURTHER IN THE JOURNEY: MAPPING THE DIRECTION FOR THEOLOGICAL CONSTRUCTION

Convinced of the importance of the theology of struggle, primarily for the struggle of the oppressed and the struggle within theology itself, I am challenged to continue what the theologians of struggle have started and

---

[33]Mario Bolasco, "Notes on Theologies of Liberation as Politics," in *Liberation Theology and Vatican Document,* vol. 2. Compiled by Claretian Publications (Quezon City, Philippines: Claretian Publications, 1986), p. 110.

pursue some areas that I believe are important. The main concerns that I pursue and expound are as follows.

When the majority of those who are suffering have already interpreted their plight as *kapalaran* or the way things are, I believe that there is a need to challenge this assumption and emphasize the historical character of the people's plight, which means that it is a creation of people, not by God. The idea of *kapalaran* – a form of fatalism – has been deeply engraved among the oppressed communities, as my experience in community organizing testifies, that there is no end to the task of enabling these communities to realize that the situation is alterable. Although fatalism may not be totally absent among those whom society consider to be "successful," fatalism is a disease prevalent among those who have felt themselves powerless for so long. Although theology of struggle is an expression that the people have awakened from their fatalistic slumber, the need to combat this disease has to continue without ceasing. This is an area that theology of struggle can contribute to the people's awakening and is the reason why I am focusing on it in this work under eschatology and history.

With the experience of struggle as long and protracted, along with a history that seems not to progress smoothly from one epoch to another (salvation history model), there is a need to assert the point that the act of struggle itself is an experience of God's presence, a foretaste of liberation in the making (sacramental character), a new spiritual experience. Theologians of struggle have hinted at this and I would like to pursue it.[34]

If *kapalaran* is an easy escape for most of the suffering Filipinos, the same could be true of symbols associated with eschatology, like salvation, heaven, and resurrection. Because eschatology has been interpreted in a way that supports the existing oppression of the people, I have deemed it necessary to incorporate for the theology of struggle an eschatology interpreted in light of suffering (theodicy) and struggle (politics), rather than a search for immortality. Conversely, suffering, from which the theology of struggle must start, needs to be interpreted in light of eschatology and struggle.

In a situation in which the so-called separation of politics and religion has become instrumental in the perpetuation of the domesticating status quo, I have no other choice than to pursue the discourse on the theology of politics with the hope of disclosing the nature of the reigning politics and of equipping those who are struggling. Chapter III, which is to commence my theological construction, deals with the above-mentioned concerns.

Another concern that I pursue is the people's quest for humanity or

---

[34]See Feliciano Cariño, "Reflections on Culture and Religious Symbols," *Kalinangan,* vol. 8, no. 3 (September 1988), p. 25. Ruth O. Cortez, in her brief article on the theology of struggle, has picked up this sacramental character of struggle when she spoke of struggle as the "locus of God's salvific act" – as a Christ event, which is an act of incarnation now in the lives of those who are involved in the struggle. See her essay, "Theology of Struggle: Some Notes and Reflections," *Branches* (Fall/Winter, 1990), p. 6.

subjecthood. A theology of a struggling people must necessarily include their quest and struggle for humanity. This has been a long quest and struggle of the Filipinos, but one to which the existing theology of struggle has not yet given much focus and articulation. I pursue this concern in Chapter IV.

Although the figure of a passive and meek Jesus has been propagated by the conquerors and their local conduits to abort the people's struggle for humanity, the struggling Filipinos have also evolved a christology that is expressive and supportive of their struggle. This is one point that theologians of struggle have started to develop and that I pursue (Chapter V).

Furthermore, with the important role that the church plays in the lives of the Filipino people, I, like the rest of the theologians of the struggle, am not yet willing to give up the church. A struggle has to be waged inside the church, and new expressions of ecclesiology have to be explored. Chapter VI is my search for new ecclesiological expressions.

Lastly, when theology itself has become instrumental in the subjugation of the people, theology is one area where struggle has to be waged. This concern falls within the ambit of what is commonly called theological method, an area that has remained weak within the emerging theology of struggle. Many theologians of the struggle have mentioned method but have not really pursued it, except for Abesamis who has written about it in a limited way.[35] Here I explore further the basic questions on methods that have plagued theology for so long and argue for its hermeneutical character, with all its logical theological consequences.

It might be in the area of method and my pursuit of the hermeneutical character of theology to its fullest consequences that I may run into disagreement — which I believe can be clarified through explanation — with some theologians of the struggle who are very much shaped by the theological approach of Barth (especially among Protestants), notwithstanding their avowal of theology as sociologically shaped and contextual. This I sensed is particularly true on the issue of norm (readily identified as the Gospel), which is often impliedly understood as a "pure noninterpreted essence" in which everything is to be judged in relation to it, but not the other way around. In other words, it is in danger of suffering from a theological amnesia, that is, of forgetting its own assertion of the historical and hermeneutical character of theology from start to finish. These concerns will be pursued in Chapter VII of this book.

The pages that follow are my attempt at theological construction which, as I see it, may enrich the theology of struggle. Greeting the reader at the doorstep of my constructive theological work is my chapter on the sobering theme of suffering, a theme that Filipinos know by heart, leading to its transfiguration into hope and struggle.

---

[35]Carlos H. Abesamis, "Doing Theological Reflection (Philippines)" *Loyola Papers* 9 (Manila, Philippines: Loyola Papers Board of Editors, 1982), p. 105.

3

Cry for Deliverance

Suffering, Hope, and Politics of Struggle

There lived many centuries ago, a people called Indios. They were peace-loving, patient, and simple. They also had their own way of trading, leadership and culture.

Then came to their land a king from a far-away land with his soldiers and his priests. They made the Indios accept their ways, occupied their lands, and turned them into slaves.

"Force them to work," they said, "for they are lazy!" These Indios then had to work on their rulers' encomiendas. They were forced into slavery and their lives made unbearable with hard labor, working in the fields and doing all kinds of work forced on them.

"Let us teach them our language," the Pharaoh said, "so that they will understand us." So the language of the Pharaoh was taught in all the schools in the land. The Indios learned the language of the Pharaoh well and adopted the ways of their rulers.

As the days went on, the Indios got used to the ways of the Pharaoh. Although they were treated like slaves, they grew in numbers and strength. Then the Pharaoh got alarmed and said: "These Indios have become so numerous and strong that they are a threat to us. We must be prudent and take steps for they might take arms against us."

After years of silence, the Indios finally spoke up. Knowing that their strength is in their unity, they organized to press their demands. Instead, the Pharaoh ordered their imprisonment and massacre.[1]

The story of the *indios* speaks of the plight of the Filipino people; it speaks of their suffering, their vision and hope, and their resolve to struggle. This story embodies the litany of countless stories that are hard to tell and sad to hear — stories of anguish, fear, and human brutalities — yet, stories that have given rise to the indomitable will of the people to hope and struggle. Suffering, hope, and struggle are the motifs around which the painful story of the Filipino people revolves.

---

[1] Theresa Dagdag, "Emerging Theology in the Philippines Today," *Kalinangan*, vol. 3, no. 3a (September 1983), p. 4. The last paragraph is my own revision of the original.

Guided by these three focal themes, I now set sail in this journey of theological construction starting with an interpretation of suffering in relation to the theodicy question, then of hope in relation to eschatology, and of struggle in relation to politics. Finally, I attempt to locate the activity of God in relation to the themes of suffering (theodicy), hope (eschatology), and struggle (politics).

THE PEOPLE'S CRY:
SUFFERING AS A THEOPOLITICAL QUESTION

The Theology and Politics of Suffering

To start with the theology of struggle is to start with the prior theme of suffering, as de la Torre had rightly pointed out.[2] This theme of suffering figures prominently in the Filipino people's stories, songs, poems, and artistic works. For many of these people, even the act of telling their stories of suffering is an act of suffering or represents an invitation to more suffering, for there are those who are threatened even by the mere telling of these stories. As one Filipina who dared to tell her story put it: "The telling of our situation is part of our suffering because it could mean our life, it is a risk. You are actually laying your life on the line."[3]

What adds mystery and depth to this theme of suffering is its theological character; that is, it is a question of theodicy. Deeply religious, the struggling Filipinos have always grappled with their suffering in relation to their cherished religious beliefs. However, rather than be concerned about suffering as a means of proving or disproving God's existence (*Si deus est, unde malum*), like many Western philosophers and theologians,[4] the Filipinos have come to view suffering in a different light and in the context of their experience and struggle as a people. A story of a friend of mine would help to illuminate some aspects of the Filipino experience of suffering.

On September 2, 1984, a strong typhoon dubbed "Nitang" hit hard the island of Leyte, Philippines. Aside from the devastation and havoc both to life and property that it caused, there were two events that made me always

---

[2]de la Torre, *Touching Ground, Taking Root,* p. 156; Melanio Aoanan made a similar assertion: "the poor man's outburst is a primordial datum in our understanding of spirituality and struggle." See *Witness and Hope Amid Struggle: Towards a Theology of Struggle and Spirituality of Struggle,* Book II, ed. Victoria Narciso-Apuan et al. (Manila: Forum for Interdisciplinary Endeavors and Studies [FIDES], 1991), p. 21.

[3]"Out of the Valley of Dry Bones," in *Faith in Struggle,* Book II, compiled and arranged by Sammie P. Formilleza (Quezon City, Philippines: People's Theology Publication, Ecumenical Center for Development [ECD], 1990), p. 78.

[4]See, for example, Richard Swinburne, *The Existence of God* (Oxford: Clarendon Press, 1979); Alvin Plantinga, *God, Freedom, and Evil* (New York: Harper and Row, 1974).

remember that typhoon: one, it was the day when my first child was born in a flooded hospital in Maasin, Southern Leyte; second, a friend of mine whose immediate relatives were victims of a tidal wave that hit Limasawa (an island believed to be the site of the first Christian mass in the Philippines) made a profound but disturbing remark. As he stood on the hilly side of the island overlooking the devastated barrio, his heart was pierced with sadness and anger. Sadness, we can easily understand, but anger, for many that is puzzling. He was angry, but he could not be angry at anyone for the natural disaster except at a supernatural power like God. But God was nowhere to be found, so all that he could do was sigh in anguish.

Unlike the philosophers of religion of the West, this person did not spin theories or arguments about the being of God, about proving or disproving God's existence, of a cosmological, teleological, or ontological sort. Neither was he interested in pursuing the issue of God language or theological language or in engaging in matters regarding the intellectual adequacy of belief in God.[5] Instead, he was driven by the sense of righteous indignation for the undeserved suffering of his friends. He was driven to search for the one responsible for that painful event so that the victims may be vindicated and the perpetrator held accountable. He found it hard to conceive that an all-powerful, loving, and just God would allow that disaster to happen.

Even in this natural phenomenon, which a believer would easily attribute to God (theological), the question of suffering already points to the question of justice (political). At the very heart of the theological question is a question of justice. The God question (theodicy) is a justice question (political), and the justice question is a God question, a God talk, or a theological question. But because the suffering was thought to be caused by a supernatural power through the means of the natural, all he could do was resign himself in the presence of the *mysterium tremendum et fascinosum*.[6]

As if the spoliation wrought by the natural calamities were not enough for an already suffering and agonizing people, their experience of life's adversities had been compounded by economic and political crises of tremendous proportion. After years of developmental projects, especially under the long Marcos era, the people have become poorer than ever, while the few *buayas* (literally, crocodiles—a name for those who take advantage

---

[5]See Sharon Welch, *Communities of Resistance and Solidarity* (Maryknoll, NY.: Orbis Books, 1985), pp. 1-14. Welch identified two fundamental crises of Christian theology, namely, cognitive (conceptual) and moral. Most liberal and revisionist theologies have focused on the first dimension of the crisis (though not negating the second), whereas feminist and liberation theologies have concentrated on the second. Compare the familiar rational proofs of the existence of God and the liberal responses to the theodicy issue with that of the liberation theology, e.g., Gustavo Gutiérrez's *On Job: God-Talk and the Suffering of the Innocent,* trans. Matthew J. O'Connel (Maryknoll, NY.: Orbis Books, 1987).

[6]Rudolf Otto, *The Idea of the Holy,* trans. John W. Harvey (London: Oxford University Press, 1950).

of others and enrich themselves) get richer and richer. After years of building a new society, the more the people had fallen into the quagmire of misery, the more they had experienced the loss of their freedom and dignity. A painful political jest that rings true not only during the time of Marcos but even after his notorious era reflects this: "Before Marcos' time, the Filipino children asked: '*What's* the food, Mama?' During his time [and up to the present] the question was: '*Where's* the food, Mama?'"[7] Natural disasters still continue to threaten the poverty-stricken populace: killing thousands, rendering many homeless, and sending the victims to evacuation centers. But the people have realized that "Mother" Nature's fury (the use of the "mother" nature stereotype here is intentional) pales in comparison to the "Father" system's victims, in which thousands die daily because workers are paid poorly and in which thousands go to evacuation centers, hamlet places, and slum areas of the cities because of militarization in the countryside.

It is out of this experience of a brutalizing situation that the Filipino people have realized that what they really have suffered most from is a product of history and a creation of people. This has affected a shift of focus from nature's fury to an awareness of the "anthropocentrism of suffering,"[8] more specifically of the kind of suffering that is largely the making of the power wielders. With this heightening of social awareness, the people were soon able to perceive the political nature of their suffering and even to entertain the suspicion that many of the so-called natural or inevitable calamities may have had anthropocentric or androcentric causes. This awareness of the political nature of suffering is expressed in the following parable, which the author says "is a children's story for adults":[9]

> Once upon a time there was a Big Man and a Small Man. The Big Man had a garden. The Small Man had no garden. So the Small Man worked in the Big Man's garden.
> In the beginning the Small Man was a Good Man. He worked all day long and took care of the garden. The garden yielded golden tomatoes. The tomatoes gave the Big Man nice clothes, nice cars, nice houses, and a nice wife. The Small Man did not have nice clothes, nice cars, nice houses, and nice wife. He knew he was a Small Man. He knew that the golden tomatoes he raised belonged to the Big Man.

---

[7]From "Selected Marcos Jokes," in Salvador Roxas González, *The Philippines: Democracy in Asia* (Burgos and Burgos Ltd., Inc., 1987), p. 141.

[8]Matthew Lamb, *Solidarity with Victims: Toward A Theology of Social Transformation* (New York: The Crossroad Publishing Company, 1982), p. 7, citing Johann Baptist Metz.

[9]Renato Constantino, "The Parable of the Big Man and the Small Man," *Issues Without Tears: A Layman's Manual of Current Issues,* vol. 8, ed. Leticia R. Constantino (Quezon City, Philippines: Karrel Inc., 1989), pp. 164–175.

As a reward for his good work the Big Man gave him tomatoes. The Small Man was glad. After all, he had no garden of his own. And the few tomatoes that the Big Man gave him were enough to keep him sturdy and virile so he could raise more tomatoes for the Big Man and bring up more Little Men to raise more tomatoes for other Big Men.

So the Big Man said that the Small Man was a Good Man. But one day, the Small Man became a Bad Man. He made friends with other Small Men who were Bad Men. The Small Men who were Bad Men wanted more golden tomatoes from the Big Men. That is why they were Bad Men.

The Bad Men paraded around demanding more tomatoes. They carried placards calling the Big Men names. Some of them refused to raise golden tomatoes. Many got the golden tomatoes of the Big Men. And there were Small Men who were very, very Bad Men because they wanted to have gardens, too. The Small Man became a Bad Man because he went with the Bad Men.

The Small Man broke the Big Man's heart. The Big Man asked the Small Man to become a Good Man again. He reminded him of the good things he had done for the Small Man. After all, the Small Man had no garden and he could not have gotten even a few tomatoes if the Big Man had not allowed him to work in his garden. True, he was given only a few tomatoes. But he did not need nice clothes, a nice house, and a nice wife because he was not a Big Man.

But the Small Man would not listen to the Big Man. He remained a Bad Man.

So, in the last effort, the Big Man told the Small Man that if he wanted to go to Heaven he must become a Good Man again. The Big Man asked the Black Robe Man [priest or pastor] to talk to the Small Man. But the Small Man did not want to go to Heaven with the Big Man and the Black Robe Man. He only wanted more tomatoes.

Along with the other Bad Men, the Small Man became a very, very Bad Man.

So the Big Men got very angry. They called for the Brown Men [Police or Philippine Constabulary] with Guns.

The Small Men who were Bad Men thought that the Brown Men with Guns were going to kill them and send them to Heaven.

But they did not want to go to Heaven and eat heavenly tomatoes. They wanted their own gardens to grow their own tomatoes here on earth. They have become very, very, very Bad Men.

So they fought the Men with Guns. But more Brown Men with Guns came. And the Bad Men were sent, not to Heaven but to jail.

In jail, the Small Man learned that the Big Man is always right.

The two stories narrated here (typhoon Nitang that hit Limasawa and Big Man-Small Man) show the growth of people's awareness with regard to suffering from one of complete separation of theological and political suffering to the increasing awareness and conceptualization of their inextricable connection, a connection that has remained operative from the most ancient to the most modern societies.

My personal experience with a tribal community, the Ikalahans (Igorots)

in Imugan, Santa Fe, Nueva Vizcaya, testifies to this inextricable connection between theology and politics. During a Bible study that I conducted
regarding the Exodus account, one of the participants asked: *"Kung talaga
hong nagmamahal sa atin ang Panginoon, bakit pinapayagan ng Panginoon
na ang palay namin ay kakainin ng mga ibon. Ganyan ba ang pagmamahal
ng Panginoon?"* (If it is true that God loves us, why is it that God allowed
the birds to eat our *palay* [rice plant]?). Not expecting that kind of question,
I answered half-jokingly: *"Ayaw pa ninyo, hindi lang kayo binigyan ng
palay may pang-ulam pa, hulihin ninyo ang mga ibon"* (Would you not like
that, you were not only given rice, but also meat [birds]? Why don't you
catch the birds?).

Although I answered that person's question half-jokingly, I soon realized
how deep the question was: He wanted to relate to the experience of the
tribal people, in that example, the birds eating of their *palay*, with what it
means to say that God is love. But soon this problem of birds and *palay*
(natural calamity) would turn into the problem of the *palayan* (ricefield)
itself – a much greater problem (political) – when the lowlanders with their
legal documents and armed goons would come to the highland to grab their
lands. It was at this level that the relationship of the theological and the
political was all the more heightened, for the deeply religious tribal people
could not reconcile the God whom they knew with the barbarous acts of the
"civilized" lowlanders.

With an ironic twist, the *sacadas* (sugarcane plantation workers), whose
sweat makes it possible for the sweet goods (e.g., sugar) to flow to our
kitchens, have, not in sweetness but in bitterness, also raised their theopolitical sigh and questions. Hechanova, who had spent some time with the
sacadas, related that one frequently asked question among the poor was: "Is
there a God in the world?" It should be noted that this question was not
asked by a Marxist (the so-called atheist), or an academe agnostic, but by
ordinary folks steeped in religious culture; nor is this theological question
meant to prove or disprove the existence of God, but it is triggered by the
people's predicament. In other words, within their context and experience as
a suffering people, they are struggling to make sense of their faith,
especially as Christians. On the other hand, they see that their theological
question is indeed political and is rooted in politics.[10]

When Suffering Is Detheopoliticized:
Solutions that Obfuscate the Problem

Suffering "interrupts," asserted Rebecca Chopp,[11] and suffering demands explanation. Although in a crisis situation empathy may just be

---

[10]Hechanova, "The Christ of Liberation Theology," in *With Raging Hope*, p. 1.

[11]Rebecca Chopp, *The Praxis of Suffering: An Interpretation of Liberation and Political
Theologies* (Maryknoll, NY.: Orbis Books, 1986).

enough, and, in fact, there is the possibility that explanation might only disturb the sufferer, suffering needs an explanation, whereby the sufferer can at least make sense of what he or she is undergoing. There are various ways in which suffering has been explained; I only review a few for our purposes.

Nature, in spite of progress in science and technology, has not been fully under control. In fact, it fights back, causing destruction, with the dwellings of the poor badly hit. Although natural disasters are almost everywhere, they occur only to a limited degree in affluent areas. Most of these disasters — typhoon, epidemics, floods, and so on — have heavily affected the less privileged. It is troubling to see scientifically minded theologians attempt to explain suffering in a way that forgets the experiences of those who suffer most, and also in a way that tends to justify the places of those who triumph over others by subsuming the political to the "way of nature." This I perceive to be present in the writings of the evolutionist-ecologist-theologian Holmes Rolston III.[12] Rolston's explanation of suffering is the first kind of explanation to which I respond.

What purpose do the words of an evolutionist-ecologist-theologian serve by saying that "the way of nature is the way of the cross" (*via naturae est crucis*), or that "if nothing much had ever died, nothing much could have ever lived."[13] Maybe such statements have a therapeutic value, that is, they enable the person to endure suffering. But in a situation in which the people have already endured for so long because they have accepted that nature is *cruciform*, Rolston's interpretation only encourages passivity and resignation. His point also aggravates the situation of those who are already suffering because of its seeming justification of the achievement of those who have triumphed over others. Rolston does not forget that on the altar of progress many lives have been sacrificed. Surely nature (which includes politics and the progress of history) is cruciform, but Rolston refuses to ask the questions: Who crucifies whom? Whose existence is meant? Whose death? Whose life? Whose life is being sacrificed for whom? Maybe it is the life of an anemic Filipino to that of a diet-conscious North American.

Another attempt to explain suffering remains limited to the existential and ontological level. Theological reflections that have employed existential analysis of human estrangement have for some time made a deep influence on theology because they have addressed at a deeper level the human predicament. However, one of their limitations, as pointed out by Johann Baptist Metz, lies in their attempt to abbreviate *history* to *historicity*, which means withdrawing from the contradictions of history to "a secret, unavailable and inexpressible point of identity in the subject or in existence itself."[14] By withdrawing from history into historicity, that is, to the terrain

---

[12]Holmes Rolston III, *Science and Religion* (New York: Random House, 1987).

[13]Ibid., pp, 135, 146.

[14]Johann Baptist Metz, *Faith in History and Society: Toward a Practical Fundamental*

of the *ontos* or essence, they have failed to take seriously the concrete sociopolitical expressions of human suffering. When they speak, for example, of human alienation and estrangement, they beautifully articulate the way human beings have been alienated from their true beings and from each other; they speak about the truth in that in the situation of estrangement, neither of the persons involved is truly human. However, because they do not swim in the political water, they fail to analyze that in an alienating condition there are those who oppress and there are those who are oppressed. The alienation of the oppressed and the oppressor from their humanity is not the same.

Obfuscating further the problem of suffering is when explanation tries to absorb this historical suffering into God's very own eternal suffering in the form of the trinitarian character of God.[15] For Metz, this only "leads either to a dualistic gnostic eternalization of suffering in God or to a condescending reduction of suffering to its concept."[16] C. S. Song added to this chorus of criticism in pointing out what seems to be a gnostic "divine masochism."[17] In addition to being a very speculative interpretation, it does not really face the negativity of suffering. To say that in the very constitution of the trinity God has been eternally suffering portrays a God who has internalized the suffering of humankind, but it moves too quickly from the suffering of millions to the suffering of God, thereby blurring clarity as to the location of suffering and the demand to opt with those who suffer now.[18] Furthermore, what does it serve to those who are undergoing suffering? Maybe it is a source of comfort and strength to know that someone is in the same boat, especially to think that that companion is God. Though this notion of a suffering God may be a source of strength to the victims and a desirable corrective for an absolute and transcendent God,[19] it may add to the sufferers' passive acceptance of their situation, unless this

---

Theology, trans. David Smith (New York: The Seabury Press, 1980), p.131. Cf. Welch, *Communities of Resistance and Solidarity,* in which she criticizes those theologies that claim to be concerned with history but locate its truth in an "ahistorical" realm (p. 85). In a similar vein, see also Cornel West, review of *Philosophy and the Mirror of Nature,* by Richard Rorty, In *Union Seminary Quarterly Review* 37 (Fall/Winter 1981-1982), p. 184.

[15] Jürgen Moltmann, *The Crucified God: The Cross of Christ as the Foundation and Criticism of Christian Theology* (New York: Harper and Row, 1974).

[16] Metz, *Faith in History and Society: Toward a Practical Fundamental Theology,* p. 132.

[17] C. S. Song, *Third-Eye Theology,* rev. ed. (Maryknoll, NY.: Orbis Books, 1979), p. 78.

[18] Cf. Chopp, *The Praxis of Suffering,* p. 116.

[19] See Dorothee Sölle, "God's Pain and Our Pain," in *The Future of Liberation Theology: Essays in Honor of Gustavo Gutiérrez,* pp. 326-333. The understanding that God is someone who is absolute makes God really incapable of suffering and, therefore, of compassion, argued Sölle. Instead of stopping with a suffering God, Sölle proceeded to speak of this suffering God as one with the people of God in their suffering and struggle (pp. 326-327). For an excellent exposition on the danger of an absolute God, in spite of contrary claims that the notion of an absolute God would serve to relativize human absolutizations, see Sharon Welch, *A Feminist Ethic of Risk* (Minneapolis: Fortress Press, 1990), pp. 111-122.

suffering is construed in relation to their struggle. Vicarious suffering must lead to the protest of undeserved suffering.

However, the most common explanation for the people's suffering is to put the blame on the victims themselves, or on nature (the way things are), and finally on God. For many Filipinos who have not gained the consciousness of struggle, their plight is reflexively explained in terms of *pagbuot sa Dios* (will of God), *kapalaran* (lines on one's palm), and *kinaiyahan* (nature or *kinaiyahan*, interestingly enough, means not simply the natural world, but also the social realities). On top of this, churches preach the gospel of passivity and greater subservience to those whom the people call *dagko ug tai* (Cebuano) or the elite (literally, people with large manure).

The Cry for Total Deliverance

The unity of faith and politics in matters of life and death only points to an understanding of deliverance that encompasses political and theological notions, or what I would call total deliverance. I prefer the term *deliverance* because it can be interpreted to mean liberation (political connotation) and redemption or salvation (theological). Although there have been changes in understanding the notion of deliverance, many still cling to the notion of deliverance as salvation of the soul in heaven (*fuga mundi*). One has to be good in this life in order to go to heaven; heaven being the final destination. In this notion of deliverance, the gospel or Christ has acquired the imagery of a "life jacket" that people have to wear in order to be saved from the sinking ship (the world).[20] The ship's captain (priest or pastor) has sounded the call to abandon the ship, thus the people must not delay in putting on their life jackets — that is, accept Jesus Christ as their personal Savior — if they want to be saved.

Those who consider this notion of deliverance to be repulsive have proposed their own version of salvation, but most often they have not advanced to a significant degree from the first position. Deliverance still belongs to another world, although they give some concessions to emancipatory praxis as a preparation of the gospel.

The notions of deliverance just mentioned still operate on common basic presuppositions: they still operate on the idea of "two histories," and the christendom notion of deliverance is still in force.[21] They continue to be guided by the understanding that outside of the church there is no salvation. The church continues to be the depository of God's grace and its ordained ministers the dispensers of this salvific grace. Because it is only through the witness of the church that the saving power of Christ is experienced, everything considered liberating by secular movements or by other religions

---

[20]I first heard of the "life jacket" imagery from Dodong Reyes during a seminar sponsored by IDEA (Inter-Church Development Education Agency).

[21]Gutiérrez, *A Theology of Liberation,* pp. 86–97.

is seen only as a preparation of the gospel. Even calling believers of other religions "anonymous Christians" can still be classified as preparation of the gospel.[22]

Now, I would like the theology of struggle to move to a notion of deliverance in which, instead of saying outside the church there is no salvation, it can say: outside of the world there is no salvation. The church is still part of the world no matter how it claims to be the "Christified portion of the world."[23] The church has no other deliverance apart from the world; the world is the locus of God's presence and salvific activity. Even before the gospel is uttered by the church through its missionaries, God is already present. Furthermore, even the so-called "pagans" and people's movements can be the loci of God's salvific manifestation and heralds of the good news.[24]

The notion that there is only "one history" is something that would also strengthen the theology of struggle. To think that there are "two histories" would only lead the theology of struggle to devalue the present struggle of the people as *pre-evangelization*. In this *ordo salutis* (order of salvation), the *spiritual* would still appear as the *proper function* of the church. When history is viewed as one, it is but proper to construe that action in behalf of justice is *constitutive* of the gospel.[25] This means that acts of justice or people's development are not simply preparation of the gospel (*praeparatio evangelica),* but the gospel itself at work; not simply pre-evangelization, but essentially a part of the salvific process, although not all of it. It is not a question of one being "temporal" and the other "spiritual," but, for Gustavo Gutiérrez, only of "partial fulfillments" and "total fulfillment."[26]

I would still continue to use Jürgen Moltmann's[27] framework in referring to *partial fulfillments* as the "immanent side" of "salvation" (Gutiérrez) or *redemption* (Metz) and *total fulfillment* as the "transcendent side" of "liberation" (Gutiérrez) or "emancipation" (Metz). However, rather than "reducing" the transcendent to nothing more than the immanent, as Alfredo Fierro has done,[28] I still maintain the transcendent but follow a course that

---

[22]Song, *Third-Eye Theology: Theology in Formation in Asian Settings,* p. 8. Song contends that calling believers of other faith as "anonymous Christians" is not complimentary.

[23]Pierre Teilhard de Chardin, cited in Gutiérrez, A Theology of Liberation, p. 147.

[24]The proponents of the theology of struggle understand the people's movement as a locus of God's redeeming and liberating activity. See Noriel Capulong, "Towards a Prophetic Theology of History for the Filipinos," *Tugón,* vol. 10, no. 1 (1990), p. 89; also Elizabeth Dominguez, "Signs and Countersigns of the Kingdom of God in Asia Today," *Kalinangan,* vol. 4, no. 4 (December 1984), pp. 10–12, 32.

[25]1971 Synod of Bishops' Document, "Justice in the World."

[26]Gutiérrez, *A Theology of Liberation,* p. 96.

[27]Alfredo Fierro, *The Militant Gospel: A Critical Introduction to Political Theologies,* trans. John Drury (Maryknoll, NY.: Orbis Books, 1977), p. 268, citing Jürgen Moltmann, Esperanza y planificatión del futuro (Salamanca: Sígueme, 1971), p. 343.

[28]Fierro, *Militant Gospel: A Critical Introduction to Political Theologies,* p. 293. Fierro

tries to avoid the error of "leaping outside history"[29] or suggest a reality beyond this world that in part coincides with the earthly reality. Instead of thinking of something beyond the world, the transcendent side serves both as a negative and a positive critique: first, as a reminder of the limitations of any project of liberation and, second, to maintain the openness of the future.

HISTORY AS ESCHATOLOGY:
ESCHATOLOGY AS THE HORIZON OF HOPE

The eschatologization of history is, I believe, an offspring of those who have suffered most in life; however, instead of getting cynical and falling into hedonistic play, they have retained a ray of hope, even hope against hope. Out of the wounded, bruised, mangled, and anemic bodies of history's victims, an eschatologized understanding of history has blossomed, which is the wider horizon of hope. Those who live by the present, that is, those who are enjoying the blessings of the present and those whom they have deceived, cannot truly bear to peek at the future, much less to welcome the presence of the future, for they are only bent on maintaining what they have at present. Because it is from those who suffer that the longing for the future has truly sprouted, I think it is appropriate and reasonable that I journey from suffering to hope, from theodicy to eschatology. Following this course is a fitting theological rendering of the experience of those who have suffered but struggled. At the same time, this also encourages those who are suffering because they do struggle.

As early as the closing period of the 19th century and the inception of the 20th century, there has been a resurgence of interest in eschatology (e.g., Schweitzer and Weiss).[30] This resurgence created theological ripples that led to various proposals on how eschatology is to be interpreted: (1) apocalyptic-

---

criticized Moltmann as falling into supernaturalism. The same could be said of Rubem Alves. The issue that political eschatology and the theology of hope must decide, for Fierro, is: (1) Whether they rigorously maintain that salvation and resurrection are nothing more than the transcendent side of historical liberation and do not really add anything, or (2) that they contain something more to which there is no corresponding reality in this world. Political theology, in Fierro's judgment, falls within the second position, whereas liberation theology remains ambiguous. Fierro has opted for the first position.

[29]Hope theologians, for Fierro, still "leap outside history." God is still imported from the outside. Fierro takes the position that "faith and the Holy Spirit are not different things but rather two aspects of one and the same happening." See *Militant Gospel: A Critical Introduction to Political Theologies,* p. 293.

[30]Johannes Weiss, *Jesus' Proclamation of the Kingdom of God,* eds. Richard H. Hiers and D. Larrimore Holland (Chico, California: Scholars Press, 1985, reprint); Albert Schweitzer, *The Quest for Historical Jesus: A Critical Study of its Progress from Reimarus to Wrede* (New York: Macmillan, 1959); also see Claude Welch, *Protestant Thought in the Nineteenth Century, 1870-1914,* vol. 2 (New Haven: Yale University Press, 1985).

otherworldly thrust, (2) prophetic-this-worldly thrust, (3) eschatology as an existential presence (present), (4) eschatology as that which is yet to come (future), (5) and the notion that any alternative is a false one.[31]

Although there has been a renewed interest in eschatology, Fierro argues that it has been an "apolitical eschatology." It was only with the appearance of political theology, he proceeds, that eschatology acquired a political interpretation—historical, collective, and truly future-directed. Within the perspective of political theology, all eschatological theology needs to be transformed into a political theology, that is, a theology serving as a criticism of society.[32] It is in this direction that my own views move.

From Theodicy to Eschatology

As I started to articulate at the beginning of this section, it is from the wounds of the forgotten people that the eschatologization of history and a real hope for a new day can truly blossom. From the wounds of the rejects of society eschatological hope has arisen and is going to arise; they are the bearers of eschatological hope. When eschatology is detached from the soil that has been fertilized by the suffering of the rejects and the blood of their martyrs, I can only say that it is doomed to serve as a form of escape to another world beyond, or as a private affair between God and the individual, or as a way of extending the ego even to eternity.

To say that the suffering of victims is the springboard or the wellspring for interpreting eschatology is, I believe, profoundly liberational, thus I have opted for this interpretation. In a similar vein, Moltmann asserts that the theodicy question (suffering) is the basic question from which eschatological images of the future arise.[33] And this theodicy question does not focus on proving the existence of God, but on God's righteousness vis-à-vis the evil world.

Suffering, not the search for immortality, is the womb from which the notion of resurrection was born, asserts Rosemary Radford Ruether.[34] For her, the Hebraic idea of resurrection was intended not to support immortality, but to bridge the gap between the present suffering and the future vindication of those who have suffered unjustly. Detached from the question of the suffering of the downtrodden and their longing for

---

[31]Carl Braaten, "The Kingdom of God and Life Everlasting," *Christian Theology: An Introduction to its Traditions and Tasks,* rev. and enlarged edition, eds. Peter C. Hodgson and Robert King (Philadelphia: Fortress Press, 1985), pp. 328–352; see also Wendell Willis, ed., *The Kingdom of God in 20th Century Interpretation* (Peabody, Massachusetts: Hendrickson Publishers, 1987).

[32]Fierro, *Militant Gospel: A Critical Introduction to Political Theologies,* p. 258.

[33]Jürgen Moltmann, *Religion, Revolution, and the Future* (New York: Charles Scribner's Sons, 1969), p. 45.

[34]Rosemary Radford Ruether, *Sexism and God-Talk: Toward a Feminist Theology* (Boston: Beacon Press, 1983), p. 243.

vindication, eschatology becomes skewed only to support the quest of individuals who want to extend their personality even to eternity or to support their "posthumous egoism."[35] Detached from its base in the suffering of the marginalized, eschatology would only become an ideological tool of those who want to control not only the earth, but even the heavenly abode. Not content with their control in this world, those in power still want to extend their control in heaven. And because the church has, even up to the present, devised some ways in which one's space in heaven can be secured (sacraments and masses), it appears that the will of the powerful is going to be fulfilled not only on earth, but also in heaven.

Eschatologization of History: Horizon of Hope

People who have suffered the most but have continued on hoping are people who have an eschatologized view of history and have been empowered by it. Those who have resigned themselves, the romanticists of the past, and those who have been fattening themselves from the fleshpots of the present do not really have an eschatologized view of history. They all have one thing in common: they have lost the sense of expectation, the sense of active waiting for the not yet, and the sense of anticipation.

Contrary to the notion that the eschatologization of history is putting history into a straitjacket,[36] an eschatologized view of history maintains a posture of openness to the future, a sense of expectation and anticipation. While for the romanticists the past tends to expand, and for the defenders of the status quo the present, people who are imbued with an eschatologized notion of history are people who take seriously their past as they anticipate the future through active engagement in the present. *"Paningkamot dong/ day para sa imong ugma,"* as the Cebuano people would say (literally, "Work hard now my child for your tomorrow"). By viewing history eschatologically they have ceased to be prisoners of the past, they have refused to be lulled by the monotony of the present, and they have declined to be pigeonholed into an inevitable future. A Filipino saying combines this sense of expectation of what is yet to come with the wisdom of the past: *"Ang hindi lumingon sa pinanggalingan, ay hindi makararating sa paruruonan"* (literally, "She or he who does not look back at where she or he comes from cannot reach to her or his destination").

Hope or Flight: Escape from Freedom

Sprouting from the experience of suffering, eschatological hope has been interpreted by many as a form of escape or illusion; it is only an exit for

---

[35]Ibid., p. 236, citing Charlotte Perkins Gilman, His Religion and Hers (New York: Century, 1923), pp. 46–47.

[36]See Carol A. Newsome, "The Past as Revelation: History in Apocalyptic Literature," *Quarterly Review,* vol. 4, no. 3 (Fall 1984), p. 40.

history's losers. This accusation contains some truth. For if we can say that suffering is the mother of hope, it can also be the mother of illusion. There is a Filipino proverb for this: *"Ang taong nagigipit kahit sa patalim kakapit"* ("A desperate person or a person in deep crisis will grasp anything, even a sharp bladed object").

Eschatological hope is not, however, an escape or a refusal to face the reality of this world. To the contrary, the person who hopes has done his or her homework and knows the hard facts of history, that is, that the historical is not eternal, that the plight of the people could be made better because it belongs to the realm of the alterable. And because something could be made better, the person who is full of hope is committed to live in the present the promise of the future; the person who is empowered by hope is committed to make her or his dream come true. Oppressed people know the power of their hopes and dreams and the possibility that their dreams will lead them to martyrdom. Even those who are fattening themselves in the present know that the dreams of the oppressed have a threatening power. José F. Lacaba's poem articulates this point:

> Sila'y nangarap din nang gising,
>   subalit ang mga pangarap nila'y
> matalim na bituin;
>   ang mga berdugo't panginoon
> ay natakot sa kanilang
>   mga pangarap,
> natakot na baka ang kanilang mga
>   pangarap ay magkatotoo,
> at dahil dito, sila'y wala na
>   sa ating piling.

> (They also dreamt while awake,
>   but their dreams were like
> sharp-bladed stars;
>   the cruel masters
> were afraid of
>   their dreams;
> they were afraid that
>   their dreams might come true,
> and so they are no longer
>   in our midst.)[37]

People who are imbued with the power of eschatology are people who already live in the presence of the future, although only proleptically. Because they are open to the future, they are hurt all the more by the necrophilic bias of society. The goad of a promised future always inexo-

---

[37]Cited in Gaspar, *How Long? Prison Reflections from the Philippines,* p. 115.

rably reminds them of every unfulfilled present. Living at the threshold between the promise of a better future and the agony of the life-negating present, they are driven not to the posture of passive waiting, like Juan Tamad (Johnny-the-Lazy),[38] but of active waiting and active hoping. This is precisely what it means to hope or to have a sense of the future: It means active involvement, for to truly love the future means full generosity to the present.[39] I have observed many poor Filipino parents who, out of their resolute desire to send their children to college to get a better future, would endure working from dawn till dusk with only a *bagoong* (salted fish) and *gulay* (vegetable) most of the time for a meal.[40] Still they are called lazy because they are poor. Although we can easily observe poor lazy people, actually they have more reason to be lazy than those lazy government officials who are "busy" enriching themselves. With only a *bagoong* or *tuyo* (dried fish) for a meal, they have to play lazy, says Charles Avila, if they are not to go crazy.[41]

To hope, as I understand it, is not to escape or resign. Escape is not the posture of those who believe that their miserable situation is not eternal. Those who resign themselves, such as those who have accepted their plight as natural and those who engage in hedonistic play, are not really capable of real hope because they see the future as simply the continuation of the present. Life for them is simply a business of *"kaon, kalibang, higda lantay, patay"* ("eating, excreting, sleeping, and dying"). Besides, it appears that to think of the future as nothing more than an extended time that has not yet come provides a form of security, although a false one at that. These people enjoy the comfort of a closed future—which is not a future—because it relieves them of freedom and responsibility to forge a better tomorrow. It is actually an "escape from freedom," to use the title of Erich Fromm's work.[42] Fatalism or resignation, a disease common among those who have been subjugated for so long, is a form of not facing the open future. The future, by its being a future, is open. However, people in submerged conditions do not see this future as a possibility for something new and better. Domesticated, they would rather remain in Egyptian captivity than journey into the wilderness where new possibilities as well as risks await. Refusal to face the open future is a form of refuge for these people because everything that is associated with the open future—freedom, decision, and responsibility—are already relegated to someone else, to those who dominate them.

---

[38] Juan (Johnny in English) is a name oftentimes used for Filipinos, like Uncle Sam for U.S.

[39] Gutiérrez, *A Theology of Liberation,* p. 125, citing Albert Camus.

[40] To be a vegetarian is an option for many in North America. Among many poor people in the rural Philippines, to eat vegetables almost everyday is not a choice but a product of poverty. To have meat for a meal is a real treat.

[41] Charles R. Avila, *Peasant Theology: Reflections by the Filipino Peasants on their Process of Social Revolution,* Book no. 1 (Bangkok: WSCF Asia, 1976), p. 43.

[42] Erich Fromm, *Escape from Freedom* (New York: Holt, Rinehart and Winston, 1941).

I think this helps to explain why, in spite of the years that the Filipinos were plundered under the Marcos dictatorial regime, many have remained loyal even long after the collapse of his reign. This helps to explain why the poor people in the rural churches in Leyte where I worked would be contented to have others, that is, the pastor and the more educated and monied church council members, think and decide for them. I can recall one occasion when I heard someone say, "Whatever is agreed upon, I will follow," to which I retorted quickly, "Suppose we will agree to sell your carabao or waterbuffalo" (there was laughter). This is not simply for the sake of convenience or because of a hectic schedule but due to a deep feeling of inferiority and powerlessness. By fleeing from the open future which calls them to act in freedom, they escape from freedom and fall prey into the hands of an authoritarian power. But in becoming *mga tuta* (puppies or puppets) of an authoritarian power, they participate in some way with the power of the powerful, that is, they participate in their strength and glory. In fact, they pretend to be much tougher than their bosses and turn out to be equally avid defenders of the present. That is why the *bata-bata* system (patronage) works well in the Philippines. The Cebuano people have a saying that illustrates this point: *"Ang langaw nga nakatungtong sa bukobuko sa kabaw, magpakakabaw na pod"* ("A fly who happens to rest on the back of a carabao, thinks and acts like a carabao").

But how about those who busy themselves amassing wealth and strengthening their political power? They, in another sense, refuse to face the reality of the future and also escape from freedom. They always speak of the future, but they do not really want to face the reality of the future, and the future does not belong to them. Their only future is the maintenance of their dominant status. In this sense they are like the oppressed. But unlike the oppressed who seek security by being swallowed, they swallow others in order to secure their present from the incursion of a threatening future.

Hope and the Resurrection of Subjugated Memories

Hope, at first sight, seems to be identified only with the future and memory with the past. This is not exactly true. In fact, those who are impassioned by active hoping are also those who are deeply immersed in the memories of the past, specifically painful memories that wounded the community. Those who hope are also those who have not forgotten or who have not lost their sense of memory.[43] The powers-that-be would do everything within their means and might to see oppressed communities lose their memories because this is an effective way of controlling the people.

---

[43]Robert N. Bellah et al., *Habits of the Hearts: Individualism and Commitment in American Life* (New York: Harper and Row, 1985), pp. 152-155; José Comblin, *Retrieving the Human: A Christian Anthropology,* trans. Robert Barr (Maryknoll, NY.: Orbis Books, 1990), pp. 129-130; also Song, *Third-Eye Theology,* pp. 163-164.

But a community that hopes has maintained the dangerous memory of suffering. When the oppressors are successful in effacing this memory, the powerless become captive to a kind of rationality governed by the rules of exchange—a "pragmatic rationality."[44] What has become important is something that can be exchanged for something: a commoditization of relationship. This is a rationality that does not remember the dead and has lost the sense of idealism, both of which are shaped by the past and the expectation of the future.

When the oppressed community remains deeply rooted in its tradition of suffering, it could be said that it has still retained the sense of being wronged. When the oppressed community still remembers its suffering and knows how to cry, this indicates an awareness on the part of the subjugated that things are not right. When the oppressed community still sighs and dreams, this indicates that a ray of hope is still alive. When this capacity to remember suffering, to cry, to sigh, and to dream fuses with the realization that the oppressive plight and social structures are not eternal, the "consciousness of freedom"[45] bursts from the bleeding side of history. At this bleeding point of history, subjugated memories experience a resurrection. What were once the subjugated memories now arise into dangerous and subversive memories, subverting the order that has buried these memories in ignominy and oblivion.

Negation of the Negative: Refusal to Accept the Finality of the Present in Favor of the New Tomorrow

Anger and Denunciation: Negation of the Negative

When the consciousness of freedom emerges, that is, when the capacity to remember suffering, to cry, to sigh, and to dream fuses with the realization that the oppressive condition is not eternal, anger and denunciation are inevitable. Anger and denunciation are the early outpourings of the emergence of the consciousness of freedom. Anger borne out of the consciousness of freedom is an early sign of a people trying to regain their lost dignity and self-worth. Unless the slave can *spit* on the face of the master, asserts Cariño, the slave has not yet been freed from the master's control.[46] A long time ago, John Calvin, the Genevan Protestant Reformer, unleashed a similar sharp attack against the corrupt officials of his time:

---

[44]Metz, *Faith in History and Society: Toward a Practical Fundamental Theology*, pp. 36–39, 170.

[45]Rubem Alves, *A Theology of Human Hope* (New York: Corpus Books, 1969), p. 11.

[46]Feliciano Cariño, "Towards a Culture of Freedom: On Saying 'No' to the American Bases," *On Wastes and National Dignity: Views and Voices on the US Military Bases* (Quezon City, Philippines: International Affairs Desk, National Council of Churches in the Philippines, 1988), p. 74.

"We ought rather utterly to defy them [*conspuere in ipsorum capita*, literally, to *spit on their very heads*] than obey them."[47] Only a subjugated consciousness does not know how to get angry in spite of obvious oppression.

While the immediate reaction after this realization of oppression is anger, that anger should not be thought of as temporary or fleeting. Anger plays a positive role in the long and protracted struggle; it nourishes the oppressed to keep on resisting. "I am a believer in anger, well-focused anger," says William Coffin, because "if you lower your anger at oppression, you lower your compassion for the oppressed."[48] Anger is an expression of a people who are hurt and still care, not only for themselves but also for others, not only for the immediate future, but also for the hoped-for future. Anger is also an expression of hope. We should not only be angry because we are hurt or others are hurt, or because we care, but also because we hope. A people imbued with hope know how to get angry. Anger is a daughter of hope, as is courage, says Augustine. We need both: "anger so that what cannot be may not be," and "courage so that what must be, will be."[49]

Our society needs people who still know how to get angry because they care and because they are hurt. People who have been calloused or have lived their lives in conformity to the dominant mindset are not capable of crying anymore or of getting angry, except when a waiter in a restaurant gives them the wrong order for their *hors d'oeuvres* or main menu. With "state terrorism" running amok in many so-called Third World countries with the support of the affluent West, it is really time to get angry. What is disgusting is when people are not disgusted anymore with the disgusting situation.

When the oppressed people start to get angry, the powers-that-be are the most threatened. All that they see is the impatience and hatred that the poor have toward them. Threatened, they only see anger in the form of hatred; however, they fail to see that the anger of the poor, expressed in their resistance, is not necessarily the opposite of love, that in it lies the potential for healing through which the humanity of both can be restored. This anger, guided by a proper analysis of society and a humanizing orientation against an oppressive system, may be properly called *passion*.[50]

---

[47]John Calvin, *Calvini Opera, Corpus Reformatorum*, edition XLI, 25, quoted in John McNeill, "John Calvin on Civil Government," *Calvinism and the Political Order*, ed. George Hunt (Philadelphia: The Westminster Press, 1965), p. 40. Emphasis added. .

[48]William Coffin in Tonnya M. Kennedy, "Using Anger to Promote Compassion," *Vanderbilt Register* (3–10 February 1992), p. 2.

[49]Augustine, cited by Sharon Ruiz, "A Search for a Relevant Asian Ecclesiology: Philippine Perspectives," *Tugón*, vol. 9, no. 3 (1989), p. 222.

[50]See Susan Brooks Thistlethwaite, *Sex, Race, and God: Christian Feminism in Black and White* (New York: Crossroad, 1989), pp. 22–24.

From Anger to Passion for Justice: Annunciation

Anger, born out of suffering, realization, and hope, not only expresses itself in the negation of the negative or in denunciation, but also in annunciation. This anger denounces the claim to finality of the present order of things as it announces the possibility of a new tomorrow. When anger, born out of suffering and hope, is guided by proper tools of social analysis, it is transformed into a passion for justice. In this conversion of anger to passion, anger, hope, and reason intersect in order to achieve a worthwhile goal. What we have here is not a mere expression of pent-up feelings or the desire to be destructive, but a desire to be constructive; what we have here is the proclamation of the good news.

Eschatology as a Critique and Subversion of Order

Eschatological hope not only generates denunciation of the negative and the annunciation of the coming future, it also calls for a critique and subversion of the dominant order. The annunciation of the new undercuts the foundation of the old and questions its basic presuppositions. Oppressed people who are capable of hoping threaten the established powers because hoping for the new and better is actually to proclaim the death of the old; it is actually to subvert the old. The foundation in which the old oppressive order finds its legitimacy is questioned and subverted. Appropriating Paul Lehman and José Míguez Bonino's thoughts on the issue of the critique of order, I would say that eschatological hope subverts the priority given to law and order in favor of freedom (Lehman), that eschatological hope subverts the priority given to order in favor of justice (Míguez Bonino).[51]

The established power by its very logic is driven to preserve the order. It will attempt by any means available to prevent the coming of the new; it will attempt by any means to hold at bay the coming of the future. For the established powers, order and law are given prioritization. The establishment logic, asserts Lehman, operates on the understanding "that order is the presupposition and the condition of freedom; that law is the foundation and the criterion of justice." [52] Freedom operates within a given order and does not question the order. Likewise, justice has to be justice only within the parameters set by the existing law — a law that supports the order, a law whose foundation is power and authority. And through ideological blindness, the prioritization of law and order finally leads to the belief that the

---

[51]Paul Lehman, *The Transfiguration of Politics* (New York: Harper and Row, 1975), pp. 238-290; also José Míguez Bonino, *Towards a Christian Political Ethics* (Philadelphia: Fortress Press, 1983), p. 86. See, for more discussion, Oscar S. Suarez, "Theology of Struggle: Reflections on Praxis and Location," *Tugón,* vol. 6, no. 3 (1986), pp. 47-60.

[52]Lehman, *The Transfiguration of Politics,* p. 238.

reigning law and order is the unquestionable given, as if descended from heaven. The existing law and order, which in reality is a product of history, has now acquired the status of the natural—it is God given. This is an apotheosis of idolatry.

Liberating consciousness, which is expectant of the new, calls for a reversal of the establishment logic. For liberating consciousness, continues Lehman,

> freedom is the presupposition and condition of order: order is not the presupposition and the condition of freedom; justice is the foundation and the criterion of law: law is not the foundation and the criterion of justice.[53]

The above point finds a similar note with Míguez Bonino as he asserts the priority of justice over order, that is, that the right question is not "what degree of justice (liberation of the poor) is compatible with the maintenance of order?" but "what kind of order, which order is compatible with the exercise of justice (the right of the poor)?"[54] The controlling hermeneutical key is justice, not order.

When the priority of justice to order is inverted, along with the acceptance of the present order as God-given, God has taken the side of the defenders of the order. To work for the transformation of the present order is a crime not only against humanity but against God, thereby justifying a crusade against those who are working for meaningful change. Tortures, "salvagings" (extrajudicial executions), and various forms of coercion and repression are perpetrated against the people without the slightest compunction because of strong religious and moral justification. It should not surprise us that the perpetrators of these most abhorrent and detestable crimes against humanity are very religious; they usually sit in the front pews during worship services and masses and volunteer as *hermano/a mayores* of fiestas. What the Gospel of John says is true, "the hour is coming when whoever kills you will think he is offering service to God" (John 16:2).

On the other hand, behavior that conforms to the established order is encouraged. The conformist is a well-adjusted person. *"Maayo 'ning tawhana kay walay libog"* ("This person is good, because she or he does not complain"). "To approve without thinking" the "wrongking" instead of the "ranking" and to believe that the "boss does no wrong" are encouraged.[55]

---

[53]Ibid., p. 240.

[54]Miguéz Bonino, *Towards a Christian Political Ethics*, p. 86.

[55]I owe these ideas and expressions from Benoni Yepes, an active church member of the United Church of Christ in the Philippines, San Isidro, Tomas Oppus, Southern Leyte. The political teaser on "wrongking" instead of "ranking" is a popular complaint among the public school teachers. For further understanding of what the dominant society considers as "good" behavior as well as "mal-adjusted" behavior and for an interpretation of the notion of "adaptation" vis-a-vis "integration," see Paulo Freire, *Education for Critical Consciousness* (New York: Continuum, 1973).

THE TRANSFIGURATION OF SUFFERING AND HOPE INTO THE POLITICS OF STRUGGLE

What Kind or Which Kind of Politics/Theology?
The Relation of Faith and Politics Reinstated

Suffering is the arena in which the theological and the political interact. It is a life and death issue, and when death and life matters or when death and life questions are raised, they are questions both political and theological. When I say life and death I am not focusing on what is called the "existential limit dimensions" understood existentially or phenomenologically or through "eidetic" reductions of everyday experience.[56] Questions about where to get the next meal, about health, work, life, and living are questions of theology and politics. Religious and political questions intersect, interact, and interweave because, as Ruiz said, they are at their profound depths questions of life and death, of faith and unfaith.[57]

If suffering is a question in which theology and politics intersect, this is certainly true with dreaming and hoping. If suffering is theopolitical, and suffering propels the people to dream and hope, then it is sound to conclude that dreaming and hoping are also theopolitical. Dreaming and hoping are attempts of the human to deny that which denies life and craves for something better, therefore they are matters of life and death, hence theopolitical.

When the sighs, longings, aspirations, and hopes of the people for that which is different from their current experience—which is a matter of life and death—lead to the quest for what is fundamentally new and better, the interweaving of the theological and political becomes more and more pronounced. In this search for something new and better, I would say that the interweaving of the political and religious is more apparent, for the theological becomes clearly constitutive of the political and the political emerges as a mediating nexus in the realization of the theological. Gutiérrez

---

[56]See David Tracy, *Blessed Rage for Order: The New Pluralism in Theology* (New York: The Seabury Press, 1975), particularly pp. 91–118. In these pages Tracy carefully analyzes the religious dimension through the idea of "limit" to delineate it from other dimensions of human experience. Paul Tillich's "ultimate concern" can be classified as a "limit" concept. See Paul Tillich, *Systematic Theology,* vol. 1–3 (Chicago: The University of Chicago Press, 1957). Also Langdon Gilkey, *Naming the Whirlwind: The Renewal of God-Language* (Indianapolis and New York: The Dobbs-Merrill Company, 1969). Cf. Welch, *Communities of Resistance and Solidarity: A Feminist Theology of Liberation,* specifically pp. 38–39, in her criticism of theologies that are preoccupied with the task of disclosing the universals of faith and correlating these to the ontological structure of existence, but that fail to address the particular and concrete issues.

[57]Ruiz, "Towards a Theology of Politics: Meditations on Religion, Politics, and Social Transformation," *Tugón,* p. 32.

asserted a similar point when he emphasized that faith and political action enter a correct and fruitful relationship only through the project of creating a new type of human being in a different sort of society.[58]

Suffering, hope, and struggle for the new and better are all matters of life and death; therefore, they are theopolitical questions. In these questions theology and politics interact, intersect, and interweave. For the Filipinos, one of the quintessential idioms of this inextricable link between religion and the affairs of everyday life is the people's popular religiosity. If popular religiosity, which is actually the religiosity that has been practiced by the people, is thrown out, the privatization of Christian faith or the dichotomization of theology and politics would gain ground. With the capitalist and secularist worldview and ethos saturating the texture of Filipino life, the dichotomization of the political and the theological is already on the way. Consistent with secular society is the confinement of the realm of religion to the inner chamber of the private, perhaps a concern of women.

But to speak of the dichotomization of religion and politics and the privatization of religion is actually misleading and deceptive. It is deceptive because it hides the operative "faith" that runs societies that claim to be secular; it conceals the faith or belief of the Western world, said Gibson Winter, "in progress through domination and accumulation."[59] On top of this, the dividing of religion and politics actually works to the advantage of the reigning social arrangement on two counts, argued John Kavanaugh: It destabilizes the transformative power of religion and it "seduces the religious impulse into a stance of mere accommodation to political and economic power."[60]

It appears here that dichotomization actually works to the advantage of preserving the status quo and of effectively concealing the reality that politics and religion continue to interweave. Status quo politics is in actuality the kind of politics that is at work in the dichotomization, not only because religion has accommodated to politics by its silence, but also because the status quo politics has become natural. Thus, what is considered the meddling of religion in what is political is only applied against those who question the dominant political order, not against those who support the status quo. Bishop Francisco Claver's letter to the Roman Catholic Bishops of the Philippines is useful on this point.

When a churchman praises martial law [referring to the martial law in the Philippines] as good, even as the will of God for our people, that is not

---

[58]Gutiérrez, *A Theology of Liberation,* p. 138.

[59]Gibson Winter, "Notes for a Socio-Political Religious Biography," *Religious Studies Review,* vol. 10, no. 4 (October 1984), p. 329. See a similar point by Ruiz, "Towards a Theology of Politics: Meditations on Religion, Politics, and Social Transformation," *Tugón,* p. 24.

[60]John F. Kavanaugh, *Following Christ in a Consumer Society* (Maryknoll, NY.: Orbis Books, 1981, revised 1991), p. xii.

politics (I use the word here in the disparaging way it often is used among us)? When another churchman criticizes the conduct of martial law as subversive of human rights, that is politics?[61]

It appears then that the question is not so much the meddling of the theological in what is political and the political in what is traditionally construed as theological, but what kind or which kind of politics, what kind or which kind of theology. This does not mean of course that we have to go back to the old unity of religion and politics under the Constantinian or theocratic paradigm, but it does point to the fact that meddling in political matters has been applied only to that which threatens the status quo and the interest of the power wielders. Christian charity or giving food to the hungry is acceptable as well as not meddling in politics, but when concerned Christians, like Bishop Dom Helder Camara, ask why the poor are poor, that is political, at worst, communist inspired.

Because the primary question is what kind or which kind of theology and what kind or which kind of politics, a politics of struggle must necessarily choose in the Philippine context the theology of struggle as its *kasama* (companion). And this means not just the awareness of the political character of one's religious beliefs, but a politics that chooses for transformative praxis. Linked with transformative praxis, it means that theology has become a political theology; it means that the truth of faith is linked with a world-transforming practice. To this politics of struggle I now turn.

From Suffering and Hope to Politics of Struggle

Extreme suffering may lead to fatalism, cynicism, and despair; it may lead to flight or daydreaming either by romanticizing the past or by projecting a place of total comfort above (space) or beyond (time). With the emergence of the consciousness of freedom, the sufferer is saved from resignation and despair and is caught by the power of hope. Because hope is not based on the dream of the perfectability of the future but in the nonnecessity of the present,[62] it points to the future as it grounds one's feet, not on the quicksand, but on the hard rocks of the present.

Because hope sees the present reality in light of a better future, it encourages the oppressed and those in solidarity with them to critically analyze the forces that block the coming of the desired future. In other words, it girds the oppressed for the concrete politics of struggle. Only in struggle and by struggle are suffering and hope saved from being a futuristic escape; only by struggle will the oppressed forge a better tomorrow; only by struggle will heaven come to dwell on earth; only by struggle will the

---

[61]Bishop Francisco F. Claver, *The Stones Will Cry Out: Grassroots Pastorals* (Maryknoll, NY.: Orbis Books, 1978), p. 154.

[62]Alves, *A Theology of Human Hope,* p. 15.

memory of the dead be resurrected; only by struggle can parents truly love their children and future generations. It is thus fitting that after my account of suffering and hope the theme of struggle should follow. The theology of struggle, as I analyze it, points in this direction.

The Vocation of the New Person:
A Spirituality of Political Engagement

Emerging from the ravages of a history that has left them without a future, we can sense here a new "conversion experience" (spirituality) that the people are undergoing.[63] The theologians of the theology of struggle or "TOS" have emphasized this new conversion experience (spirituality), especially as made explicit by Bishop Julio Labayen when in the later publications "TOS" expanded into "TSOS" (Theology and **Spirituality** of Struggle).[64] We have here the signs of a new person embodied in the community who has come to realize that the creation of a new tomorrow is her or his vocation. This "new consciousness believes that the new man and the new tomorrow," claimed Rubem Alves, "are to be created in and through the activity which is political in character. Politics would be the practice of freedom, the activity of the free man for the creation of a new tomorrow."[65] From the start of this chapter I introduced the notion that suffering and hope are political, but nowhere is this clearer than in the shaping of a new tomorrow. Shaping the new tomorrow means a concrete political praxis inspired by those who have been marginalized but who have arisen from their oppressed condition.

This conversion experience that I have referred to is the kind of conversion experience that people involved in the struggle have undergone. Basically, this spiritual journey starts with the common belief, especially among those long exploited, that their situation is natural or the will of God. When you ask them "How are you?", the usual response is *"Asya la gihap"* (Waray) or *"Mao gihapon"* (Cebuano), "as usual" or "nothing new." Later on, through the long process of expanding their horizon and awareness, the people come to the understanding that their situation is a product of history, but they are overwhelmed by the immensity of the problem. So they say: *"Tinuod na, pero wala tay mahimong mga mayuk-mok"* ("Yes, there is a problem, but we, lowly people, cannot do anything about it"). Oftentimes, one hears the remark: *"Ayaw na gani pagpa Rizal Rizal kay mahal na ang semento"* ("Don't play like Rizal [a national hero

---

[63]The theology of struggle sees this "conversion experience" to the task of social transformation as a new spirituality. See a similar point in Gustavo Gutiérrez, *The Power of the Poor in History*, trans. Robert Barr (Maryknoll, NY.: Orbis Books, 1983), p. 21.

[64]Bishop Julio Xavier Labayen, "Introduction," in *Witness and Hope Amid Struggle: Toward a Theology and Spirituality of Struggle*, Book 2, pp. ix-xi.

[65]Alves, *A Theology of Human Hope*, p 16.

who was executed by the Spaniards] because we cannot afford to build a monument for you [the cement is quite expensive]"). A new conversion is achieved, although this is not the end, when an individual or a community can say, "Yes, there is something wrong, and through our unity and with the *awa* (grace or help) of God, we can change it."

Empowering the De-Peopled People:
Awakening the Sense of Peoplehood

People who have gained the consciousness of freedom are people who have discovered power in themselves. As longtime "absents" in history, they now assert their presence in reclaiming their power to "reread" the social realities and "remake" their destiny, a destiny that has been imposed on them from on top.[66] This makes it clear that a new sense of conviction and peoplehood has engulfed the people. Regaining this sense of peoplehood is not, however, enough. The oppressed people should not only be empowered by right principles and strong convictions, but must also know the principle of power. To engage in the shaping of a new tomorrow—a political activity—is facing the principle of power itself. Politics is primarily a question of power relations. This means understanding the basis of power and how it operates, that this power may not only be converted from a power without love to a power with love, but also to a power with love that is politically viable. Knowledge of the locations of power would help to demystify it and bring it down to the banal, to show that the question of power is a question not only for kings but for the common people as well.[67]

Furthermore, understanding the sources and the principle of power is necessary in the task of empowering people. Although it is usually understood that there are a few who control power, this power could also be undermined by the people in the direction of the common weal. Only an empowered people can do this, and only an empowered people can really be called a people. It appears here that empowerment is both a means (also a task) and a goal. Shaping the future involves the task of empowering people, so that a people may emerge; it involves the building of "people's power."

Empowering the people, which is both a means and a goal, is a necessary move for them to abandon misery and to prevent hope from becoming an escape. When the direction of the supposed empowerment of people moves

---

[66]Gutiérrez, *The Power of the Poor in History,* p. 21.

[67]Míguez Bonino, *Towards a Christian Political Ethics,* pp. 94–95. Power, for Míguez Bonino, has four locations: (1) the power to affect matters related to economic decisions, (2) the power to affect matters related to political decisions, (3) the power to affect and control matters related to ideological decisions, and (4) the power to affect and control matters regarding force. These four locations of power actually include all the angles: economics, politics, culture, and the military.

contrary to the interest of the people, it is not people's empowerment and not "people's power," but "people power."[68] It means the use of the power of the people against their interests for the benefit of the powerful. This phenomenon stands out in the Philippines, where the achievement of people's power—such as that of the formation of basic Christian communities, people's cooperatives, and people's revolt against the dictator Marcos—is countered by "people power" or is bastardized into right-wing vigilantism, like the use of religious fanatical groups (e.g., Alsa Masa, Tadtad, Nakasaka, etc.) by the ultra rightists in their counterinsurgency campaign.

We should not confuse people's power and people power, for the empowered people do not give finality to the present oppressive power but remain open to the new and better. Fanatical groups, unlike the empowered people, can be charged with betraying hope and the fundamentally new. These groups have not really been empowered by the eschatological hope because they are being used to forestall the future and defend the present, a present that is not their own but that of their masters. On the contrary, wounded by oppression and energized by hope, the rising people refuse to become instruments of the power wielders, something to which the ultra-rightist religious fanatics have succumbed. Hugo Assmann helped to elucidate this emphasis when he said: "The dialectical polarity set up by eschatological 'dissatisfaction' on account of what is not yet an effective anticipation of what can and should be, disqualifies the Christian from any form of accommodation to the status quo."[69]

A Political Incarnation of the New-Found Freedom for the "Not Yet": Freedom for Ideology

A person of principle is a person with power, but this power of principle is not enough, as I pointed out earlier. A person of principle must also learn the principle of power in order to handle properly the powers-that-be and help form the "powers that will be" for the service of the common weal.[70] But the harnessing of power to a desired goal must further lead to political specificity, and for this a choice has to be made between competing political platforms. This choice has to be made because the desired tomorrow cannot be actualized by mere generalizations. This is where commitment takes a specific shape, which many of the well-intentioned Christians are not willing to make. But the choice has to be made despite the risks involved,

---

[68]See Ponciano Bennagen, "People's Power as an Evolutionary Process Toward Social Transformation," in *Nagliliyab: The Burning Bush* (Quezon City, Philippines: Claretian Publications, 1986), pp. 79–83.

[69]Hugo Assmann, *Practical Theology of Liberation,* foreword by Gustavo Gutiérrez, preface by Ernesto Cardenal, trans. Paul Burns (London: Search Limited Press, 1975), p. 68.

[70]See de la Torre, "The Philippines: Christians and the Politics of Liberation," *Tugón,* p. 64.

even the risk of error. It is possible that one can break the egg without producing an omelette, but it is already absolutely certain that no omelette can be produced without breaking the egg.

Many well-intentioned Christians who are sympathetic to the plight of the people and see the need for some changes do not operate with the same motivation as the defenders of the status quo. However, because what seems to occupy their sights are the imperfections of the people's movement in light of the kingdom of God, they contribute to the people's reluctance to search for alternative ways of human dwelling and relating; they tend to pour cold water on the enthusiasm of the people even before it has taken hold. In a situation in which the people are still beginning to regain their strength and to figure out a political platform that best serves their interest, the "eschatological proviso" may contribute to the people's reluctance to take a specific political option.[71] Eschatological proviso de-ideologizes, commented Juan Luis Segundo, "because it wields the sword of criticism even before ideologies have time to be effective and arouse real enthusiasm."[72] Though the eschatological proviso seems progressive, de la Torre considered that, in effect, "it accepted the existing system, at least by default."[73] A people suffering under an oppressive status quo will not be encouraged to look for alternatives if they are always told that all systems are imperfect.

This criticism of the eschatological proviso should not be viewed as a total rejection of it, for I believe in its importance. The imperfections of the people's movements are more than enough for us to realize that they should not be given absolute status, that they should always be put under judgment. At this juncture, however, the eschatological proviso can be used to discourage the needed political option. It is because of this danger that I would like to put the relevance of this proviso within the purview of one's commitment for social transformation rather than outside of this specific political commitment. Outside of this commitment, it only discourages political choice. Within the commitment for transformation, it serves a positive purpose by way of negative critique. Rather than giving weight to

---

[71] Johann Baptist Metz, *Theology of the World,* trans. William Glen-Doepel (New York: Seabury Press, 1969), p. 114. Cf. Juan Luis Segundo, *Liberation of Theology,* trans. John Drury (Maryknoll, NY.: Orbis Books, 1976), pp. 125–153. See a similar criticism by de la Torre, *Touching Ground, Taking Root,* p. 179. Cf. Welch, *A Feminist Ethic of Risk,* pp. 106–111. The question of eschatological proviso is a point in which liberation theology has accused political theology of falling into. "European theology," as Assmann observed, "seems to find great difficulty in embracing this positive form of ideology [political platform] as an indispensable tool in choosing an instrument of analysis." And "this constantly incapacitates them in their efforts to marry the data resulting from analysis with the references provided by faith" (Assmann, *Practical Theology of Liberation,* p. 93.).

[72] Segundo, *Liberation Theology,* p. 126. Segundo's criticism includes Moltmann and Alves and the whole of political theology. Alves is accused by Segundo of being in close affinity to political theology.

[73] de la Torre, *Touching Ground, Taking Root,* p. 179.

the "pause" before embracing ideology, I would emphasize the other side of Levi Oracion's point, that "we should embrace any ideology in an eschatological sense," because the question is no longer that we should have ideology or not.[74]

What does embracing any ideology in an eschatological sense mean? It frees the person from absolute choice, but not to abdicate choice; it is to embrace ideology or an ideological platform without giving it an absolute status, that is, that it is *provisional* although not *arbitrary*.[75] But, how can one be encouraged to take the risk of social transformation in what is provisional? Here de la Torre is insightful. He quoted a nun who in his judgment had set forth a proper stance: "What I choose to give myself to is imperfect. I have no illusions that it is perfection. But it is in this and through this that I commit myself to perfection."[76]

There is no illusion that a political project is perfect, but it is a sign of maturity to give oneself to the provisional, hoping that one contributes in the journey toward perfection. It is not easy to hold beliefs for which one is willing to die and still entertain some shades of doubt, yet this is what precisely the *quaerens* in the scholastic formula *fides quaerens intellectum* mean, asserted Dorothee Sölle.[77] It is not easy to die for one's belief and still be open to new insights, said Ian Barbour, "but it is still precisely such a combination of commitment and inquiry that constitutes religious maturity."[78] Commitment without the element of doubt has no defenses against dogmaticism and its most destructive cousin — fanaticism. Rollo May is right in advancing the idea that

> commitment is healthiest when it is not **without** doubt, but **in spite of** doubt. To believe fully and at the same moment to have doubts is not all a contradiction: It presupposes a greater respect for truth, an awareness that truth always goes beyond anything that can be said or done at any given moment.[79]

If there is one sickness that the ultra-rightist sectarian and the ultra-dogmatic leftist sectarian share in common, in spite of the fact that they are engaged in mortal combat, it is that "they both suffer from the absence of doubt."[80]

---

[74]Levi Oracion, "God's Dialectic of Liberation," *ATESEA Occasional Papers,* no. 2.

[75]de la Torre, *Touching Ground, Taking Root,* p. 84.

[76]Ibid., p. 180.

[77]Dorothee Sölle, *Thinking About God: An Introduction to Theology* (Philadelphia: Trinity Press International, 1990), p. 4.

[78]Barbour, *Myths, Models and Paradigms: A Comparative Study in Science and Religion,* p. 136.

[79]Rollo May, *The Courage to Create* (New York: W. W. Norton and Company, 1975), p. 21.

[80]Paulo Freire, *Pedagogy of the Oppressed,* trans. Myra Bergman Ramos (New York: Herder and Herder, 1972), p. 23, citing the journalist Marcio Moreira Alves. Cf. Welch, *Communities of Resistance and Solidarity: A Feminist Theology of Liberation,* in which she cautions liberation theology's lack of skepticism. This skepticism, for Welch, is not based on

DISCERNING GOD'S PRESENCE IN THE SUFFERING, HOPE, AND STRUGGLE OF A PEOPLE: OPTION FOR THE VICTIMS

In the manner that I pose the issue of eschatological proviso within one's option for political praxis, I also pose God's activity within the commitment of those who are giving themselves to the project of a better tomorrow. It is not because God comes last; in fact, all along I have made it known that the struggle has always been construed as theological as much as it is political. The purpose of putting this notion of God at the end of this chapter is to avoid the pitfall of "supernaturalism"; it is to avoid the impression of making God a "substitute" for human activity, rather than a "plus," to use Assmann's language.[81] God is not outside of the struggle for a better tomorrow or outside pulling the people to act (Aristotelian *primum movens*),[82] but is present through human activity. Filipinos know that *"Nasa Diyos ang awa, nasa tao ang gawa"* (literally, "God gives grace, human beings do the labor"). Neither is this God "above" doing something for the people (*deus ex machina*) or in the "gaps" and "existential limits," but in the "shapes" and "spaces" of freedom by way of human activity.

The interest in any God-talk in this work is not primarily for God's sake but for human sake; it is not to prove the being of God and God's existence (God's reality is presupposed) but for the sake of human living; it is because a notion of God, in spite of problems involved, affects how we view the world and organize our lives (ethical implications).[83] The nonpersons, after centuries of living under the culture of silence, are now erupting. They have emerged from the captivity of suffering without hope to a suffering that generates hope, and have struggled so that this hope may come to concrete fruition. This, as I see it, is the proper locus in which to discern God's liberating activity—a liberating activity not in spite of the people, but through the people.

---

the idea of "eschatological reservation," but on the awareness of the limitation of discourse (pp. 84–85). For more discussion on this issue see Michel Foucault, particularly his stance that he described as "hyper-and pessimistic activism," in "On the Genealogy of Ethics: An Overview of Work in Progress," *Foucault Reader,* ed. P. Rabinow (New York: Pantheon Books, 1984), p. 343.

[81]Assmann, *Practical Theology of Liberation,* p. 96.

[82]Alves, *Theology of Human Hope,* p. 59.

[83]See Gordon Kaufman, *The Theological Imagination: Constructing the Concept of God* (Philadelphia: The Westminster Press, 1981). Because one's understanding of God affects how one lives, an exploration on a possible construction of the concept of God is useful. For Kaufman the God concept is "mythical" —that is, it organizes how we view the world and consequently our lives. Regarding the ethical implication of a theological statement, Leonardo Boff gives an example in the notion of God as "Father" [also as mother], which ethically would mean that we are all brothers and sisters. To say that God is our parent is to speak of a new sense of community. See his book, *The Lord's Prayer: A Prayer of Integral Liberation,* trans. Theodore Morrow (Maryknoll, NY.: Orbis Books; Melbourne: Dove Communications, 1983), pp. 30–31.

Consistent with my identification of the suffering, hope, and struggle of the people as the theological loci, I would propose as my first point in construing God, drawing some insights from Peter Hogdson's recent book *God in History: Shapes of Freedom*, that this God should be discerned in the *interweaving* of the *actual* condition and the *possibility* of the new, of the is and the ought, of prefiguration and refiguration, of fact and fiction.[84] God is discernible not simply as a God of the future, or of the past, or even of the present, but in the intersection, at the point where the weft of the actual (product of past and present) and warp of the possible (future) meet.

In our world, where we have seen encouraging signs that the people's struggle has succeeded in creating some "democratic spaces," but is also constantly undermined by the forces of "closure," it appears fitting to speak of God in the interweaving of the actual and the possible. Locating God at this interweaving is, I believe, a valid stance, because we can discern God's presence in the very concrete, but also not fully disclosed. Furthermore, this stance also prevents us from identifying the actual with the absolute, while we continue to thirst for what is to be.

Following the first point of locating God at the interweaving of the actual and the possible, I would add as the second point that where the interweaving occurs, a "space" is created, a breathing (spirit) space, or what the Filipinos have been fond of describing after the ouster of Marcos as a "democratic space." This is the space where we can discern God's activity, the space where we can see God, though only dimly. However, this space is not an empty space but a "clearing" in which freedom is taking shape. God as *Geist* (Spirit) is never without a gestalt (shape, figure, or form), claims Hodgson, as he appropriated the insights of Hegel via the thoughts of Ernst Troelstch.[85] Yes, God is not without a shape, but is discernable in the "shapes of freedom," that is, in the transformative praxis of the struggling communities. To search for these shapes of freedom, one need not raise one's eyes to lofty places, but look rather in the "margins" or in the "cracks" of the dominant social order. Making these "cracks" bigger would be a participation in the liberating activity.

Finally, to speak of God in the shapes of freedom through the interweaving of the actual and the possible is not enough if it is not explicitly stated that consistent with the people's struggle for a better tomorrow is to speak of God as taking sides; God is not neutral. The victims must have this kind of God, not a neutral God in the face of injustice. Rebecca Asedillo made this point so movingly via the story of a peasant:

---

[84]Peter C. Hodgson, *God in History: Shapes of Freedom* (Nashville, Tennessee: Abingdon Press, 1989), p. 161. The idea of prefiguration, configuration, and refiguration is Hodgson's appropriation of Paul Ricoeur's thoughts. For additional background see Ricoeur's work, *Time and Narrative,* trans. Kathleen McLaughlin and David Pellauer, 3 vols. (Chicago: University of Chicago Press, 1984, 1985, 1988).

[85]Hodgson, *God in History: Shapes of Freedom,* p. 207.

One peasant was talking to his priest: "I'm fighting to get my proper share of the harvest, so I have taken my landlord to court. But when I bring him to court, I fight with him. When I fight with him, I get angry with him. When I fight with him, I am told, 'You're not a very good Christian, because Christians are not supposed to get angry and to fight.' Then I go to church and I ask what they have to say. And the Church would say, 'Do you not see, I am a mother and you are my children — the landlord is my child and the peasant is my child — and I cannot take sides.' What kind of a mother is that? When a young, weak child is being beaten by an elder child, the mother takes sides. In so doing, she does not stop from being a mother."[86]

Consequently, to speak of God taking sides means that the *Geist* has taken form through the humanity of the society's victims. This enables us to say that the voice of the victims is the voice of God (*vox victimarum, vox Dei*), to construe God in the people's journey as animating hope, and, lastly, to speak of God as struggle. God has taken the form of humanity's victims in the gestalt of their struggle, not because they are morally better, but because they are "dying before their time," to use a phrase from Gutiérrez.[87]

Thus the option for the poor is the way to know God. And because the poor are the ones who have remained open to the fundamentally new, to opt for the victims is actually to opt for the coming of a new day; it is to opt for the possibility of the emergence of a new humanity. By way of the poor, not despite the poor, we should start seeking our authentic humanity. This chapter allows us to turn to the next chapter of this study, which focuses on the search for an anthropology that is supportive of the dream and aspirations to forge a new Filipino.

---

[86]Asedillo, "Faith in Struggle," *SPI Faith and Ideology Series,* p. 16.

[87]Gutiérrez, answering the question, Why must the Christians take the side of the poor? Cited in Ruiz, "Towards a Theology of Politics: Meditations on Religion, Politics, and Social Transformation," *Tugón,* p. 21.

4

Struggle for Historical Selfhood
and Humanity

Suffering, yet hoping and struggling for the creation of a new community, is the mark of a people who has experienced the foretaste of a new humanity or a new historical selfhood. In the suffering and struggling Filipino people this new historical selfhood and humanity is taking expression; in the Filipino struggle to construct a life-giving community this new humanity is now taking shape. This emerging new humanity and selfhood cannot be fully discerned outside the struggle toward a liberating community, and, conversely, apart from this struggle and experience of an emerging community this selfhood and humanity cannot be fully grasped. Thus, the search for humanity and community is inseparable, for there is no humanity outside of a community.

Focusing at this juncture on the search for selfhood and humanity, I would say that our concept of humanity bears upon the kind of dwelling we all long for. This point was echoed by the participants of the Consultation on Theological Education for Christian Ministry in Asia (Philippines, 1977):

> The yearning of Asian peoples for a truly democratic order, as opposed to highly centralized if not totalitarian regimes, is an expression of a search for authentic sense of humanity and this can be interpreted by the Christian community as an encounter with the Holy in the realm of politics.[1]

Selfhood and the search for a community, from this quote, are inseparable. Selfhood and community interweave with each other, with selfhood often understood as the "soul." Anwar Barkat, speaking of Asia, advanced the interpretation that Asian struggle is a revolution within the soul as it is for national independence. As he put it: "It is because of this [Western colonization] that the struggle for national independence in Asia was a

---

[1]Emerito Nacpil and Douglas Elwood, eds., *The Human and the Holy: Asian Perspectives in Christian Theology* (Quezon City, Philippines: New Day Publishers, 1978), p. 7.

struggle for the 'discovery' of Asia in terms of its own *historical selfhood* which had been totally submerged under colonialism."[2]

If there is one thing that people from the right, left, or center of the political spectrum in the Philippines are in agreement with, it is I think the point that one's view on anthropology bears on how the human dwelling is to be organized and the cosmos construed. What Barkat refers to as historical selfhood, Ruiz speaks of as *political subjecthood*, which he interprets as the soul of the politics of social transformation. For him, the struggle for a better society is a question of "who we are, what we are, and what we hope for." Speaking of the Philippine society in particular, Ruiz asserted that the struggle for the creation of a democratic society is at the same time a struggle for "authentic political subjecthood."[3]

Although coming from a different ideological persuasion, Emerito Nacpil spoke of the need for the formation of a new Filipino which, theologically speaking, is a search for a new anthropology.[4] Nacpil seemed to suggest that if a desirable Philippines is to come, a new Filipino must be born. For him, the Christian gospel has something to say in the search for a new Filipino, a new humanity.

The dictator Ferdinand Marcos also perceived the connections between building a new society and building a new humanity—a new Filipino. Marcos's vision of a new society certainly required a new Filipino, and he used the various machineries of the state, even for repression, to create a new Filipino under a new society. His new society's slogan reflects this: *"Bagong buhay sa bagong lipunan"* ("New life under the new society"). His critics however were quick to reword his slogan: *"Mabahong buhay sa mabahong lipunan"* ("A stinking life under the stinking society").

Although there is an agreement on the need to search for a new anthropology, the way this anthropology has been construed is varied and, consequently, with varied political implications, that is, with various notions of how the human dwelling is to be organized. I know that the supermarket is already saturated with various brands of theological anthropology, yet in spite of this cacophony of interpretations, I advance a notion of anthropology with the intention that this may promote the Filipino struggle for selfhood or subjecthood and for a dwelling that is not only democratic but also "biocratic."[5]

---

[2]Anwar M. Barkat, "Reconstruction of Political Ethics in an Asian Perspective," in *Perspectives on Political Ethics: An Ecumenical Enquiry,* ed. Koson Srisang (Geneva: World Council of Churches Publications; Washington, D.C.: Georgetown University Press, 1983), pp. 54–55. Emphasis supplied.

[3]Lester Edwin J. Ruiz, "Philippine Politics as a Peoples' Quest for Authentic Political Subjecthood," *Alternatives,* 11 (1986), pp. 505–534.

[4]Emerito Nacpil, "The Gospel for the New Filipino," *Asian Voices in Christian Theology,* ed. and with an introduction by Gerald H. Anderson (Maryknoll, NY.: Orbis Books, 1976), p. 124.

[5]It has been suggested by ecologists that we need to be concerned not only with "democracy"

In unfolding this quest — a quest that is both theological and political — I argued at the very outset of this chapter that the quest for humanity is constitutive of the search for a dwelling that is liberative and liberating. From this starting premise I embark on a deconstructive critique by exposing the "universalist" pretensions of the dominant anthropologies that have emerged from the centers of global power, contending that these anthropologies are of one mind with the political vision and project of the dominant centers. Moreover, I point out that these conceptions of the human being in the dominant centers of the world have found their way into the periphery through conquest and colonization. Taking the understanding that conquest is totalistic, even the subjugated people's understanding of their humanity and historical selfhood has been overhauled — Westernized.[6] Unfortunately, Christianity has played a pivotal role in the formation of this confused historical selfhood.

Subsequently, I proceed to expound the new humanity that is emerging among the subjugated peoples and races. I contend that it is from these subjugated peoples that we can find a new humanity in the making. Christian symbols are explored to support this claim.

Finally, I connect this quest for authentic humanity to the Filipino people's struggle, the appropriate anthropology that the struggling Filipinos, I suggest, should adopt, and the political dwelling that this notion of humanity projects.

Instead of approaching anthropology by focusing on the realm of human essence, I push the issue to the experience of real people in their historical situatedness. Whenever I attempt to expound some abstract categories, I make sure that the connections are established with specific communities of people who would bleed when wounded, cry when hurt, laugh when in joy. In other words, I deal with anthropology in the way it is manifested in history, with all its sociopolitical configurations. Maulana Ron Karenga conveys my point:

> Man is only man in a philosophy class or a biology lab. In the world he is African, Asian or South American. He is a Chinese making a cultural

---

but with "biocracy." Democracy as a concept is basically anthropocentric (considers "man" as the measure of all things) and fails to see the interdependence of all life forms in our planet. The move to a biocratic perspective is an expression of a new worldview and a new sensibility. See, for example, Jay B. McDaniel, *Of God and Pelicans: A Theology of Reverence for Life* (Louisville, Kentucky: Westminster/John Knox Press, 1989); McFague, *Models of God: Theology for an Ecological, Nuclear Age*, pp. 3–28.

[6]One lasting legacy of colonization is the colonized people's confusion as to their "historical selfhood." Basic to the struggle of these colonized people then is the search for historical selfhood. See, for example, Barkat, "Reconstruction of Political Ethics in an Asian Perspective," in *Perspectives on Political Ethics: An Ecumenical Enquiry*, p. 54.

revolution, or an Afro-American with soul. He lives by bread and butter, enjoys red beans and rice, or watermelon and ice cream.[7]

Only those who are comfortable can stay at the level of abstract ontological analysis. For someone who is worried about the next day's meal, or eviction, or massacre, a discussion of anthropology at the level of ontological categories is highly irrelevant. In fact, it is by remaining at the abstract level that people who profess to be civilized can engage in a crime that kills many innocent lives through a war completely detached from the sight of actual death by means of computerized sophisticated technologies.

ANTHROPOLOGY FROM THE CENTER TO THE PERIPHERY

Totalizing Anthropology: "The Human Nature"

I do not totally reject the idea that there is something in common among peoples of the world that makes it possible for us to speak of basic human dimensions, "elemental passion," or "tragic elements of human existence," as Edward Farley has carefully argued.[8] But to start from here is methodologically dangerous, especially for the subjugated peoples, for these "universals" of human existence most often are accompanied by unstated notions of what it means to be human based on a particular but dominant worldview and ethos. Although universal categories, argued Thomas Ogletree,

> enjoy formal clarity and precision, they always carry with them unstated and even unacknowledged meanings and assumptions of a more concrete sort. The accompanying meanings and assumptions tend, moreover, to affect decisively the specific applications of the principles themselves. When moral principles are applied without critical awareness of the concrete meanings associated with them, they are apt in their universalistic grandeur to serve as ideological cover for what is actually going on.[9]

---

[7]Maulana Ron Karenga in Archie Hargraves, "The Meanings of Black Power," *Register, The Chicago Theological Seminary,* vol. 59, no. 2 (December 1968), p. 31, quoted by James Cone, *A Black Theology of Liberation,* 2d ed. (Maryknoll, NY.: Orbis Books, 1986), p. 86.

[8]Edward Farley, *Good and Evil: Interpreting a Human Condition* (Minneapolis: Fortress Press, 1990), specifically pp. 1–29. This work tries to defend the method of "reflective ontology" against the so-called postmodern criticisms. Farley, although acknowledging the relevance of criticisms coming from deconstructionists, feminists, and liberation theologians against "ontological universals" (my language), thinks that their criticisms do not warrant absolute rejection of the ontological universals; instead, they are relative criticisms.

[9]Thomas Ogletree, *Hospitality to the Stranger: Dimensions of Moral Understanding* (Philadelphia: Fortress Press, 1985), p. 98.

Because most often we are not aware of the particular dimensions of our universal claims and, in particular, our anthropological notions, we impose on others what for us is human. I point out later how this anthropology from the center has been imposed on the periphery, and for a long time the people of the periphery have been living in a kind of anthropology that is not their own.

People in the center would usually argue that universalist claims are often made by all people. Although ontologically we can say that this is present in all people, what is politically naive about this statement is that this does not take into consideration the question of power and the ability to impose one's worldview and ethos. On the world scale, who can really impose their worldviews if not those also with power? This is also ignorant of the fact that in most third-world countries, such as the Philippines, the perspective of the West has come to be viewed as the ideal. How then could these people project their inferior understanding of themselves in a universalistic fashion? In relation to the powerful West, this is unlikely, although within the national boundary the national center behaves as if it were the universal norm.[10]

In fact, it has been the case in history that the dominant groups always claim that their views are universal, and this is true of anthropologists. They project something "universal" or they project an image of being defenders of "internationalism" over narrow "nationalism" or "regionalism." Even such movements as Western feminism is subject to this suspicion by feminists of "color."[11] Delia Aguilar pointed out in her article on "Feminist Internationalism" that "colonialism can lurk in the shadows of [international] sisterhood," especially through the "essentialist" premises of Western feminism.[12] But who benefits from this bogus internationalism if

---

[10]In the Philippines, Manila has captured that power of a center and establishes itself as the norm. While it is the tail of the elephant in relation to the West, it is the head of the mouse in relation to other provinces in the Philippines. People from this center behave as if their way of life were the norm and expect that other regions follow suit. When people from the provinces cannot follow their expectations, they usually say in a condescending mode, *"Bisaya kasi"* or *"Ilocano kasi"* (because she or he is from the Visayas or Ilocus). This is also evident in matters of language. They consider it strange that there are Filipinos who do not know how to speak Tagalog: "The provincial mice adopt the ways of the city mice." This is a microcosm of the global problem. When a French person (First World) attempts to speak the American English (first-world language), although not in a North American accent, North Americans say, it is "cute," but when a Filipino (someone from a Third World) cannot properly pronounce the North American English (first-world language), it is "garbage."

[11]I am not quite certain if it really helps the liberation struggle to call "nonwhites" as "people of color." Are we suggesting that white is not a color? I recall an interesting comment during the Martin Luther King, Jr. Celebration in Nashville (1992), in which a woman said that whites are people of color too. In fact they have many colors: when exposed to cold weather, they become pale; when they go sunbathing they become tan; when they are angry they get reddish; when they die they become purple.

[12]Delia D. Aguilar, "Feminist Internationalism," in *Solidaridad,* vol. 13, no. 3 (1989–1990), p. 32. Elizabeth Schüssler Fiorenza's essays offers a corrective to the "essentialist" pitfall. See

not the powerful. In fact, by projecting themselves as the *avant garde* of internationalism, the powerful nations give a deceptively benign camouflage to their interventions. Now it is time to expose the kind of anthropology that has taken on a universalizing face, an anthropology that has also become the anthropology of third-world peoples through their anthropological conquest.

The Ontological Foundation of the Liberal Bourgeois Subject

As early as the ninth century, says Dussel,[13] a certain kind of person, neither feudal nor ecclesiastical, emerged. This person was called *burgher* or bourgeois and began to build a new culture and emerged on top in the French Revolution of 1789, replacing the feudal person. This is the kind of "man" that has been described as the "essential man" — the human; the kind of "man" that philosophy speaks about, the kind of "man" that the field of anthropology has for a long time established as the norm or the "civilized" man vis-à-vis other races; the kind of "man" who is the main bearer of the revolt against the powerful church that once controlled both earth and heaven. But it is also the androcentric "man" and the kind of "man" that has accompanied colonial conquest and the subjugation of other races. This is the "man" of Descartes, Hobbes, Locke, the national security states; the "man" of monopoly capitalism; the modern "bourgeois man."[14]

Here, one finds an interplay between the actual domination of the peripheries and the emergence of the bourgeois "man." Descartes's *ego cogito*, asserted Dussel, is the *ego conquiro*, which is the practical foundation of the "I think, therefore I am." The *ego cogito* is the theoretical foundation of the *ego conquiro,* and the *ego conquiro* is the practical expression of the *ego cogito*. In actual history, the *ego cogito* is not simply the *homo sapiens* or the *homo faber,* but the *homo homini lupus,* which is the political definition of the *ego cogito*: the person who is personified in the bourgeois "man" of global capitalist domination.[15] "To consider modern ideology (individualism in all its ramifications) apart from its histo-

---

her essay, "The Politics of Otherness: Biblical Interpretation as a Critical Praxis for Liberation," in *The Future of Liberation Theology: Essays in Honor of Gustavo Gutiérrez,* pp. 311-325.

[13]Enrique Dussel, *Ethics and the Theology of Liberation,* trans. Bernard F. McWilliams (Maryknoll, NY.: Orbis Books, 1978), p. 7.

[14]This point is beautifully developed by Dussel in his two books, *Philosophy of Liberation* and *Ethics and the Theology of Liberation.* See also C. B. Macpherson, *The Political Theory of Possessive Individualism: Hobbes to Locke* (Oxford: Oxford University Press, 1962); Ruiz, "Philippine Politics as a Peoples' Quest for Authentic Political Subjecthood," *Alternatives;* Comblin, *The Church and the National Security State.*

[15]Dussel, *Philosophy of Liberation,* p. 5.

rical agent (the bourgeoisie)," asserted Gutiérrez, "would falsify sociology, philosophy, and theological as well as secular history."[16]

Following the lead of Dussel, Ruiz picked up the *ego conquiro* and further took account of its "transvaluation" into the Hobbesian-Lockean "possessive-acquisitive individual." The "I think, therefore I am" of Descartes has now become the "I **possess**, therefore I am."[17] Possession has become the basis or the ontological foundation of the "I." Pursuing the transvaluation of the not innocent "I" of Descartes, or even that of Pizarro, Ruiz found its practical consummation in President Ronald Reagan's "Star Wars" program which, for him, became the example par excellence of the *ego conquiro*.[18]

If I have to pursue further the series of transvaluations that Dussel and Ruiz have started, I would say that this "I" of Pizarro, of Descartes, and this possessive-acquisitive "I" of Hobbes and Locke, is also the "Eurocentric-American I," the "patriarchal I," the " racist I," "the capitalist I." This "I" is the conqueror of my people, the exploiter of our natural resources, who rapes women and even children; this "I," said Chopp, "has been erected on the back of others."[19]

The emergence of the Euro-American "I" is synonymous with the birth of modernity, which is usually dated as early as the year 1492.[20] Modernity, from the eyes of many, is associated with Enlightenment, pluralism, and progress. But such an assessment is blind to the fact that the age of modernity is also an age of violence, conquest, colonization, exploitation, bigotry, and fanaticism of various sorts, unsurpassed in the long history of the human race.[21] The age of modernity is also the age of the emergence of the conquering and devouring "I." Outside of this Euro-American "I" is a "faceless" "other," whom the Europeans have not thought of as "human."[22]

---

[16]Gustavo Gutiérrez, "Two Theological Perspectives: Liberation Theology and Progressivist Theology," in *The Emergent Gospel: Theology from the Underside of History*, p. 231.

[17]Lester Ruiz, "After National Democracy: Radical Democratic Politics at the Edge of Modernity," *Alternatives* 16 (1991), p. 172.

[18]Ruiz, "Towards a Theology of Politics: Meditations on Religion, Politics, and Social Transformation," *Tugón*, pp. 18–31. See also Chap. I, n. 3.

[19]Chopp, *The Praxis of Suffering: An Interpretation of Liberation and Political Theologies*, pp. 124–125.

[20]Enrique Dussel, Cole Lecture, Vanderbilt University, February 5, 1992, "1492: The Apparition of the Other – Conquest and Prophetical Criticism in the Origin of Modernity." Cf. Peter Eicher, "The Consequences of God's Humanity for the Problem of Christian Humanism," in *Is Being Human a Criterion of Being Christian?*, Concilium, eds. Jean-Pierre Jossua and Claude Geffre (New York: The Seabury Press; Edinburgh: T. & T. Clark Ltd., 1982), pp. 1–9, especially pp. 2–3.

[21]Bellah et al., eds., *Habits of the Heart: Individualism and Commitment in American Life*, p. 277.

[22]There are a few exceptions, like Antonio de Montesinos and Bartolomé de Las Casas (although at first, before his "conversion," he actively introduced black slavery into the "New" World), who saw the Indians as "the scourged Christ of the Indies." See Andrés G. Guerrero, *A Chicano Theology* (Maryknoll, NY.: Orbis Books, 1987), pp. 5–10. Here Guerrero takes

Even their so-called objective and neutral scientific disciplines did not really escape from this Eurocentric bias. Anthropology as a discipline, for example, according to Gerrit Huizer, is a child of Western imperialism, with roots of the humanist vision in the Enlightenment. And it became instrumental in the conquest of other peoples.[23]

The "Euro-American Ego" Goes on the Project of Conquest and Colonization

The Euro-American ego does not doubt its humanity, but this humanity could not see any humanity in "others" than itself. By depriving "others" of their humanity, the Euro-American ego has prepared the ideological grounds for the "others'" conquest and colonization, including whatever form of genocide. By depriving "others" of their humanity, the Euro-American ego has also paved the way for its supremacy and the subordination of the "others." If peoples of other races are given humanity at all, they have to be civilized and christianized. Because their culture is inferior, it has to be killed (cultural genocide/ethnocide) and replaced with a "civilized" one.

In the history of the Filipino people, this Euro-American ego became real with the so-called "discovery" of the Philippines and the arrival of the first conquering forces (Spaniards) and subsequent colonization by the United States. In their history of conquest and colonization, the face of this conquering "I" has shone forth brightly. It can be considered a classic expression of a conquering and devouring subject, and a subject that engages in conquest for more *Lebensraum*.

Although Spain and the United States were at war, each one claiming to liberate the Filipinos, they had something in common vis-à-vis the Philippines: They were both the incarnation of the European ego — the conquering ego. Due to this commonality, they also had something in common with regard to how they viewed the *indios*: The *indios* were an inferior race. They were so inferior that from the point of view of the Spanish friars they were even considered "congenitally unfit" for the priesthood.[24] When the Span-

---

account of Montesinos's contribution to Las Casas conversion from that of an oppressor into a defender of the slaves. See also Julio Barreiro, "Rejection of Christianity by the Indigenous Peoples of Latin America," in *Separation Without Hope?: Essays on the Relation Between the Church and the Poor During the Industrial Revolution and the Western Colonial Expansion,* ed. Julio de Santa Ana (Geneva: World Council of Churches, 1978), pp. 127–136.

[23]Gerrit Huizer, "Anthropology and Politics: From Naivete Toward Liberation?" in *The Politics of Anthropology: From Colonialism and Sexism Toward a View from Below,* eds. Gerrit Huizer & Bruce Mannheim (Paris: Mouton Publishers, 1979), p. 3, citing Kathleen Gough, "New Proposals for Anthropologists," in *Social Responsibilities Symposium. Current Anthropology,* vol. 9, no. 5 (1968), 403–407.

[24]Peter Gowing, "Christianity in the Philippines: Yesterday and Today," p. 3, in a reprint from the *Silliman Journal,* vol. 12, no. 2 (Second Quarter, 1965).

iards were almost defeated by the Filipino revolutionary forces, and knowing the timely arrival of U.S. forces, they chose to surrender to another imperial power, for they considered it an ignoble act to surrender to an inferior race.[25]

Like its predecessor, the United States did not sail across the Pacific Ocean without the noblest of motives. But more than its predecessor, deeply ingrained in its soul was the notion of "manifest destiny," that is, that God formed this great nation whose "divine calling" was to spread the three pillars of Western civilization: civilization, Christianity, and democracy, or science, democracy, and Christianity.[26] The Spaniards came to liberate the Filipinos from paganism; the United States came as a liberator of the Filipinos from Spanish decadence and to bestow the so-called three pillars.

However, concealed and deeply embedded under the cloak of spreading the three pillars was the intrinsic distortion of the North American project, for in the triadic interaction of civilization, democracy, and Christianity, which were thought to be noble goals, the exploitative drive of the "new liberator" was made more cunningly effective. Concealed under the notion of civilization was the cultural subjugation of the Filipino people and the formation of colonial mentality and the use of Christianity for the colonizer's interest. The equation of capitalism and democracy, which is another form of concealment, was accurately exposed by C. B. Macpherson. As he put it:

> Western democracy is a market society, through and through; or, if one prefers to confine the term democracy to a system of government rather than a kind of society, Western democracy is for market society.[27]

The speech of Senator Albert J. Beveridge, an advocate of American expansionism, did not fail to mention the acquisitive and exploitative drives along with its God-given duty. In his speech before the U.S. Congress to support the expansionist move, he said about the Philippines:

> I have gold dust washed out by crude process of careless natives from the sands of the Philippine stream, indicating great deposits. . . . The mineral wealth is but a small fraction of the agricultural wealth of these islands. . . . And wood, hemp, copra, and other products of the Philippines supply what we need and can not ourselves produce. And the markets they will themselves afford will be immense.[28]

---

[25]Abaya, *The Untold Philippine Story,* pp. 1–2.

[26]Comblin, *The Church and the National Security State,* p. 77, citing General Golberydo Couto e Silva, *Geopolitica do Brasil* (Rio de Janeiro: José Olympio, 1967), pp. 101ff.

[27]C. B. Macpherson, *Democratic Theory: Essays in Retrieval* (Oxford: Clarendon Press, 1975), p. 25.

[28]Speech of Albert J. Beveridge cited in Frank H. Tucker, *The White Conscience* (New York: Frederick Ungar Publishing Co., 1968), pp. 149–150.

Also concealed was the racist character of the Western project which constituted as a strong ideological force that enabled the conqueror to disregard the humanity of the Filipinos. This racist and moral arrogance can be garnered from the words of soldiers involved in the Filipino-American war. One soldier had this to say:

> The old boys will say that no cruelty is too severe for these **brainless monkeys**, who can appreciate no sense of honor, kindness or justice. . . . With an enemy like this to fight, it is not surprising that the boys should soon adopt "no quarter" as a motto, and fill the blacks full of lead before finding out whether they are friends or enemies.[29]

Furthermore, with the alliance of Christianity and capitalism, the United States added another trend—the church's antagonistic stance against those who are critical of the capitalist system, oftentimes labeled as communists (Spain started to bring the first form of antagonism: Filipino Christians versus Muslims). Spain started the trend of foreign exploitation, especially with its gift of Christianity, but it has been through the United States by means of its triadic thrust that the exploitation of the Filipinos penetrated deeply, even disorienting how they view their identity.

When the early Filipinos encountered their second conqueror, the kind of ego they encountered was the *ego conquiro*—possessive individual, space-dominating organism, infinite appropriator, the morally and racially superior ego; the Filipinos were conquered by this Euro-American "I." This conquest and colonization has resulted in an inferior view of themselves and in making their colonizer the ideal of true humanity.

The National Security Doctrine and its Anthropology

While the rhetoric of manifest destiny, the symbolic bearer of the Euro-American *ego conquiro*, seems to have died out, it continues in the present under a different name and face, a different ideological cover. Yet the conquering anthropology is ever more subtly present, conquering the peoples of the Third World. Political analysts call this new ideology the *national security ideology*—an ideology that undergirds the North-South conflict, the Low Intensity Conflict, and the continuing exploitation of third-world countries.

What is the operative anthropology that underlies national security ideology? When we analyse it closer we can see the basic Hobbesian-Lockean and Machiavellian roots. Although the national security doctrine

---

[29]Letizia R. Constantino, "Recalling the Philippine American War," in *Issues Without Tears: A Layman's Manual of Current Issues,* vol. 8, ed. Letizia Constantino (Quezon City, Philippine: Karrel Inc., 1989), pp. 157–158, citing Stuart Creighton Miller, *Benevolent Assimilation,* p. 189. Emphasis supplied.

tries to smokescreen its Machiavellian roots, in essence and logic it is shaped by Machiavellianism. The morality of any ruler, be it ruling elite or military junta, is not based on doing what ought to be done, which when pursued will only undermine the power of the ruling few, but is solely based on the maintenance of power and the survival of the state.[30] Indeed its rationality is founded on *Realpolitik*.

National security anthropology is primarily based on the deep-seated insecurity of the individual. The "other" is always viewed as a threat, as an imagined, potential, or real enemy of whom the individual has to be constantly watchful. The human as *homo homini lupus* is the kind of anthropology operative in this doctrine. In order for persons to proceed unhampered in the pursuit of their interests and happiness, some amount of social harmony, at least, must exist, which justifies the creation of the state. Mutual insecurity is the basis of the state, which has to be created in order to adjudicate the competing interests, not on the basis of the need for belongingness or community.

If the "other" is always viewed as a threat to one's interest, then the atmosphere is that of constant war. Whether there is the naked use of military force or of political means, war is an instrument of state policy. Even peace is nothing more than the conventional name given to the "continuation of war [struggle] only by other means," according to the well-known parody of Clausewitz.[31] Or, as one writer said, "Peace: a period of cheating between two periods of fighting."[32] Cheating was certainly present throughout the "peace talks" (1986–1987) between the NDF (National Democratic Front) and the government of the Republic of the Philippines during the presidency of Corazon Aquino when, after the collapse of the talk, some NDF representatives fell into the hands of the armed forces.[33] There is not only a *constant* war, but a *total war* – using economics, politics, and culture.

In what way is freedom viewed in this kind of anthropology? It is a kind of individual freedom that does not take into consideration the weal of the whole community. The Visayan people have a riddle that fits this: *"Dakong tawo dili kantigo mangilo. Tubag – kalabaw"* ("What is the name of that adult who does not know how to clean her or his anus? Answer – carabao"). President Reagan's favorite line struck a similar note: "A government is like a baby's alimentary canal, with a healthy appetite on one end and no responsibility at the other."[34]

---

[30]Niccolo Machiavelli, *The Prince*, eds. Quentin Skinner and Russell Price (New York: Cambridge University Press, 1988), p. xviii.

[31]Carl von Clausewitz, *On War*, ed. with an introduction by Anatol Rapoport (New York: Penguin Books, 1968).

[32]Cited in Jovito R. Salonga, "Christ our Peace: Building a Just Society," *Tugón*, vol. 11, no. 3 (1991), 468.

[33]"Interview with Mr. Satur Ocampo," in *Kalinangan*, vol. 12, no. 3 (1992), pp. 19–21.

[34]Ronald Reagan, cited in Alan Geyer, "Towards an Ecumenical Political Ethics: A

The freedom that this dominating world knows is a freedom that is viewed in relation or, more properly, in proportion to one's power. The more power you have, the freer you are, the freer you are to impose your will on others. Power is understood here as the ability to impose one's will or the ability to make one's will real. "Without power," argued José Comblin, "freedom is nothing."[35] This is not simply a textbook analysis but finds contemporary expression in the words of the U.S. Secretary of Defense, Richard Cheney, in an interview during the Pearl Harbor anniversary. Cheney conveyed the idea that if we (North Americans) want to remain "free," we should "invest a tremendous amount in defense."[36] Filipinos know this well. When a Filipino says: *"Hindi mo yata ako kilala"* ("Perhaps, she/he has no idea of what I can do"), this means that one has to watch out, for that is a hint that she/he is powerful or has connections (*malakas*) with someone powerful.

In this case, it becomes clear that freedom is only the freedom of the strong and puts the weak at the mercy of the freedom of the powerful. The weak have no freedom, except to be an object of mercy and charity. The law, as it is usually argued, should protect the weak. But the question is: Who makes the law and whose interests is it serving? Who has the means to make full use of the law and hire the services of brilliant lawyers to find loopholes in the law? Not the weak and the poor, but the strong and the powerful. Indeed, as the oppressed Filipinos would say: *"Batas na maraming butas"* (law with many [loop] holes). Indeed, even laws can be discarded (martial law situation) if the ruling elite considers them as impediments to their full control. And *according* to Cicero, "when arms speak, the laws are silent."[37] Or, if there is any law at all, the "sons of a gun" have turned it into the "law of a gun" (*batas ng baril*).

A THEOLOGICAL READING OF ANTHROPOLOGY: ALIENATING AND LIBERATING ANTHROPOLOGIES

Totalizing and Alienating Theological Anthropologies: A Critique of the Necrophilic Trend of our Society

The centers of power, more specifically at the global level, have transformed the cooptation of theology into an instrument of the center in

---

Marginal American View," in *Perspectives on Political Ethics: An Ecumenical Enquiry,* p. 127.

[35]Comblin, *The Church and National Security Doctrine,* p. 93.

[36]Pearl Harbor Anniversary Interview of Richard Cheney by Harry Smith of CBS/CBN News, Morning Edition, December 12, 1991.

[37]Cicero, quoted in Jovito R. Salonga, "Why Did They Kill Juan?", in *Suffering and Hope: An Anthology of Asian Writings,* 2d. ed., prepared by Ron O'Grady and Lee Soo Jin (Singapore: Christian Conference of Asia, 1978), p. 16.

the imposition of its views on what constitutes humanity on the peripheries. When theology became identified with the powerful of the world, said Comblin, "it had to claim to present a total view of human beings and their place in the world."[38] Although challenged by the emergence of various scientific disciplines, theology tried to regain center stage by acting as synthesizer of the insights of various disciplines. "Even after having de facto lost control of Western society," continued Comblin, "[Western] theologians continued for several generations to maintain an idealistic, totalizing vision of human beings—one that could offer at least the equivalent of the great ideologies whose ambition was the intellectual conquest of the world."[39]

Theological totalization of anthropology, which in reality is particular, is more than an academic matter or a failure in theological methodology: it is itself an expression of human alienation, a form of conquest and domination, a violation of the rights of others to be human, a form of an idolatrous, self-securing act. As Kerry Whiteside put it: "In a world where meaning is plural, the temptation always exists to reestablish univocal meaning through domination. To treat others as objects is to gain unquestioned security in one's world view."[40]

Anthropology that Blames the Victims: Madness in the Age of Reason

The emergence of the modern ego, although a factor in the breaking of the feudal structures and the birth of individual rights, also brought with it the atomization of individuals—like billiard balls—and the eclipse of the community,[41] the commoditization of relations and the triumph of the instrumental-calculative reason or instrumental rationality over the gentler passions of life.[42] Although in a different vein, I think Michel Foucault is right to cast a shadow of "madness" in the age of "reason."[43] At the heart of modern reason is madness; it is oriented toward the love of death—a

---

[38]Comblin, *Retrieving the Human: A Christian Anthropology*, p. 1.

[39]Ibid.

[40]Kerry Whiteside, *Merleau-Ponty and the Foundation of an Existential Politics* (Princeton, New Jersey: Princeton University Press, 1988), p. 87.

[41]See Elizabeth Dodson Gray, *Green Paradise Lost* (Massachusetts: Roundtable Press, 1981), for a critique of the Newtonian and Cartesian anthropologies. The two seem to be a team: one, mechanistic, thinks of human beings as billiard balls moving through empty space; the other emphasizes the dualism of mind and matter.

[42]Martin Heidegger, *The Question Concerning Technology and Other Essays,* trans. William Lovitt (New York: Harper and Row, 1977); Hans-Georg Gadamer, *Reason in the Age of Science,* trans. Frederick Lawrence (Cambridge, Massachussets: MIT Press, 1981); Gibson Winter, *Liberating Creation: Foundations of Religious Social Ethics* (New York: The Crossroad Publishing Company, 1981).

[43]Michel Foucault, *Madness and Civilization: A History of Madness in the Age of Reason* (New York: Vintage Books, 1973).

necrophilic bias. To say that at the heart of modern reason is madness is swimming against the current, for the "educated" and the "rational" have been considered in our modern society as the epitome of human achievement. While during the Renaissance madness was at least considered as the other side of reason and people entertained the "instructive" character of madness, as pointed out by Foucault, in modern times reason has confined madness. The reasonable citizens of our time are confident that they are not mad, that they have found the solutions to today's problems if the ideas of the "think-tanks" are just carried out without much interference from those whose participation they consider to be irrelevant, like the poor.[44]

Because our society no longer suspects that at the heart of modern reason can be madness, the evils of the modern age are simply viewed as acts of mad persons and marginalized communities—the less than human. The sick, the poor, the insurgents, and the mad get blamed for all society's evils by the "sane" and "reasonable" human beings. Although the poor are the people with problems, in the final analysis the dominant mindset views them as the problem people. What remains out of sight is that the most heinous crimes against humanity, the poor, small children, women, the environment, and the people of color have been committed by our so-called reasonable and educated human beings, people who do not experience any sense of guilt because they are far removed from the consequences of their own decisions. We are at war, a war not of the making of those whom psychiatrists call mad or the poor, but a war waged by our "sane" and "reasonable men," whom society has identified as the real human beings.

The Violation of the Others' Right to be Human: On "Naming" and "Misnaming"

Theology has long asserted that the power to "name" is constitutive of being human: It is very intrinsic to being an *imago Dei*. Biblical symbols speak of the power to name as a gift from God to all human beings. To human beings belong the power to name, that is, to organize society in such a way that it can fulfill human needs and nature's integrity. To name is more than what is commonly understood as giving a name to something; it is intrinsic to human dignity and constitutive to the very survival of a human community and its identity.

But this capacity to name is also the capacity to "misname." Kosuke Koyama, in his article, "Adam in Deep Sleep,"[45] spoke of this "misnaming" as "miscosmos," that is, creating chaos. To engage in a *mining* business (a term coined after Imelda Marcos's "that is **mine** or grabbing business"), for

---

[44]The views of Roy Golez (Developer, Asia World City) is a glaring example. See Wesfall, *On Borrowed Land.*

[45]Kosuke Koyama, "Adam in Deep Sleep," in *The Human and the Holy: Asian Perspective in Christian Theology*, pp. 36-39.

example, is to misname and create miscosmos/chaos. In the history of misnaming and miscosmos, Christianity has often been used to justify the misnaming. It has been used to misname the Filipinos, to create crisis upon crisis, and to drive the people into submission. Christianity has been used to enrich the power wielders, to rob the lands from the people (like the use of sacraments in exchange for reward in heaven), to capture revolutionary forces (e.g, confession), to create a worldview of fatalism and resignation, to blind the people to the fact that what has been construed as natural is actually a product of history, and therefore can be changed, and to create justifications for the reigning social arrangements (*pagbuot sa Dios* — will of God).

Not only have the victims been misnamed, but they also have been dispossessed of their right to name their world, to name their experience and history, to name or decide what is good for them as a people, and to name their destiny. The oppressed peoples of Asia, Africa, and Latin America have been deprived of this power to name; they can only echo what the dominant groups have named and decided, like calling themselves third-world peoples in relation to the First World, or calling their nations "developing," as if the first-world nations were the models of real development. Even in their resistance, oppressed peoples are constrained to use the language and rhetoric of the dominant groups.

Subjugation and Alienation from the Fruits of One's Labor: Fetishism of Commodities and the Commoditization of Human Beings

The subjugation of the other also takes expression in the exploitation of human labor and the laborers' alienation from the fruits of their labor. Labor has to be exploited to produce maximum profit and to create more capital. Ironically, the more the worker produces or "the more value he creates the more worthless the worker becomes; . . . the more civilized the product the more barbarous the worker."[46]

While there is no need to romanticize the life of early Filipinos, it was not until the advent of the Euro-American ego, and in the later period, the Japanese, that the Filipino workers were more alienated from the fruits of their labor, and their working conditions became so miserable. Yes, the Filipinos who lived in *barangays* (small social units) did not have *surplus* to cover the worst times (natural calamities), but they did not have to create *surplus* for an exploitative class.[47] This was radically altered with the coming of the conquerors.

---

[46]Karl Marx, "Economic and Philosophical Manuscripts," in *Early Writings,* trans. T. B. Bottomore (New York: McGraw-Hill 1963), p. 123. Marx's analysis of alienation in the context of alienated labor includes threefold alienation: from the product of labor, from the activity or labor itself, and from species or life (pp. 120-134).

[47]See Constantino, *The Philippines: A Past Revisited,* vol. 1, pp. 26-41.

Under its first colonial rulers, they were forced to produce surplus for the consuming class and to plant cash crops for export, with enormous profits going into the hands of the few. The *encomienda,* and later on the *hacienda* system, was introduced to extract tributes from the local inhabitants. Forced labor was extracted from the people to build churches, houses for the colonizers, public buildings, ships for the galleon trade, and so forth. When Governor General Guido de Lavesares was ordered by the King of Spain to explain the abuses, he flatly explained:

> We have collected large amount of gold as tribute in Ilocos and Camarines without benefit to the natives, but you must understand that in order to eat we need to be supported by the natives.[48]

What the first colonizers of the Filipinos did, the succeeding neocolonizers made worse, although in a subtle and complex way, and this of course could not have happened without the collusion of the local elite. As part of the package deal to entice transnational corporations to invest in the country, the Philippine government has offered cheap labor, controlled labor unions, and tax breaks. Indeed, this is prostitution of Filipino labor at the hands of the government.

Adding more pain to the alienation of the Filipino laborers from the fruits of their labor is that even the small salary that belongs to them does not arrive on time, and the cost of commodities continues to spiral. Where will the workers go if their salary is delayed? The majority of them become victims of "loan sharks." This situation has sent many to the streets shouting, *"Itaas ang sahod, ibaba ang presyo!"* ("Raise the wages, lower the prices!"), or to go abroad in various capacities as entertainers, domestic helpers or "DH," technical workers, and professionals.[49] While many are fortunate, a good number of them become victims of "recruitment agencies," thus they are alienated all the more from the fruits of their labor.

While palatable words are often heard in praise of labor as a partner to capital, profit-oriented society makes it a mockery. Labor creates a value but, in the process, labor (alienated labor), which is the creator of value, becomes a commodity serving the product of its alienated activity, that is, capital. The product of alienation further estranges the laborer because it is already in the hands of people whose interests are opposed to those of the producers. Capital, which is nothing other than a surplus value of one's labor, has now become a value that sucks and kills the value-creating

---

[48]Pedro Salgado, "National Sovereignty, A Historical Perspective," *Kalinangan,* vol. 10, no. 2 (June 1990), p. 8, citing Guido Lavezares, "Tribute in The Christianization of the Philippines," Historical Conservation Society, University of San Agustin, Manila, 1965, p. 351.

[49]In the Middle East alone, before the final outbreak of the Gulf War, there were 250,000 contract workers. See "Editorial," *Philippine Resource Center Monitor,* no. 9 (November 1990), p. 2.

power. Dead matter, a product of human labor, dominates living people. This situation is the story of the "metamorphosis of value." As Bertell Ollman said:

> Metamorphosis of value is a tale about man, his productive activity and products, and what happens to them all in a capitalist society.[50]

In the metamorphosis of value or in its merry-go-round journey, the products of labor get ossified into independent forms and appear in the form of capital, commodity, landed property, profit, interest, rent, wages, and money. To these are given independent life and the subordination of the creator of value. It is as Franz Hinkelammert put it, "the subjugation of the human being and human life to a product of human labor, with the consequent destruction of the human being per se through the relationship that is established with an idol."[51]

It is out of this long experience of alienation from the fruits of their labor that Filipino workers struggle and hope along with the prophet Isaiah of the Old Testament: "They shall not build and another inhabit, they shall not plant and another eat . . . my chosen shall long enjoy the work of their hands" (Isaiah 65: 22). The Filipino workers also long for a day when labor becomes truly a fulfillment of their humanity.

Patriarchal Hegemony: The Subordination and Exploitation of the "Woman Other"

Patriarchy can be construed as an ideology based on the power of the male to impose its worldview, making itself the norm of humanity and justifying the domination of the "woman other." However, patriarchy can be understood not only in the limited sense of the domination of women by men, but as a prism with which to view the various forms of exploitation and their interstructuration.

Patriarchal anthropology is a form of hegemony, a totalizing anthropology, which reduces and devours the other. The modern *ego cogito-ego conquiro* can be viewed through this patriarchal prism, as feminist theologians have done. Patriarchal anthropology is not a relic of the past that can be found only in the museum or a reality existent only in a feudal society, but it is operative in the modern period, in the world of the modern market, in the proliferation of national security regimes, in apartheid systems, and wherever we encounter the exploitation and plunder of nature.

This androcentric and patriarchal ego plunders and devours not only wealth, but is also engaged in the *erotic domination* of women. Women are

---

[50]Bertell Ollman, *Alienation: Marx's Conception of Man in Capitalist Society* (Cambridge: Cambridge University Press, 1976), p. 195.

[51]Franz Hinkelammert, "The Economic Roots of Idolatry: Entrepreneurial Metaphysics," in *The Idols of Death and the God of Life: A Theology,* ed. Pablo Richard et al., trans. Barbara E. Campbell and Bonnie Shepard (Maryknoll, NY.: Orbis Books, 1983), p. 191.

viewed as objects of sexual gratification, a form of commodity, by both local elite and foreign tourists. The Euro-American conquerors, upon their arrival in a colonized country like the Philippines, lived in concubinage with the colonized women. The *mestizo* or *mestiza*, such as the "Amerasians" (mixed-race children of Filipinos and usually North American military men), is the child of this exploitative and illicit relation.[52]

Although there was resistance at first to this erotic domination, the colonized people soon began to think of their conquerors as their benefactors and as models of desirable traits and beauty. Without putting the blame on the victims themselves, those who belong to the lower rung of society, especially when their chances of getting someone from the local elite is slim, marrying this conqueror-turned-benefactor is perceived as the only way to share what the conqueror possesses: power, greatness, wealth (seems to be the primary reason), and to a certain extent beauty — blue eyes, blond hair, and light skin.[53] Construing this relationship with the foreigner and conqueror as something that provides prestige and most of all financial security, women from the rural areas flock to the cities and to places where the foreign military bases are located with the hope of marrying G.I. Joe, his dollars, and the possibility of coming to the "States." However, many of them are unfortunate (given their purpose), for Joe's promise of marriage was meant to be broken.[54]

Now that the U.S. bases are closed (although the U.S. still has access to them), it appears that Japanese men are taking the lead in the project of erotic domination and exploitation. Experiencing economic boom, many Japanese tourists come to the country for business and sexual deals. In the hope of improving their situation in life, Filipinas, usually recruited by "production and promotion organizations," also flock to Japan, but in many instances they land in the Japanese "flesh markets."[55]

Whether it be erotic domination or cheap labor or the belief that a woman's place is at home, women have been viewed as an object, a commodity, and of a subordinate status in relation to Filipino and foreign men.

The Christian tradition has contributed much in the perpetuation and legitimation of various forms of patriarchal exploitation. It is clear that the church itself is an enclave of androcentrism and oppression of women. The

---

[52]For an essay on the "Amerasians" and their plight, see "Near Subic Naval Base: U.S. Babies for Sale," *Kalinangan,* vol. 8, no. 4 (December 1988), p. 18.

[53]See Franz Fanon, *Black Skin, White Masks,* trans. Charles Lam Markmann (New York: Grove Press, 1967), pp. 41–62.

[54]See *In Their Own Words: Four Philippine Profiles* (Manila: Jeman Productions; and General Board of Global Ministries, United Methodist Church, U.S.A.), n. d. Videocassette.

[55]"The Sex Trade: Women Pay for National Debts," in *Weaving New Patterns: Women's Struggle for Change in Asia and the Pacific,* ed. Jennie Clark for WSCF Asia/Pacific (Hong Kong: World Student Christian Federation — Asia/Pacific Region, 1986), pp. 9–13. Originally from an audiovisual entitled: *Reaping the Whirlwind: The Importation of Women into Japan* (Singapore: Christian Conference of Asia).

Bible and the writings of the early church Fathers are replete with references to the patriarchalization of the human norm and the subordination of women. The *imago Dei*, among many Christian theologians, was equated with "maleness."[56] Known personalities of the Christian faith—like Augustine, Aquinas, Luther, Calvin—as well as contemporary male theologians are all products of their age; thus their theological reflections are not totally sanitized from the influence of patriarchal culture.[57]

Conquering Anthropology and the Exploitation of Nature

The way anthropology is construed surely has some bearings on one's relationship with nature. If people of other races are not spared from exploitation, the same holds true for nature. The conquering ego does not just exploit the inhabitants of one area, but also their natural resources. If women are raped, nature, which is closely identified with a woman's body, will surely suffer a similar fate. Or as Ruether put it, "through the raped bodies the earth is raped."[58]

Destruction of nature has been ongoing, like the *kaingin* (slash and burn) method of farming in the Philippines. Sean McDonagh cited the case of Dodong Balayon, a Filipino farmer in the island of Mindanao, who, in his scramble to make both ends meet for his family's *present survival needs*, had to practice the destructive *kaingin* and had to close his eyes to the destruction of nature and what the *future* may bring.[59] The attitude of Dodong reminded me of a story of a hungry boy who was ordered to keep quiet during a *barangay* meeting or else he would be put in prison. Not mindful of the horrors of prison, all that he asked for was food *now*: "Doon po ba sa loob mayro'n bang pagkain" ("Is there food in the prison house?"). While Dodong's crime against nature is basically bound with his family's *survival,* for the loggers, it is more a case of *greed* and *profit*.

Not to exonerate the poor Filipinos, but never in their history has nature been so exploited and devastated (not for mere survival) than with the coming of the Euro-American ego onto their shores in the name of development and modernization, backed by an efficient and destructive technology. With the triumph of instrumental rationality and the captivity of the Filipino elite to this *Weltanschauung*, the conquest of nature was all the more facilitated and, with it, catastrophic consequences: denuded forest, destruction of breeding grounds for fish and other marine life, polluted

---

[56]Ruether, *Sexism and God-Talk: Toward a Feminist Theology,* p. 93.

[57]Ibid, specifically pp. 93-115; also Jane Dempsey Douglass, *Women, Freedom, and Calvin* (Philadelphia: The Westminster Press, 1985), especially regarding Calvin's view; Anne Carr, *Transforming Grace: Christian Tradition and Women's Experience* (San Francisco: Harper and Row, 1988), p. 7.

[58]Ruether, *Sexism and God-talk: Toward a Feminist Theology,* p. 263.

[59]Sean McDonagh, *The Greening of the Church* (Maryknoll, NY.: Orbis Books; London: Geoffrey Chapman, 1990), pp. 9-12.

rivers and ocean, and so forth. When nature is exploited it has a way of fighting back, like the flash floods in Ormoc City (Leyte) on November 5, 1991 (6,000 dead and 3,000 unaccounted for) and Oras (Eastern Samar), and many more.[60]

In the name of development, which in reality is "developmental aggression," nature and people's dwelling have to be destroyed. The struggle of our tribal communities against the construction of dams that are meant to supply electricity to transnational industries, but that will also bury entire villages of tribal communities, is a glaring example of this violent disrespect for the life of people and for nature.

This violent disrespect of nature and people's dwelling, I believe, would not have been so quickly carried out without the backing of the Christian religion. While the early Filipinos had more respect for nature, even attributing some spiritual power to it (understandable since it can give life and death), the Christian gospel, modern instrumental rationality, and capitalism all conspired in the domination of nature. In this unholy alliance, Christianity has always provided the theological-ideological undergirding by removing all trace of the association of God with nature, or anything sacred in nature, so that it could be exploited for profit.

Growing up in a small barrio of Hinunangan, Southern Leyte, I observed how the name of Christ was used to ward off the spirits of nature before a place or mountain could be bulldozed for so-called development. On one occasion our neighbor buried a wooden cross in a lot where a movie house was soon to be constructed. While I can understand the importance of Christianity in liberating the people from the spirits that have enslaved them, the capitalist bourgeois *ego conquiro* brought another spirit (god) of the worst kind in the name of Christianity to dominate the spirits of nature. In the name of the bourgeois capitalist god — Profit — nothing has been spared to be sacrificed. As long as this god continues to dominate, nothing is sacred, not even the burial sites of the natives, for example, the Igorots of the Philippines.

Christianity, interpreted by the conquering bourgeois, has turned around the Genesis creation account as a support for the domination of nature. With individuals detached from nature because they believe their true home is in heaven (although they want to control both earth and heaven), there are people who are ready to conquer the earth, rather than save it. Entrusted by God to exercise "dominion" (Genesis 1:26), the *ego conquiro* has easily turned dominion into "domination" of nature. Although not everything can be heaped on the shoulders of Christianity, Lynn White's indictment that "Christianity bears a huge burden of guilt"[61] is, I believe, appropriate.

---

[60]See "Ecology: An Ecumenical Perspective," in *Tugón,* vol. 12, no. 2 (1992), p. 216.

[61]Lynn White, Jr., "The Historical Roots of our Ecologic Crisis," in *Western Man and Environmental Ethics,* ed. Ian G. Barbour (London: Addison-Wesley, 1973), p. 27.

Anthropology from the Periphery:
The Humanity of the Oppressed

Due to conquest and colonization, the anthropology of many third-world peoples is the anthropology of their conquerors. As Paulo Freire put it:

> Every act of conquest implies a conqueror and someone or something which is conquered. The conqueror imposes his objectives on the vanquished, and makes of them his possession. He imposes his own contours on the vanquished, who internalize this shape and become ambiguous beings "housing" another.[62]

The vanquished person, in the long history of oppression, without his or her knowledge, has become a *house* of the soul of the conqueror. In the case of conquered people in the Third World, they are housing the soul of the Western bourgeois subject. This is glaring among the Filipino people who have begun to think of themselves as "little brown Americans" — comparable to the "black white men" of Africa or what Franz Fanon has called "black skin, white masks" — and are confused regarding their identity as a people.[63] A poem helps to articulate this Filipino malady:

> We are a brown race
> with white gods
> and whitened soul.
> We are aliens
> in our land,
> hostage by our past.[64]

Thus, essential to the liberation of the Filipino people is a new awareness and a different perspective from which to interpret anthropology — the anthropology of the subjugated and struggling Filipino.

---

[62]Freire, *Pedagogy of the Oppressed,* p. 134.

[63]Many Filipinos have been deceived into thinking that U.S. interest is identical to Philippine interest. This "colonial mentality" or "culture of prostitution," as Cariño put it, has erased from the people's memory the countless instances of U.S. barbarity to the Filipinos. See his essay, "Towards a Culture of Freedom: On Saying 'No' to the American Bases," in *On Wastes and National Dignity: Views and Voices on the US Military Bases,* pp. 71-75. Cf. Sam M. Kobia, "The Christian Mission and the African Peoples in the 19th Century," in *Separation Without Hope?: Essays on the Relation Between the Church and the Poor During the Industrial Revolution and the Western Colonial Expansion,* p. 165. In a similar way, black Carribeans have been also conditioned to "think white." See Noel Leo Erskine, *Decolonizing Theology: A Caribbean Perspective* (Maryknoll, NY.: Orbis Books, 1981), p. 11, citing Ashley Smith; also Fanon, *Black Skin, White Masks.*

[64]"Aliens in our Land," *Philippine Resource Center Monitor,* no. 9 (November 1990), p. 2.

Viewing Anthropology from the Subjugated
and the Mutilated

For a long time the conquerors have made it their sole prerogative to explain what is human, depriving the Filipinos of the right to see themselves as they are. For a long time they have been led to believe what their conquerors have told them: that they are born physically weak and mentally inferior and that they are generally lazy. Their plight has always been attributed to their very nature and culture. Never have they been made to understand the forces that have dehumanized them, forces that are not due to their nature or their genes.

The restoration of the humanity of the struggling Filipinos requires that they themselves realize their dehumanization, that anthropology takes as its new interlocutor not the bourgeois subjects, but the "nonpersons." With the eruption of the subjugated peoples around the world, there have been some attempts at trying to recover the humanity of the conquered. Liberation theologians have been trying, with much success, to bring the history of the subjugated as central to the theological agenda, or as a *locus theologicus.* Speaking of this emerging anthropology, Antonio Moser claimed that

> the man envisaged by the ethic of liberation is a man marked by suffering, suffering caused by deep poverty, widespread and deliberate. . . . The starting point for an ethic of liberation cannot, therefore, be either man in the abstract or man marked by success. . . . This represents a greater revolution by far than that brought about by Vatican II.[65]

When theology tries to interpret anthropology from the experience of the suffering poor, it cannot do otherwise but change its approach and method. It should try to interpret anthropology not idealistically, but through the disfigured bodies of the poor, through the mangled bodies of those mutilated.[66] If we have to speak of human dignity, let us look to the poor and their undernourished and ailing bodies; bodies of peasants agonizing from the excruciating heat of the sun; bodies that have been subjected to back-breaking labor from dawn till dusk; and tortured bodies of community organizers and human rights advocates. It may appear to be an oxymoron, but the privileged forget their bodies even as they care so much for their health and body shape. As Comblin again put it:

> Bodies remind us that they exist when they suffer. This is when we are forced to remember them. No one who has never been truly hungry will fully understand that a human being is first and foremost a being who needs to eat. No one who has never been sick will know what health is. For the poor, the

---

[65]Antonio Moser, "The Representation of God in the Ethic of Liberation," *Concilium,* eds. Dietmar Mieth and Jacques Pohier (Edinburgh: T. & T. Clark LTD, 1984), pp. 43, 46.
[66]Comblin, *Retrieving the Human,* p. 4.

liberation of humanity is the liberation of suffering, crushed, humiliated bodies.[67]

The Epistemological and Salvific Significance of the Poor: The Poor as Prism for Understanding the Human

It is common to hear that both the oppressed and the oppressor are alienated because neither of them is truly human. I agree, but with certain qualifications. First, the alienation of the oppressed and that of the oppressor are not the same. Second, the alienation of the oppressed has salvific significance; it plays a positive role in the humanization of society.

The idea that the oppressed play a positive role in the struggle toward humanization has been advanced by several writers.[68] There is no need to rehearse in full the literature on this topic, but a rough sketch is enough for our concern here. It has been argued, and rightly so, that the oppressed, by virtue of their marginalization in the system, have still retained the consciousness of being outsiders to the system; thus, their alienation is not as complete as those who are fattening inside the system and whose consciousness has been fully sold to it. The marginalization of the op-pressed has prevented them from fully identifying with the system, and it is only from this position of marginalization that "prophecy is possible," hence, the possibility of liberating change.[69]

When we say that the oppressed are the bearers of humanity, it does not mean that the oppressed are already fully human, for how can they be fully human who are still living in oppression? But we see in the critical spirit of the oppressed the seeds of humanity in the process of unfolding, for although still oppressed, they have started to negate the negative;

---

[67]Ibid.

[68]This has been one of the central insights of Marxism and liberation theology. To cite a few examples, see this point expounded by Gregory Baum, *Religion and Alienation: A Theological Reading of Sociology* (New York: Paulist Press, 1975); also Freire, *Pedagogy of the Oppressed;* Dussel, *Philosophy of Liberation; Moving Heaven and Earth,* p. v. In a more detailed fashion, Comblin has identified four positive roles of the poor in the emergence of the new person. First, the poor act by the simple assertion of their presence. The cry of the poor obliges the whole of society to search, to innovate, to create something new, to burst barriers; it is an ongoing ferment of destabilization and invention. Second, the beginnings of human community develop among the poor, where freedom and service are one at last. The poor generate the expressions of communion that constitute the promises of a new humanity. Third, as the vanquished of history, the poor bear within them the remnants of an ancient legacy of humanity accumulated over the centuries: the legacy of all history's attempts to build a life of community and partnership. Fourth, when the poor receive the cooperation of the more privileged sectors of society, who help them to organize, they come together in social and political movements, religious and secular at the same time, that are struggling for the transformation of an alienated humanity. These movements, in spite of limitations, express in history the liberation promised by the God of the oppressed *(Retrieving the Human,* p. 37).

[69]Baum, *Religion and Alienation: A Theological Reading of Sociology,* p. 31.

although still oppressed, the oppressed consciousness is no longer domesticated. What we have in the oppressed but struggling people is a new emerging humanity; in the struggling victims we are witnessing the emergence of new historical subjects. This means, according to Alves, that a "new man is born into history."[70] Although not yet complete, the emergence of historical subjects is an expression of humanity restored, and in this process of struggle the human also continues to discover new dimensions and criteria of humanhood. That is why the language of humanization can be spoken only "on the way," in the historical context in which human beings find themselves and from the concrete commitments that today and tomorrow may require.[71]

However, in order to avoid any naive romanticism of this new humanity, which may result either in absolutism or cynicism toward the people's movements, it must be recalled that the old and new self still exists in the new historical subjects that I am speaking about. The truth is that the new person cannot subsist except as enfleshed in imperfect, ambivalent actions and movements. This notion is important if we are to realize the weakness of our own perceived strength and if we are to approach properly the weaknesses of *kamanlalakbay* (co-journeyers).

I am in debt again to de la Torre as he related the story of an Italian journalist who wrote of the Vietcong cadres. This journalist admired highly the courage of the Vietcong cadres, but he was scared too because, as he put it: "Would men who took such risks and made so many sacrifices understand human weakness when they came to power?" In referring to those who had given up during torture or imprisonment, de la Torre proceeded: "You have to know weakness in order to forgive and restore a person. In prison we know human limitations. Young people in the movement don't. In prison you are more tolerant and human. Don't crush the bruised reed."[72]

People who have not perceived the danger and weakness in their strength can hardly be expected to understand the weakness of others. If we identify the people's movements by their leaders, who in some instances behave as if they own the movements, we would end up leaving the people's movements, because we can surely find individuals whose lives obscure the noble cause that the movements espouse. Yet, far from being a definitive obstacle, imperfection is precisely the path of the Spirit of God to reach final liberation.[73]

---

[70]Alves, *A Theology of Human Hope,* p. 11; see a similar point that reverberates in the work of Comblin in *Retrieving the Human.*

[71]Alves, *A Theology of Human Hope,* p. 17.

[72]de la Torre, *Touching Ground, Taking Root: Theological and Political Reflections on the Philippine Struggle,* p. 162.

[73]See Comblin, *Retrieving the Human,* p. 34.

Finding One's Humanity Through Solidarity with the Victims of Inhumanity: Option With the Poor

If the poor are the bearers of the new humanity and their struggle is an expression of this humanity coming into being, to stand in the way of this struggle is in a sense to stand against the realization of this humanity and one's own humanity. On the other hand, if the struggle of the poor is an expression and anticipation of a new humanity, it would also mean that one can only find one's humanity in solidarity with them. To be in solidarity with the poor or to opt with and for them is in a deeper sense to opt for humanity. The solidarity stance is a stance of a humanity in the making and an anticipation of that which is yet to fully come. Apart from this option with the poor, the grace of humanization that comes by way of the poor cannot come to the nonpoor, not even to pious Christians.

When I say solidarity with the victims, I am not simply talking about a general posture that leans toward the poor or about some universal denouncement of human rights violations. Solidarity must specifically manifest – like defending a particular victim – a victim with a name. Solidarity with the victims entails risk, which is almost totally absent in universal assertions or denouncement, hence, a highly questionable index of authentic solidarity.

Human Rights as Rights of the Poor: Moving Beyond Human Rights

The struggle for humanization in a situation in which even the basic "human rights" of individuals have been violated has, in one dimension, taken the form of human rights advocacy. Many churches have even put up human rights desks to promote human rights consciousness and to actively defend the basic rights of individuals. Likewise, theological reflections about human rights issues have blossomed.

In giving theological undergirding to human rights advocacy, the question of what is truly human or theological anthropology has all the more come to the forefront. It appears here that the issue of human rights is intrinsically a question of anthropology. And, because rights are defined, violated, upheld, and defended only within the context of a wider society, the question of human rights links us not only to the question of being human – of who we are, where we are, and what we hope for – but also to the "character of human dwelling, i.e., how peoples are constituted as historical communities" – a question of social order.[74] The struggle for human rights links us then to the question of anthropology and the question of society.

Thanks to the contribution of human rights advocacy, many victims of human rights violations have been given justice. However, human rights

---

[74]Ruiz, "Philippine Politics as a Peoples' Struggle for Authentic Political Subjecthood," *Alternatives*, p. 516.

advocacy, in spite of its positive points, has serious limitations, especially when viewed from the humanity of third-world peoples. Basically, its conceptual framework is derived from Western anthropology, from Western notions of rights, freedom, individuality, and social organization that do not properly take into account the world of most third-world peoples. Although it appears that the assertion of individuality has been paramount in human rights concepts, for peoples of third-world countries, such as Asia, the sense of unity is more foundational. Song has pointed out that the assertion of the principle of the separation of individual identities is typical of a Western approach to community, but for Asia, it is for him the reverse, that is, the principle of unity comes first.[75] This is not to say that the priority of the communal does not have weaknesses associated with it, but our knowledge of how the rise of the modern Western subject has meant the eclipse of the human community and the commoditization of relations should help third-world peoples to cherish what they have and build from there the dreamed community.

Deeply embedded in the concept of human rights, but often escaping the scrutinizing eye, is the principle of individuality—the same principle that makes the contractual way of relating possible and keeps the capitalist market operating. Individual rights, founded on the Western mode of comprehension, particularly its notion of individuality, could equally support two conflicting points: "the commitment to equal right to dignity of every individual" or to "justify inequality of reward, which, when extreme, may deprive people of dignity."[76] If one is observant with how the rhetoric of individual rights has been used by many Western bourgeoisies, it is not difficult to perceive the connections between individual equal rights and the justification of inequality.

The generally accepted approach to human rights, although in a sense useful to pressure violators of human rights in various sociocultural settings, may tend to cover the particular presuppositions of human rights concepts. One can observe that secular humanists and religiously motivated advocates of human rights both approach human rights based on transcendental and universal principles. It is common, for example, among Christian interpreters to use the concept of *imago Dei* to establish a transcendental principle of human dignity.[77] For this purpose, the creation account in Genesis is often cited as the biblical basis of human rights over those who deny it.

While it can be granted that the defense of human dignity can be sup-

---

[75]Song, *Third-Eye Theology,* p. 21.

[76]Bellah et al., *Habits of the Heart: Individualism and Commitment in American Life,* p. 150; Aloysius Pieris, "Human Rights Language and Liberation Theology," in *The Future of Liberation Theology: Essays in Honor of Gustavo Gutiérrez,* p. 303.

[77]Noriel C. Capulong, "Human Rights: A Theological and Historical Basis," in *Human Rights: Biblical and Theological Readings,* ed. Liberato Bautista (Quezon City, Philippines: National Council of Churches—Human Rights Desk, 1988), pp. 19–39.

ported by biblical passages, it is in my judgment questionable to call the transcendental-universalist approach to human rights biblical or, more precisely, Hebraic. What I think the Bible clearly witnesses, if we have to speak of rights, is the "rights of the poor" and God's liberating activity through them. The measure for the true fulfillment of rights is when the rights of the poor are served; in a similar manner, what is done to the poor becomes the measure of justice.[78] This is where we should be moving, and where human rights advocacy, as commonly understood, finds its limitations.

Human rights concepts do not fully account for the radical nature of the oppression of the people in the peripheries. Many human rights advocates in third-world countries, and more particularly in the Philippines, are aware of this limitation, although they support human rights programs. The extent of the violation of the humanity of the poor cannot be contained by the concept of human rights because the marginalization of the many is a structural disease. This disease needs a surgical operation that human rights cannot provide. Human rights still falls within the orbit of *juridico-procedural* struggle, whereas what is needed is a *substantive* critique and therefore a substantive treatment, to employ the concept of Ruiz.[79]

While useful when properly appropriated, human rights can be an imposition of a worldview and notion of human dwelling on third-world peoples. It can be and has been, as pointed out by Aloysius Pieris, an instrument of Western imperialism, of intervention, against those who would not conform to the Western mindset.[80]

Important as such an issue as human rights is, such attention runs the danger of leaving untouched the further issue of what can be called social rights, that is, the rights of people to survival, to food, clothing, shelter, health care, education, and sustainable development. These rights, which most of the people of the northern hemisphere define as privileges and available for those who can afford to pay them, are rights for survival. Short of these social rights, which in essence represent the right to life of the poor, the human rights of the poor continue to be violated. In the emphatic words of Robert McAfee Brown,

> But as long as children are growing up in a society where their parents cannot get jobs, so that children grow up undernourished, as long as people cannot get decent housing or education and health care for their children, human rights are being violated, and such rights must be the focal point of human

[78]Míguez Bonino, *Toward A Christian Political Ethics,* pp. 84–86; Comblin, *Retrieving the Human,* p. 57.

[79]Ruiz, "Philippine Politics as a Peoples' Quest for Authentic Political Subjecthood," *Alternatives,* p. 517.

[80]Pieris, "Human Rights Language and Liberation Theology," in *The Future of Liberation Theology: Essays in Honor of Gustavo Gutiérrez,* pp. 306–309.

endeavor in this area. . . . Measured against such a yardstick, there is a long way to go.[81]

PHILIPPINE POLITICS AND THE QUEST FOR THE NEW HUMAN BEING: FILIPINO IMAGE, IMAGE OF GOD

Political Quest for a New Human Being

Earlier in this chapter I cited Freire's analysis of an oppressed people who, after centuries of domination by the conquerors, are actually beings housing the soul of the conqueror. In other words, the oppressed is the house of the spirit of the conqueror; the being of the conqueror is the one controlling the humanity of the oppressed; the oppressor has been internalized. The oppressor has gained a foothold in the very being of the oppressed and, in spite of the physical absence of the oppressor, the being of the oppressor lives within. What was an external imposition of worldview has now become internal.

With the subjugation and colonization of the Filipino people, we have an example par excellence of a people housing the being of the conqueror, specifically the being of the Western bougeois subject—the modern individual. Ruiz, who is extremely helpful in developing this section, strongly argued that "the history of the Enlightenment project of self-assertion as it was appropriated by Filipinos is well established, going as far back as the Revolution of 1898."[82] The appropriation by the Filipinos of the Western bourgeois subject is very clear, especially with the ruling class and among the *ilustrados*. Coopted and trained by the conquerors—the West—they were molded according to the worldview of the West more than the oppressed people of the countryside. In this case they are among the most alienated of all the Filipinos; they think that the interests of the Filipino people are identical with those of the foreigners.

With the formation of the Filipino bourgeoisie, the conquerors were able to establish effective conduits in their continuous exploitation of the people and the rich natural resources of the country. Grabbing the leadership of the government, which they ran like a private enterprise for profits, the elite politicians promoted a development that has reduced many to abject poverty and propagated an education that has further deepened the control of the West among the majority. A schoolboy offers us his wisdom in characterizing the Filipino elite politician when asked to distinguish between

---

[81]Robert McAfee Brown, "Preface," in Gutiérrez, *The Power of the Poor in History,* pp. xiv-xv.

[82]Ruiz, "After National Democracy: Radical Democratic Politics at the Edge of Modernity," *Alternatives,* p. 162.

a politician and a statesman: "A statesman is a man who belongs to the State; a politician is the man who thinks that the state belongs to him" (the radical left calls this man a bureaucrat capitalist).[83] Turned into bourgeois subjects, they have become agents of the *ego conquiro* of the West and its capitalist enterprise. It is against this imposition of a "bourgeois vision" of human life and dwelling that the Filipino struggle finds itself.[84]

What kind of human dwelling comes out of this liberal bourgeois subject, taking into consideration that one's view of anthropology shapes a notion of human or societal dwelling? A democratic society is the most likely response, for democracy has always been associated with the Western modern project. However, when we look deeper into the nature of the *ego cogito-ego conquiro*, which stems from modernity, the appropriate name of its social project would rather be *elite democracy*. It is democratic in many respects, but also at its heart is an elite democracy based on control of wealth and power. At the heart of the core capitalist-democratic countries, like the United States, is a "secret government" that runs the country, even contrary to the policies set by the U.S. congress.[85] In the third-world countries the project may appear in the form of crony capitalism. At its worst, elite democracy can easily turn into the most brutal form of dictatorial regime.

It may be difficult for others to see how Western democracy, sublated into elite democracy, could turn into dictatorship. But dictatorship is not foreign to liberal democracy and, in fact, is consistent with its logic. Elite democracy and dictatorship come from the same concept, except that in elite democracy you have dictatorship by the few—the wealthy and the powerful. The fact that in the confrontation of emerging people or popular democracies and right-wing dictatorships in third-world countries, the United States, as the guardian of Western democratic heritage, has chosen to support right-wing dictatorships, is proof enough that dictatorship is logically consistent with the capitalist-liberal democracy — a project of the liberal bourgeois subject. Of course, the threat of communism is always used to justify dictatorship, but in reality it is afraid of the people for whom it claims to exist; it is afraid because it is an elite democracy. "Liberal democracy" asserted Ruiz, "with its anti-democratic consequences, as a way of life, has been one of the most deceptive and elusive obstacles to radical transformation in the Philippines."[86]

Deceptive and elusive are fitting descriptions of liberal democracy — the modern bourgeoisie project. In spite of the system's crimes against the

---

[83]Cited in Salonga, "Christ our Peace: Building a Just Society," in *Tugón,* p. 467.

[84]Ruiz, "Philippine Politics as a Peoples' Quest for Authentic Political Subjecthood," *Alternatives,* p. 524.

[85]One recent example is the Iran-Contra Affair.

[86]Ruiz, "Philippine Politics as a Peoples' Quest for Authentic Political Subjecthood," *Alternatives,* p. 529.

people, it has survived because of its ability to hide, even to blame the victims; it has successfully hidden from many the fact that exploitation and the rise of a dictator are consistent with an elite democracy, in which the ultimate supreme value that guides society is gold, not God. It has concealed from many the fact that the Western project of liberal democracy, as appropriated by the peoples of color, in its very depth is antipeople, continuing to siphon the wealth of the people for the few and to make them powerless. What needs to be uncovered is that the modern subject is an essential part of elite democracy, and that no amount of changing the leadership of the country can change the plight of the people under the human dwelling constructed by the liberal subject.

Filipino traditional leaders, politicians, and scholars are human houses for the liberal bourgeois subject who do not really have the spectacles to critique society outside the framework of liberal democracy or elite democracy. They have been blinded by their own position and have failed to see that the system itself has relegated many to the margins. Ruiz considered the response of traditional politicians against the Marcos dictatorship as "actor oriented." They played the same rules of the game that Marcos had been playing. In other words, there was nothing substantive in their critique, just juridicoprocedural. As houses of the modern bourgeois subjects, they could not be expected to see the issues from a more substantive level.

When analysis of issues is not seen at the substantive level, solutions also do not address the roots of the matter. Juridicoprocedural analysis offers some palliative measures, in many instances even blaming the victims. It focuses on the weakness of the Filipinos, like fatalism and resignation (*gulong ng palad, bahala na*), but it does not seek to deal with the causative factors of fatalism and resignation. Since these ailments are common among the poor, the poor get the blame. Because the elite are more progressive and forward looking in their outlook, the "modernizing elite" become the paradigm of human beings or of the "new Filipino," while the poor — also the sluggish, the lazy, the fatalistic, and the "contented cow," as Nacpil suggested — are encouraged to become like the modernizing elite, a "type of man" who is "free to decide."[87] Like other bourgeois analyses, Nacpil failed to consider the relation of the freedom to decide to the socioeconomic condition of the poor and the whole presence of "institutionalized violence."[88]

Antonio Ledesma and Edmundo Garcia's critique of institutional violence in relation to freedom is an insightful corrective to the liberal bourgeoisies' notion of freedom. For them, the existence of "institutionalized" violence constitutes a hindrance to what is called *freedom of decision,*

---

[87]Nacpil, "Modernization and the Search for a New Image of Man," *The Human and the Holy: Asian Perspectives in Christian Theology,* p. 297.

[88]Ibid., pp. 298, 300–301.

especially their point that a tenant who has been perennially indebted to the landlord is, *de facto,* really not free.[89] Would it be that easy for a poor tenant who is dependent on the landlord to freely decide, even for whom to vote during elections when she or he knows of "no vote *ibot*" (not to vote for the landlord's candidate means eviction)? I do not think so, if one is really familiar with the tenants' level of oppression and how the social system functions to put them continually in an exploited status.

It is only when we see anthropology from the experience of the poor, that is, of those who are hurt by the system or those who are nonparticipants of the system, that we can expect a substantive critique. Only from the experience of the poor can a different notion of human dwelling—popular democracy—be discerned; only from their experience, along with Filipinos who have become traitors to their class, can a new Filipino humanity and dwelling be born.

It should not be construed, however, that the quest for Filipino humanity and dwelling is the romanticization of the "original" Pinoy or *"sariling atin"* (indigenous and truly Filipino) because the quest for the "original" is even questionable,[90] or a return to the Malayo-Polynesian culture, as Miguel Bernad would say. [91] In fact, as suggested by C. G. Arevalo, we need a "new eschatology" to counter the weight of the "dead and unfree past," so that we may move forward.[92] A more balanced approach, however, would involve "integration" and "self-determination,"[93] borrowing a concept from Vitaliano Gorospe, creatively integrating the various influences that have molded the Filipino, but I would insist that it be guided by the criterion of what is liberating for the popular majority, not only by the notion of human dwelling conceived by the Filipino bourgeoisie.

Just like the name *Filipino,* a name that emerged only as the national consciousness of the people developed,[94] the humanity of the Filipino is not a timeless essence, but a humanity emerging to become full historical subjects; a humanity not "in spite of" or on the "hither side of" ambiguities,

---

[89]Antonio Ledesma and Edmundo Garcia, "Toward a Filipino Social Democracy," in *The Filipino in the Seventies: An Ecumenical Perspective,* eds. Vitaliano R. Gorospe and Richard L. Deates (Quezon City, Philippines: New Day Publishers, 1973), p. 39.

[90]See the work of Michel Foucault, "Nietzsche, Genealogy, History," in *Foucault Reader,* pp. 76-100; also Welch, *Communities of Resistance and Solidarity.*

[91]Miguel A. Bernad, "Philippine Culture and the Filipino Identity," in *The Filipino in the Seventies: An Ecumenical Perspective,* p. 16.

[92]C. G. Arevalo, "Some Prenotes on 'Doing Theology': Man, Society, and History in Asian Contexts," in *The Human and the Holy,* p. 190.

[93]Vitaliano Gorospe, "The New Christian Morality and the Filipino," in *The Filipino in the Seventies: An Ecumenical Perspective,* pp. 367-368.

[94]Horacio de la Costa, *The Background of Nationalism and Other Essays* (Manila: Solidaridad Publishing House, 1965), p. 27. It has been suggested, for instance, that our national history ought to begin in the middle of the 19th century because that is when we began to have a national consciousness and hence when we began to be a nation.

to paraphrase Maurice Merleau-Ponty,[95] but even in the ambiguities of oppression. Perceptible only in the current ambiguities of struggle, Filipino humanity can only be construed as a humanity in the making. Although it is already a present experience, it is also humanity as a foretaste and as a vision, that is, the vision of a suffering people seeking liberation from enslaving forces within and from enslaving forces without, that seeks to impose and totalize a notion of humanity and a project of human dwelling. The Filipino humanity is a humanity rooted in its third worldness and Asianness, shaped by the past, marked by generous struggle in the present, in light of the hoped-for future.

The Image of God Is a New Filipino

What does it mean to be created in the image of God for the Filipinos? I cannot exhaust its implications but I can point out some basic thoughts. If we can say that "Christ must be a Filipino in order for Filipinos to be Christians," we can say in a similar fashion that the image of God must be a Filipino if Filipinos are to be in the image of God — not in the image of its conquerors and their Filipino cohorts. Against the backdrop of the intrusion of the Western bourgeois subject and project, this means the attainment of a genuine *pambansang kasarinlan* (national sovereignty) and identity and openness to the self-determination of cultural minorities within the country. This means freedom from the shackles of "colonial mentality" and the formation of a national consciousness that is liberating to the Filipinos. Its formation will constitute the regaining of political power of the majority, the restoration of the fruits of the labor of the suffering Filipinos that have been snatched away both by local leaders and foreign powers, and engagement in the project of popular democracy and sustainable peace. Moreover, it is the regaining of the Filipino popular idioms — the non-Western indigenous and "proletarian/populist" assumptions[96] — that have been devalued by the coming of scientific instrumental rationality, including the Filipinos' deep bond to nature.

The Struggle for Filipino Humanity and Dwelling Goes On

Because the humanity of the Filipino is not something fixed but a humanity-in-the-making through the way of suffering and struggle against

---

[95]Maurice Merleau-Ponty, *The Phenomenology of Perception* (London: Routledge and Kegan Paul, 1962), p. 455.

[96]Ileto, *Pasyon and Revolution: Popular Movements in the Philippines, 1840–1910;* Ruiz, "Towards a Theology of Politics: Meditations on Religion, Politics, and Social Transformation," *Tugón,* p. 42; Cariño, "Some Recent Development in Asian Theology," *Kalinangan,* p. 10.

suffering, the search for this humanity is also a continuing challenge. *"Sapagkat ako ay tao lamang"* ("because I am only human") is not an excuse, as those who are resigned are fond of saying. The search for a new humanity is a challenge that Filipinos know, as expressed in the saying: *"Madaling maging tao, mahirap magpakatao"* ("It is easy to be born, but it is not easy to be human"). It is only by way of struggle, through struggle, in being in and of the struggle, that this new humanity is to be born and find its present expressions.

5

The Christo-Praxis of a People

The "Pasyon," Death, and Resurrection of the "Sambayanang Pilipino"

Christian believers, so far as their faith is concerned, have always affirmed Jesus as a paradigm of authentic humanity or as the way to be human.[1] If Jesus is a way to be human, then it can be said that the christological question is an anthropological question and the anthropological question a christological question.

Without denying that the Bible is replete with texts asserting Jesus' divinity, my concern in this chapter is to see the christological question as an anthropological question. I concur with scholars[2] who affirm that more foundational for christology is not so much the fact that Jesus as Christ is God, but that Jesus reveals the way of human beings toward God. Or, if I say that he reveals God, I say this because in his life God can be found, and not in the Nicean (*homoousios* question) and Chalcedonian (one person in two natures — *verus Deus/verus homo*) fashion.[3] Further, my interest is not on the issue of the relationship between christology and orthodox soteriology and, consequently, on the so-called "scandal of particularity."[4]

Every context shapes what is considered urgent and relevant by the people. This is certainly the case with christological dogmas that are often couched in abstract philosophical language. "Christological dogmas," said

---

[1]In spite of questions raised regarding the maleness of Jesus, Asian women, said Virginia Fabella, view Jesus' maleness as "accidental" or "functional," and not essential to the salvific process. See Virginia Fabella, "Christology from an Asian Woman's Perspective," in *We Dare to Dream: Doing Theology as Asian Women*, p. 4; idem, "A Common Methodology for Diverse Christologies?" in *With Passion and Compassion: Third World Women Doing Theology*, eds. Virginia Fabella and Mercy Amba Oduyoye (Maryknoll, NY.: Orbis Books, 1988), p. 116.

[2]See, for example, Ruiz, "Towards a Theology of Politics: Meditations on Religion, Politics, and Social Transformation," *Tugón*, p.35.

[3]Walter Lowe, "Christ and Salvation," in *Christian Theology: An Introduction to its Traditions and Tasks*, pp. 222–248.

[4]Ibid., p. 222. This scandal is so acute in orthodox christology.

Jon Sobrino, "do not say more than can be gleaned from the life of Jesus as it is presented in the New Testament; nor do they necessarily say it better."[5] Nor can dogmas, like canons, be understood as closure, but only as a *moment* in the interpretation process of the community.[6]

For people who are not even sure where to get the next meal and whose very survival is constantly threatened, I do not see it as urgent and relevant to address the topic of christology in its orthodox and classic formulation. Neither have I seen those who can hardly make both ends meet preoccupied with questions about Christ in his very essence in relation to the trinity. The suffering and struggling Filipino Christians have always been interested in the story and life of Jesus, but they have not been preoccupied with intellectual concerns that deal with the being of Christ itself.

In this chapter I formulate a christology that is born out of the experiences and aspirations of the Filipino people, a christology that helps to illuminate the people's struggle for true humanity and peoplehood. To do this, I attempt, in the first part, to present the kind of christology that has been operative in the struggle of the Filipino people for liberation. This christology can be gleaned from the Filipino religious tradition and especially from the people's popular culture and religiosity. It is my contention that this christology resonates well with the Jesus of the gospels.

In the second part, I attempt to construct the Jesus that is portrayed in the gospels with the full knowledge that there is no single interpretation and that even the gospels portray various images of Jesus. In so doing, I am quite aware of the "constructive" character of this effort, whether one speaks of methods that claim to interpret reality "behind the text" (text as window) or "in front of the text" (text as mirror).[7]

Finally, I try to make a synthesis of the Jesus of the gospels and the Jesus that has become part of the lives of the struggling Filipinos. Here I identify the main themes that the Jesus of the gospels and the Jesus of Filipino popular religiosity have in common, which I would say represents a christology that is appropriate for the theology of struggle.

JESUS AS THE SUFFERING AND STRUGGLING FILIPINOS

I could not help but be amazed and humbled that, in spite of the fact that the Filipinos have been made to absorb the kind of Jesus that is always

---

[5] Jon Sobrino, *Christology at the Crossroads,* trans. John Drury (Maryknoll, NY.: Orbis Books, 1978), p. 385.

[6] J. Severino Croatto, "Biblical Hermeneutics in the Theologies of Liberation," in *Irruption of the Third World: Challenge to Theology,* eds. Virginia Fabella and Sergio Torres (Maryknoll, NY.: Orbis Books, 1983), pp. 152–153.

[7] Norman R. Petersen, *Literary Criticism for New Testament Critics, Guides to Biblical Scholarship,* ed. Dan O. Via, Jr. (Philadelphia: Fortress Press, 1978), p. 24, citing the metaphors from Murray Krieger, *A Window to Criticism* (Princeton, New Jersey: Princeton University Press, 1964).

meek and passive by their masters, they have made a breakthrough in their total ideological captivity. Bereft of sophisticated exegetical tools to interpret the biblical text, their interpretation of Jesus has been guided by their day-to-day experiences. Because of the closeness of Jesus' life and message to their daily struggle, they did not find it difficult to "identify" with Jesus and speak of themselves as the Jesus of contemporary times, undergoing passion, death, and resurrection.[8] Their "identification" with Jesus does not mean "empathizing" with a once-upon-a-time figure and his struggle, as if the struggle was all over, but waging their own struggle as Jesus did.[9]

What appears as an effective interpretation and appropriation of Jesus — an interpretation that has inspired several generations of struggling people — may to others be a breach of biblical scholarship, a "proof texting." The Filipinos' interpretation of Jesus could suffer a similar accusation of "proof texting," such as that leveled by Russell Pregeant against liberation biblical hermeneutics, specifically referring to Sobrino's work on christology.[10] But I do not think it is appropriate to charge the Filipinos' interpretation of Jesus with "proof texting," nor indeed liberation biblical hermeneutics itself, for I do not see it as using *direct analogy*, as Pregeant is suggesting.

What is involved, according to Clodovis Boff, is not direct analogy or a "correspondence of terms," but more of a "correspondence of relations."[11] The affinity is not a correspondence of terms or a one-to-one correspondence because the people know precisely that they are living in a different time and in a different context. In fact, for Segundo, there is always an ideological bridge involved because the text or tradition does not give an eternal blueprint.[12] What the poor people are doing is "appropriation," not proof texting.

It would be better for Pregeant and others like him to charge the fundamentalist Christians who, basically, have come out of Western

---

[8]Ileto, *Pasyon and Revolution: Popular Movements in the Philippines, 1840–1910; People's Participation for Total Human Liberation* (Pasay City, Philippines: Alay Kapwa, 1982); Fabella, "A Common Methodology for Diverse Christologies?" in *With Passion and Compassion: Third World Women Doing Theology,* pp. 108–117. See also Avila, *Peasant Theology: Reflections by the Filipino Peasants on their Process of Social Revolution,* p. 34. Avila spoke of "Christ is the people, and the people is Christ." Cf. José Míguez Bonino, *Doing Theology in a Revolutionary Situation* (Philadelphia: Fortress Press, 1975), p. 3, for his notion of "transcription." Míguez Bonino is willing to say that "Christ is the people," but not to say that the "people is Christ."

[9]Cf. Elizabeth Schüssler Fiorenza, "Remembering the Past in Creating the Future: Historical-Critical Scholarship and Feminist Biblical Interpretation," in *Feminist Perspectives on Biblical Scholarship,* ed. Adela Yarbro Collins (Chico, California: Scholars Press, 1985), p. 63.

[10]Russell Pregeant, "Christological Groundings for Liberation Praxis," *Modern Theology,* vol. 5, no. 2 (January 1989), pp. 113–132.

[11]Boff, *Theology and Praxis: Epistemological Foundations,* pp. 142–150.

[12]Segundo, *Liberation of Theology,* pp. 97–124.

denominationalism and are exporting their mess among the poor Christians in the barrios and pueblos of third-world countries. What they fail to grasp is the creativity of the people to transform the Jesus of the gospels and Christian tradition into an image of Jesus that is relevant to their lives, and this is the case especially when Jesus is transformed through the popular culture and religiosity of the people.

Jesus and the Struggle of the Filipino People

There is not one image of Jesus for the Filipinos. The early conquerors of the Filipino people, who happened to be the bearers of Christian religion, promoted an image of Jesus that was supportive of their domination. In fact, as pointed out by Hechanova, unabashedly there is in the old San Agustine Church in Manila a statue of the infant Jesus dressed as a Spanish conqueror (Sto. Niño El Conquistador or The Holy Child as Conqueror).[13] Something similar can be found in San Sebastian Church in which the Sto. Niño is dressed as a Spanish Governor General.[14] The Spanish conquerors had transformed the Jesus of the gospels into a conqueror of our people. Until the present times, the image of Jesus as passive and obedient to the powers-that-be has taken hold in the lives of many. In this chapter, this is not the kind of Jesus that I am interested in. I am interested in the Jesus that has become incarnate in the lives of the many struggling Filipinos, struggling to find a better tomorrow for the country they love so dearly.

Filipino resistance against foreign invaders, especially the earliest ones, were "nativistic," said Constantino.[15] By this he meant that the Filipinos fought the foreign invaders and their god with the resources from their own native religiosity; it was a fight between the foreign god and the native god. When they were converted to Christianity, which can be interpreted as the triumph of the foreign god, the Filipinos used Christian symbols, but transformed them into something contrary to the expectations of their conquerors. Jesus for them had become a Filipino, a struggling Filipino. Against the Christ of the conquerors, the Filipinos, through their popular culture and religiosity, had evolved a Jesus distinct from the Jesus Christ propagated by the patrons of Christianity, an indication that the control of the foreigners and their god was not total.

Retrieving the Jesus of Filipino popular religiosity, a heritage that had inspired previous generations to struggle, is very important, for I believe along with others that this spirit inspired the Revolution of 1896 against

---

[13]Louie G. Hechanova, "Challenge to the Churches." A speech delivered at the International Ecumenical Conference on the Philippines at Stony Point, New York, September 27 to October 2, 1983.

[14]Benigno Beltran, *The Christology of the Inarticulate: An Inquiry into the Filipino Understanding of Jesus the Christ* (Manila: Divine Word Seminary, 1987), pp. 119-120.

[15]Constantino, *The Philippines: A Past Revisited,* p. 89.

Spain and the most recent People's Power Revolution of 1986.[16] This "Little Tradition," as Ileto termed it (sustained by popular culture and religidsity), in contrast to the "Great tradition" (nourished by the *ilustrados,* who were influenced by the Enlightenment), has long been buried, but has actually functioned as a source of energy and inspiration in the past and in the most recent struggles of the Filipino people.[17] When this "Little Tradition" is not given its proper place in the struggle, the Filipino struggle is actually emptied of its energy, pushing again to the margin the important role of the people, even in the very struggle that claims to be for the people. Without the resources and the animating energy of this "Little Tradition," the little ones will not share again the blessings of any change.

I now identify some of the main features of christology that has been operative in the lives of the Filipino people, but that has not been given much theoretical exposition.

Jesus Who Relates with the People in a Humane Way

Filipino popular religiosity, such as that depicted in the *pasyon* and *salubong* (dawn meeting with the resurrected Jesus), portrays a Jesus that can serve as a model of a humane way of relating and dwelling. The Jesus of the *pasyon* calls his disciples *katoto* (a friend who shares one's truth), *kasalo* (a person whom one eats with), *kasiping* (someone whom one sleeps with), and also *kasambahay* (someone who lives in the same house).[18] What we have here are familial and communal images and concepts that Filipinos, used to closely knit and extended families, can easily identify with. The Jesus of the *pasyon* is not the billiard ball individual of modern society, but one who seeks to build humane relationships, relationships based on the self-worth of the individual, not simply dictated by instrumental rationality. Life in companionship with Jesus is a practice of nonhierarchical, nonpatriarchal ways of relating and a humane way of constructing a human dwelling.

As one who embodies the culture of the people, Jesus is what the Filipinos call *marunong makisama* (he who knows how to get along with people), understood in a positive sense. But this *pakikisama* of Jesus is also a critical *pakikisama*; a *pakikisama* that knows how to say *no* when things are not right. As one who is also *makiangayon* (Cebuano — just and compassionate), his *pakikisama* is a *pakikisama* guided by the sense of being *makiangayon,* which in the presence of deep structural injustice must

---

[16]Joseph P. Frary, "The Philippines: February 1986 in Retrospect," *Asian Journal of Theology,* vol. 1, no. 2 (1987).

[17]Frary, "The Philippines: February 1986 in Retrospect," *Asian Journal of Theology,* vol. 1, no. 2; Ileto, *Pasyon and Revolution;* Allan J. Delotavo, "A Reflection on the Images of Christ in Filipino Culture," *Asian Journal of Theology,* vol. 3, no. 2 (1989).

[18]*People's Participation for Total Human Liberation,* p. 32, citing Aquino de Belen.

lead to *pakikisama sa pakikibaka* (participation in the struggle) against injustice for a better society.

The Jesus Who Suffers with the People

Suffering is not foreign to most of the Filipino people. This has been the lot of many of them for centuries now. In this case it is not difficult to understand that the suffering Jesus is dominant in their Christianity.[19]

The Jesus who suffers has an important place among the oppressed Filipinos. This is therapeutic to the Filipinos in two ways: either to make them accept the harsh realities of life, like the passive Jesus, or to strengthen them in their struggle. The power wielders no doubt have used this suffering and passive Jesus to continue their domination. I oftentimes hear parents telling their children to endure suffering and not to fight back if they want to climb up the ladder of social success. As they say it in my native language: *"Kung gusto mo'ng masantos, mag-antos"* ("If you want to be a saint, you must endure suffering").

There is, however, a different twist in the Filipino sense of suffering. While there is the existing understanding of suffering that is viewed as *kapalaran* (fatalism—literally the lines on one's palm), there is another notion of suffering that is associated with *malasakit* (willingness to suffer for others or for a cause) and *pakikiramay* (vicarious suffering). This is equally common among Filipinos, in spite of the propagation of the idea of *kanya-kanya* or *iya-iya-ako-ako* (to each his or her own). Parents even give almost everything they have, undergoing suffering and extreme *pagtitiis* (willingness to undergo pain and hardships), just to get their children to school. In common Filipino proverbs we can glean the notions of *malasakit*, *pakikiramay*, and *pagtitiis*: *"Magpapaalipin ako nang dahil sa iyo"* ("I am willing to be a slave just for you"), or *"Babaliin ko ang mga buto ko sa katatrabaho upang makamit mo lang ang pangarap mo"* ("It does not matter if I will break my bones working day in and day out, in order for you to fulfill your dreams").

One expression of *malasakit* and *pakikiramay* was expressed by an old man during the funeral rites in behalf of the nuns (known for their commitment to the people) who were drowned when the ship MV Cassandra sank during a strong typhoon. In his moving testimony, he said: "If it is possible to exchange my life with those of the sisters, I would gladly do so. I am already an old man and there's little I can do for the people."[20]

Suffering as *malasakit* is an appropriate imagery of Jesus for the

---

[19]Delotavo, "A Reflection on the Images of Christ in Filipino Culture," *Asian Journal of Theology,* citing Douglas J. Elwood, "The Popular Filipino Christ," *Diwa 6* (October 1981), p. 9.

[20]Gaspar, *How Long?: Prison Reflections from the Philippines,* p. 59.

Filipinos. *Malasakit* belongs to the attributes of Jesus as can be observed in his life, death, and crucifixion. Indeed, he was a person for others, a person come of age. Even with all the risks involved, he was determined to pursue his cause. While *bahala na* (risk taking) seems to be associated with *kapalaran* (fate or wheel of fortune), the *bahala na* that is intertwined with the *malasakit* of Jesus, as proposed by Filipino scholars and theologians, forms into a *bahala na-malasakit*, that is, taking all the risks involved in struggling with the disenfranchised of society.[21]

The Jesus Who Struggles with the Suffering People

There are those who suffer but do not struggle. For these people, Jesus is also perceived as a passive sufferer. But as people begin to wake up and realize that their dehumanizing situation is not the will of God, they start to struggle. From passive suffering, they who have suffered now struggle. And even those who have not suffered, upon their experience of conversion by the neighbor, have started to struggle with the oppressed and, therefore, suffer with them as well. From these suffering but struggling people, Jesus appears as the one who suffers in the struggle; he is the one who has *malasakit* to the *kababayan* (countryfolks) and struggles with them. As a result of this commitment, he suffers even more.

The suffering but struggling Jesus, in contrast to the passive and meek Jesus, is not foreign to the Filipinos. This is the kind of Jesus that has served as a model and a source of inspiration for many Filipinos who have continued to struggle against various enslaving forces in society. The suffering but struggling Jesus, the inspirer of those who have struggled, is discernible in many instances in the history of the Filipino people.

As pointed out by Alan Delotavo, the image of the crucified Jesus was a pervasive symbol during the 1986 People's Power Revolution that toppled the dictator.[22] I see here the connection of the crucified Jesus and revolution. The image of the crucified Jesus was pervasive in the People's Power Revolution, not because the image was used to make the people become passive in their suffering, but precisely to inspire them. On the other hand, it was also used to exorcise the Marcos Loyalist soldiers. The fact that the crucified Jesus was a pervasive symbol points to the interpretation that Jesus' suffering is not a passive suffering, but a struggling suffering, encouraging others to do the same.

---

[21]José M. de Mesa, *In Solidarity with the Culture: Studies in Theological Re-rooting*, Maryhill Studies 4 (Quezon City, Philippines: Maryhill School of Theology, 1987), pp. 147–177; idem, *And God Said, "Bahala Na!": The Theme of Providence in the Lowland Filipino Context* (Quezon City, Philippines: José M. de Mesa, 1979), pp. 81–161; also Dagdag, "Emerging Theology in the Philippines Today," *Kalinangan*, p. 7.

[22]Delotavo, "A Reflection on the Images of Christ in the Filipino Culture," *Asian Journal of Theology*.

The Fiesta Spirit and the Seriousness of the Struggle:
Jesus Who Struggles with Joy

The lives of most Filipinos are immersed with suffering and struggle, but they still know how to celebrate and enjoy life. When they gather after the day's work, rural folks sing, dance, laugh, eat, and drink. Filipinos love to celebrate fiestas and other events in life. Although there are some negative outcomes of this fiesta celebration (like falling into debt in order to host a fiesta), the celebration of fiestas and other occasions is a part of Filipino life and culture; it is a part of nourishing and cementing communal relationships.

Even in what is generally considered serious business, like political rallies, this joyful spirit of fiesta is present. Many Westerners and Filipinos alike have criticized this as a Filipino lack of seriousness and determination. Again, this criticism cannot be totally dismissed, but the fiesta spirit is not incompatible with the seriousness of the Filipino people's struggle. The joy of fiesta and the seriousness of politics can go together, and this has been the case with the previous struggles of the Filipino people and the most recent People's Power Revolution. When the struggle is long and protracted and many have fallen on the way without seeing the dawn, every inch of victory has to be celebrated with joy and thanksgiving.

To portray an image of Jesus as one who struggles with joy in his heart is in consonance with the character of the Filipino people. The Filipinos have found in Jesus a person who knows *pakikisama*, as one who celebrates, even as he calls them to a higher cause that entails sacrifice, like leaving the family and facing the possibility of death. This picture of Jesus is akin to the kind of Jesus that the gospels portray.

Moving Beyond Life as Lent to Hope and Resurrection

If suffering is the daily experience of people, it is understandable why Lent occupies a prominent place in the people's religiosity. This may help explain why the resurrection seems not to be in the limelight, or maybe this is due to the predominant position of Roman Catholic Christianity. Protestants tend to give more emphasis to the resurrection or the triumphant Christ, which can be observed in most Protestant crucifixes (Jesus is not hanging on the crucifix) as compared with the Roman Catholic (RC) crucifixes (Jesus hangs on RC crucifixes). Yet the resurrection has also found expression in the lives of the Filipinos.

If the Holy Week celebration has a *pasyon*, the resurrection celebration has also the *salubong* or *sugat* (Cebuano), which means a dawn meeting with the resurrected Jesus. As practiced in some places, this is the reenactment of the meeting of Jesus and his mother in which the statues of the Risen Christ and the Sorrowful Mother are unveiled by a girl dressed like an angel and singing the *Regina Coeli*. Then the removal of the veil during the meeting is accompanied by the release of doves and *bati*, a dance of joyful celebration.[23]

The *salubong* is rich in symbolism and meaning: It expresses the profound joy of release from the lent of life, and it expresses the belief that the forces of life will finally triumph. The releasing of doves is symbolic of freedom, like the famous *Ibong Malaya* (a free bird), and the *bati* is a celebration of joy for the new life. However, in a situation in which the forces of death are still dominant, the *salubong* celebration is a source of inspiration, vision, and hope. It is founded in a strong belief that, like Jesus, the Filipino people will someday have their own resurrection.

Jesus and the Filipino Search for Humanity

As manifest in the Filipino culture and popular religiosity, like the *pasyon* and even the *salubong*, the Filipinos see Jesus as a way toward a full humanity. Jesus fulfills the thought expressed in the Filipino proverb: *"Madali ang maging tao, pero mahirap ang magpakatao"* ("It is easy to be born, but it is difficult to become fully human"). Jesus was not only born, but he became truly human; his life was an expression of authentic humanity.

Many Filipinos then and now have been striving to reconcile their lives according to the humanity of Jesus. The identification with Jesus' suffering is not difficult for most Filipinos because this has been their lot in life; to suffer and therefore struggle is a further step that the Filipinos must take, although the number of those who suffer and therefore struggle has grown in recent years.

If suffering with Jesus is something that Filipinos can easily identify with and appropriate for themselves, the resurrection of Jesus has, in a way, also been internalized by the people as part of their striving to be human. There is, however, a difficulty involved in striving to be human through the lens of the resurrection because of the usual association of the resurrection with the divine origin of Jesus rather than with his humanity. This is expressed in the following complaint:

> We are often taught that the Resurrection is the proof of Christ's divinity, but we are not shown what its implications are, especially in relation to our struggle for life and our involvement in our situation.[24]

Yet the resurrection of Jesus can be viewed according to his humanity, and the experience of resurrection is discernible in the lives of the Filipino people who have opted to struggle for a better tomorrow. This is their current situation as well as a hoped-for reality.

---

[23] *People's Participation for Total Human Liberation,* p. 36.
[24] Ibid., p. 37.

JESUS AND THE POLITICS OF STRUGGLE

The Jesus that has evolved out of the Filipino suffering and struggle resonates well with the Jesus of the gospels. I view this Jesus of the gospels as someone in conflict with the Jewish establishment who, as a Jew, had to draw from the wealth of the Jewish tradition in his prophetic ministry. To substantiate this claim, I engage in the task of interpreting the biblical text. Whatever limitations one may find in my interpretation of Jesus' relationship with the Jews, I have no intention of pitting Jesus against the Jewish people.

There are various methods that one can employ in the task of biblical interpretation. Particularly relevant for this study is the social world criticism method because it allows me to construct the Jesus of the New Testament, his politics, and the social milieu of his time. Through this method I attempt to identify the overarching symbol of the society in Palestine during the time of Jesus, assuming that the central symbol mirrors the worldview, ethos, or the total social configuration of a society. Identifying this overarching symbol is, I believe, an important hermeneutical key to unlock the inner dynamics of the Jewish society and its constitution.

The Temple as a Symbol: Symbol as Mirror

A symbol functions on at least two counts: (1) it shows forth the reality that it symbolizes, and (2) it is also an instrument in ordering that reality. I first focus on a symbol as it manifests a reality and then examine how temples can become symbols.

It has been commonly understood that major temples of different religions usually serve as important symbols. Supporting this idea is Mircea Eliade who argued that "architectonic edifices of 'traditional' cultures express a very exacting symbolism." The temple is not simply considered a holy place, but "the cosmic symbolism of the village is repeated in the structure of the sanctuary or the cultic house."[25] The temple mirrors the world around it; it is an *imago mundi*.

More than an *imago mundi*, the temple is also the *axis mundi*; the life of a society revolves around that axis and is organized according to the line of structure that emanates from the temple. This is the case with the temple of Jerusalem, for it is the central organizing symbol of Jewish society. For the Jews, the temple is not only an *imago mundi*, but also an *axis mundi*. Michel Clévenot rightly pointed out the crucial place the Jerusalem temple

---

[25]Mircea Eliade, *Symbolism, the Sacred and the Arts* (New York: The Crossroad Publishing Company, 1985), p. 130.

takes when he identified the temple as a symbol of the "entire social formation."[26]

Moving along a similar line of thought is Jerome Neyrey who had explicitly made use of the work of cultural anthropologist Mary Douglas. Neyrey strengthens my point: the "temple system . . . is a major mediation or replication of the idea of order and purity established in creation."[27] Because the order of society is replicated in the temple, an analysis of the temple system is helpful in arriving at a better understanding of the social order; it offers to the interpreter a key to comprehend the complexities of Jewish society. Hence, it is proper to ask: What is the social order that is mirrored in the temple system?

The Temple, Purity Map, and Social Order: Analyzing their Interconnections

The social order replicated in the temple system can be deciphered through what is known as a *purity map.* [28] A purity map is a symbol model for classifying things, people, places, events, and others. Purity maps or rules define what is wrong and what is right at a certain place and at a certain time. The purity map sets a "place for everything and everything in its place."[29] Rules of purity are not mere rituals, but are ways of "maintaining order" and identifying those things that are "out of order." Douglas, whose works have been particularly helpful for many biblical scholars, points out with penetrating insight the relation of pollution ideas to the social order. Expressing the relation, she said, "pollution ideas relate to social life . . . . Pollutions . . . are analogies for expressing a general view of the social order."[30] Even "ideas about sexual dangers are better interpreted as symbols of the relation between parts of society, as mirroring designs of hierarchy or symmetry which apply in the larger social system."[31] In other words, the purity map defines the social order.

If pollution ideas or purity maps define social order, then ritual uncleanliness conveys a transgression of the social order. Douglas's analysis of what is considered "dirt" reveals convincingly that dirt is a violation of order. She said,

> As we know it, dirt is essentially disorder. There is no such thing as absolute dirt: it exists in the eye of the beholder. If we shun dirt, it is not because of craven fear, still less dread or holy terror. Nor do our ideas about disease

---

[26]Michel Clévenot, *Materialist Approaches to the Bible* (Maryknoll, NY.: Orbis Books, 1985), p. 50.

[27]Jerome Neyrey, "Idea of Purity in Mark's Gospel," *Semeia* 35 (1986), p. 94.

[28]Ibid., pp. 91–99.

[29]Ibid., p. 93.

[30]Mary Douglas, *Purity and Danger* (London: Ark Paperbacks, 1966), p. 3.

[31]Ibid., pp. 3–4.

account for the range of our behaviour in cleaning or avoiding dirt. *Dirt offends against order.*[32]

Take for instance what we call "weeds." Weeds are those plants that are out of place; once they become part of a landscape they cease to be weeds. Neyrey described this purity (order) and dirt relationship in a simple but clear fashion:

> A farmer working in his field is covered with dust and chaff, his shoes caked with mud and dung. This is appropriate to the outdoors work of farming during the day; it is what is expected of fields and barns. But should that farmer come inside after the day's work, wearing those same dirt-covered over-alls and dung-covered shoes, and sit in his wife's living room, his farm dirtiness, so appropriate outside, is impurity inside. The wrong *thing* appears in the wrong *place* at the wrong *time.*[33]

The ordinary dirt that we encounter every day is indeed highly symbolic; it reveals a system or an ordering of reality. Seen from the perspective of order, dirt is that which is out of order. If one views reality from the point of view of dirt, the outcome of the reading is different: dirt is a by-product of ordering the social reality; dirt does not simply exist in itself, but is a product of ordering and classifying. In actuality, it is the order that produces the dirt. Dirt is a refuse of the established order.

The Purity Map and the Jewish Symbolic Order

The purity map of Jewish society covers various subjects such as geography, time, persons, foods, and sacrificial offerings. The map is so well defined that it can be said that Jewish society is extremely ordered. People, things, events, time, and places are classified according to the purity map and are judged impure or dirty in relation to it. All these classifications are mirrored in the temple — the center of the purity map — in which the purity map is meticulously guarded.

As the center, everything revolves around the temple or is judged in relation to its proximity to the center of purity (the Holy of Holies). And as the organizing force (temple), everything moves inward and upward through it; it is the hub of what happens on earth and what gets to heaven; it is the axis that joins heaven and earth. In this picture, the temple is not only at the center, but also at the top of the hierarchical social structure. There is no access to Yahweh (at the top) except through the hierarchical channel and no healing from impurities except as one gains access to the system of purity.

---

[32]Ibid., p. 2. Emphasis supplied.
[33]Neyrey, "Idea of Purity in Mark's Gospel," *Semeia,* p. 92.

The map of places illustrates how the system of classification based on purity pervaded Israelite society in which the temple occupied the central place. One can notice that holiness lay only within Israel's geography, never outside it. Here is M. Kelim's attempt to formulate a map of places:

1. The land of Israel is holier than any other land . . .
2. The walled cities (of the land of Israel) are still more holy . . .
3. Within the wall (of Jerusalem) is still more holy . . .
4. The temple mount is still more holy . . .
5. The Rampart is still more holy . . .
6. The Court of women is still more holy . . .
7. The Court of the Israelites is still more holy . . .
8. The Court of Priests is still more holy . . .
9. Between the Porch and Altar is still more holy . . .
10. The Sanctuary is still more holy . . .
11. The Holy of Holies is still more holy . . . [34]

Such a detailed classification of places can also be applied to foods, events, time, and people. The diet-conscious modern person may think that the elaborate food classification in Palestine is a matter of health or hygiene, when primarily it is more a question of order or a purity map. The same grid is useful in reading time and events. What Eliade meant regarding the temple of Barabudur can be applied to the temple of Jerusalem: "In building the temple, not only was the world constructed but the cosmic time as well."[35] Seasons of the year are well classified according to the standard set by the temple, and events are only considered to be of importance in their relation to the temple. History is always read through the lens of the temple; the temple's perspective of history is *the* history.

The classification of places, time, and foods is, however, not as problematic and controversial as the classification of people. Whether we use the terms *division of population, stratification,* or *class,*[36] it is clear from the purity map that Israelite society was a society subject to classification. With the priestly class closely identified with the temple and guardians of the purity map, they themselves occupied the center and the top of the purity classification. Because a society that is organized around the idea of purity has its axis in the temple, Jacob Neusner is right in his analysis that the priestly "caste stood at the top of a social scale in which all

[34]Neyrey, "Idea of Purity in Mark's Gospel," *Semeia,* citing M. Kelim, p. 95; also cited by Fernando Belo in his book *A Materialist Reading of the Gospel of Mark* (Maryknoll, NY.: Orbis Books, 1981), p. 79.

[35]Eliade, *Symbolism, the Sacred and the Arts,* p. 115.

[36]Roland de Vaux, *Ancient Israel* vol. I (New York: McGraw-Hill, 1961), pp. 68–79.

things were properly organized, each with its correct name and place. The sanctity inhering in Israel, the people, came to its richest embodiment in him, the priest."[37] Because the temple occupied the center of the Jewish social order, it is not far-fetched to say that those who controlled the temple also controlled Jewish society.

Still, one may wonder why control of a religious establishment means control of the overall social system? It should be recalled that in Jewish society control of the temple was not simply cultic, but was inseparable from economics, politics, and culture. The temple, which was the center of the purity map, was also the seat of the Sanhedrin with the High Priest as the head (politics), the seat of treasury (economics), and the holy place *par excellence* (culture).[38] As the holy place *par excellence*, there is no other place that a Jew could acquire the much-needed purity except through the temple. Through Jewish law, which regulated in "minute detail the production, circulation and consumption of products at economic, political and ideological levels (goods, people and ideas)," the priestly caste controlled the reins of society.[39] In this case, the priestly caste occupied the top of the ladder of social stratification.

Together with the priests, or the Sadducees, at the top of the social formation were the Roman nobles, the absentee landlords, and wealthy urban merchants. While the history of the relationships of these groups had not been always smooth, in many instances we can discern the merging of their interests. To preserve their position in society, the Saducean aristocracy collaborated with the Romans and established friendly relations with the landlords and the merchants.

The Pharisees, although having membership in the Sanhedrin, can be classified more with the middle class. Neusner's remark that the Sadducees were much more influential among the landlords and merchants, whereas the Pharisees influenced the middle and lower urban classes, suggests that the Pharisees were more or less attached to the middle class.[40]

The rest of the population could be classified in the lower part of the social stratification. They were the small landowners, craftsmen, laborers or wage earners, peasants, women, children, beggars, and slaves. People with physical deformities or beset with diseases also fell to the lower "rung" of social stratification. The same was true with women. Neusner did not fail to see the connection of women's place in the temple as reflective of their place in society when he said that the "women's court was set away from the holy altar itself, and that fact captured the position of women in

---

[37]Jacob Neusner, *Judaism in the Beginning of Christianity* (Philadelphia: Fortress Press, 1984), p. 37.

[38]Belo, *A Materialist Reading of the Gospel of Mark,* pp. 64–81.

[39]Clévenot, *Materialist Approaches to the Bible,* p. 37.

[40]Neusner, *Judaism in the Beginning of Christianity,* p. 28.

society as a whole." There were some instances when women played an important role, but "where the priestly tradition dominated, there, women were excluded."[41]

This cursory survey of the purity map (social map) shows an extremely classified and well-stratified Jewish society. What seems to be simply cultic purity in many ways mirrors the whole reality. Although there is no perfect one-to-one correspondence between class and purity (the Roman nobles belong to the upper class although considered ritually unclean), it can be said generally that, within the Jewish communities, the purity map was expressive of class stratification. I agree with Clévenot's bold assertion that the "temple . . . is a symbol of a society of classes."[42]

Religious Symbols and the Ideological Critique of Religion

The temple system illustrated by the purity map shows that what seems to be purely cultic can be a window to or a mirror of the order of society. The temple as a symbol did not simply float in the air, but was a part of the superstructure that lay on an economic and political foundation. It mirrored society but, on the other hand, it also shaped the society. A symbol is very much a product of the historico-material condition of society. Religious symbols are no exemptions, in spite of the claim that they transcend historical determination. Like other symbols, religious symbols mirror the historical reality of that which they symbolize; but, unlike other symbols, they purport to convey what Clifford Geertz calls "divine reality."[43] It is in the way they are construed as manifesting a divine reality that the capacity of religious symbols for good and evil converge. And in the Jewish purity map a religious symbol was used to legitimize an order that was beneficial to the guardians of the purity map. The idea that the social map — viewed within the framework of the system of purity — is a replication of the order of creation gives religious legitimation to the existing social order. The social order is understood not simply as a social construction, but as a natural or God-given order. The order is already given; what individuals do is play the roles that are assigned to them by the God-given order. When this happens, a critique of the social order becomes impossible. A hermeneutics of suspicion is necessary for people to realize that "when we say, 'that's the way things are,' we are not only making a factual statement about the mechanical appropriateness of nature, but a moral evaluation of that order."[44]

---

[41]Ibid., pp. 31–32.

[42]Clévenot, *Materialist Approaches to the Bible*, p. 79.

[43]Clifford Geertz, cited in Carol Christ, *Laughter of Aphrodite: Reflections on a Journey to the Goddess* (Cambridge: Harper and Row, 1987), p. 137.

[44]Robert Wuthnow, *Cultural Analysis* (London: Routledge and Kegan Paul, 1984), p. 87.

Sin and the Purity Map

The connections between the purity map and social order convey a particular notion of sin, something quite different than what is commonly associated with that word. From our analysis of the temple and the purity map, sin appears basically as a disruption of the purity map or of the notion of order established in creation. Sin against God is only understood properly through the mediation of a set of assumptions about the structure of social reality. Judgment that a sin has been committed is based on the society's notion of God-given order. Whoever disrupts the purity map or the social order is impure, unholy, a sinner, dirt, and an enemy of God. Here, God is identified with the given order and an enemy of those who violate the order which, in a real sense, is an order of disorder.

The above framework was applied to Jesus, his followers, the outcasts, the maimed, the blind, and the lame. In the eyes of the establishment, Jesus was the sinner among sinners. His violations of the time map (Sabbath - Mark 2:23–27), and of food prohibitions (saying that what defiles a person is that which comes out of one's mouth [Mark 7:14–23]), of pronouncing forgiveness to those classified as sinners under the purity system (Mark 2:5), made Jesus a notorious sinner, even one possessed by the prince of demons (Mark 3:22).

Righteousness and the Purity Map (Social Order)

If violation of the purity map is considered sin, then righteousness (dikaiosune) is following the details of the purity map and walking uprightly in order not to violate the order. The gospel narratives depict a kind of righteousness that is in line with the meticulous observance of the purity map by the Pharisees and the Sadducees: their strict observance of the Sabbath vis-à-vis the hungry, their righteousness/cleanliness vis-à-vis the victims (Luke 10:29–37), their exclusive banquets designed for those who are pure, their prohibitions of mixed marriages with foreigners and slaves, and the social role assigned to women. The righteousness of the Sadducees and the Pharisees fell within the maintenance of the purity map.

In the Jewish society of Jesus' time, those who were considered impure, dirty, or unholy had no other way to be restored to the social order than by undergoing the purification rites administered by the priestly class. But because their categorization as dirt was a by-product of the system of purity itself, their ritual purity was in effect only temporary and palliative. With the system of purity tied to the economic and political base, the performance of the cultic rite would only provide a temporary relief from the stigma of impurity unless there was a corresponding change in the person's economic and political situation. This connection can be seen among those people who were classified as *Am ha-aretz* and those who were living in ignorance of Jewish learning *(Am ha-aratzut).*[45]

The relation between righteousness/justice and social order (purity map) from the point of view of those who wanted to preserve it (Sadducees, wealthy nobles, and Pharisees) can be summed up as the subordination of righteousness to the purity map. Righteousness or justice (dikaiosune), in this context, was to do what the established order (dike) required. By positing order as the primary given, the notion of justice as "to each his or her due" could be applied in the Jewish context, that is, that which is due to the slave should be given to the slave, and that which is due to the master should be given to the master, but the master-slave relation must not be destroyed.[46]

Control of the Temple System and the Marginalization of the People: Symbol as an Instrument

Power and Control of the Ideological/Cultural Apparatus

After focusing on the symbol construed as a mirror, I now turn to the symbol as "instrument," an instrument that helps to order a social reality.

The practice of social agents usually determines the meaning of symbol and how it is used as an instrument. Carol Christ, although acknowledging the contribution of Paul Tillich on the idea of symbol, has made a brilliant critique of Tillich's insistence that "symbol cannot be produced intentionally" and die mysteriously. This, for Christ, only eludes the historical grounding of symbol and its interpretation in the struggles of various classes.[47] Like Carl Gustav Jung's idea of symbol, which is based on "universal archetype," an existentialist understanding of symbol obscures the fact that it "is dependent on a culture's concrete historical circumstances."[48] It obscures the fact that a symbol is politically loaded. Furthermore, Christ argued that Tillich's emphasis on the mysteriousness of symbols overlooks the possibility of its manipulation and the importance of a conscious effort to construct new and liberating symbols, as feminist scholars have attempted to do.[49]

Christ's criticism of the existentialist notion of symbol is, I believe, accurate. When detached from the specific historical circumstances, the conflicting understandings of the symbol are avoided. In concrete situa-

---

[45]Abraham Chill, *The Mizvot* (New York: Bloch Publishing Company, 1974), p. xx.

[46]See Alisdair MacIntyre, *After Virtue* (South Bend, Indiana: University of Notre Dame, 1984), p. 134.

[47]Christ, *Laughter of Aphrodite*, p. 137.

[48]Robert L. Cohn, *The Shape of the Sacred Space: Four Biblical Studies* (Chico, California: Scholars Press, 1981), p. 4.

[49]Christ, *Laughter of Aphrodite*, p. 137.

tions, however, symbols battle for supremacy because they are tied to the consciousness of various groups. Usually the dominant symbol is favorable to the interest of the ruling groups. This is true with the temple of Jerusalem and the purity map it supported. With the dominant symbol (temple) gaining control of the people's consciousness, the structure that it supported soon became an accepted reality. Unless a liberating consciousness emerges to challenge the domesticating symbol, it will always remain a strong power base for the ruling elite.

The Temple System: Its Misuse and Abuse

Control of such a powerful cultural apparatus as the temple also poses a grave risk of its misuse. Considered by the Israelites as a "redemptive media" (temple system — sacrificial rites, *mizvot*, or the "revealed prescriptions for salvation"),[50] the people viewed the performance of the temple rites as necessary in order to attain redemption. The centrality of the temple in the lives surely made those who controlled it powerful and the people quite vulnerable to its misuse and abuse.

Sheldon Isenberg, in recounting the power of those who controlled the temple, commented that they "have the closest possible relation to the power of God, a position which may be and was translated into enormous political and economic power."[51] Fernando Belo's penetrating critique of the interplay between economics, politics, and culture (ideology) gives the extent of the power of the ruling class. The priestly class controlled the treasury, the Sanhedrin, and the cultural-ideological apparatus (the temple system). Because the Sanhedrin met at the temple and the high priest was the chair, Belo was right to conclude that the "religious character of the Sanhedrin provided an ideological mask for its political function."[52] The power of the temple system was so pervasive that even minute details did not escape its control.

> Control over the sacrificial system not only affected the forms of ritual observance, both individual and collective, but also involved control over what might be considered the national treasury, for each Jew was taxed and tithed for support of the priesthood and the temple. Control over commerce went to those who interpreted the laws about what goods were permissible to be bought and sold, eaten and worn, as well as what could be planted and when.[53]

---

[50]Sheldon Isenberg, "Power Through the Temple and Torah in Greco-Roman Palestine," in *Christianity, Judaism and Other Greco-Roman Cults: Studies for Morton Smith at Sixty,* vols. 1-4, ed. J. Neusner (Leiden: E.J. Brill, 1975), pp. 27-32.

[51]Sheldon Isenberg, "Millenarism in Greco-Roman Palestine," *Religion* 4 (1974), p. 31.

[52]Belo, *A Materialist Reading of the Gospel of Mark,* p. 66.

[53]Isenberg, "Millenarism in Greco-Roman Palestine," in *Religion,* p. 31.

The Romans knew so well the power base of the ruling elite that they tried to maintain the temple system; they imposed their will by coopting the guardians of the system. To assure the complete instrumentation of the temple system to their interest, the Romans even intervened in what was once an hereditary mode of succession to the office of the High Priest.[54] The priestly class also readily collaborated with the Romans, provided the temple system was maintained and they were at the control of it. At the center of the treasury, the temple system was the instrument used to siphon the wealth of the small merchants, laborers, and peasants. It was through the temple system that the tributary system was successfully implemented. George Pixley succinctly articulated the instrumentation of the temple system and the collaboration of its guardians:

> The extraction of surplus was carried out peacefully as long as the imperial authorities recognized the special characteristics of this society and allowed the temple its dominant role in the control of and exploitation of the villagers.[55]

The Sicarii's strategy of selective assassination illustrates the collaboration, or the alliance, of the priestly aristocracy/Sadducees and the Roman imperialists. Their assassination campaign, inaugurated with the assassination of the High Priest Jonathan, was intended to create a dramatic effect, primarily on those who collaborated with the imperial masters, but also on the oppressed. The assassination of the High Priest conveyed the message that the symbol of the Jewish nation "had become a symbol of the aristocracy's collaboration with the Roman rule as well as the exploitation of the people."[56]

Through the temple system, the ruling elite and the Roman masters siphoned the wealth from the people. Various methods were employed to amass wealth from the people: gifts, levies, trade in sacrificial animals, revenues in real estate, tithes, and taxes. During pilgrimage seasons (cf. Luke 2:41), trade connected with the temple boomed. The temple had control of the sacrificial goods which the pilgrims had to buy through the acceptable channels. In addition, the priestly class controlled the inns for pilgrims and the money-lending institutions. Out of the temple treasury, a sizeable amount went to the Roman masters. Belo documented:

---

[54]John E. Stambaugh, *The New Testament in its Social Environment* (Philadelphia: The Westminster Press, 1986), p. 99; also Gerd Theissen, *Sociology of Early Palestinian Christianity* (Philadelphia: Fortress Press, 1977), pp. 70–72.

[55]George Pixley, "God's Kingdom in First Century Palestine," in *The Bible and Liberation: Political and Social Hermeneutics,* ed. Norman K. Gottwald (Maryknoll, NY.: Orbis Books, 1983), p. 382.

[56]Richard Horsley, *Bandits, Prophets and Messiahs* (Minneapolis: Winston Press, 1985), p. 206.

Judea had to pay six hundred talents a year to Rome; this was the equivalent of six million denarii, with a denarius representing a day's wages for a farm worker.

This total tax comprised: the tribute *(tributum), which was a personal tax and a land tax; the 'yearly produce' (annona),* an annual contribution to meet the needs of the garrisons, taking the forms of food and of forced labor; the 'public' tax *(publicum),* consisting of indirect taxes and duties, the collection of which was usually farmed out to 'publicans' or tax collectors.[57]

The increasing demands of Rome, the hunger for wealth of the Sadducees and the lay aristocracy, and extravagant projects — such as building the temple, Herod's palace, aqueducts, monuments, and city walls — led to a stricter implementation of the taxation system. This so worsened the situation that many were pushed to the margin. Natural calamities further pushed the people into such an extremely miserable situation that many had to borrow money at usurious interest rates or had to sell their small pieces of land to the wealthy. Thus, many of the small farmers and peasants ended up as wage earners. A great many of them were reduced to such total poverty that they fell into slavery or became beggars. The threat of expropriation of lands by the Romans placed the landed gentry in a situation of uncertainty. This uncertainty had its effect, finally, on the lower classes. Because of the constant threat of expropriation, even the landowners, as S. W. Baron put it:

developed those characteristics of servility toward political superiors and of utmost ruthlessness toward underlings which often forced the latter to flee and join the roving bands of brigands. This was the usual extreme way out for the oppressed farmers, as well as slaves, in the ancient world.[58]

Increased pressure from the Romans to protect their class interest, which had been slowly brought into question, caused the priestly class to become legalistic. Their legal rigorism actually worked to their advantage, and they promoted it with fanatical zeal. Backed by strong legal codes, the priestly class executed the collection of temple taxes, even at times with force:

The High Priests finally reached such a pitch in their arrogance and their audacity that they did not hesitate to send their servants to the threshing floors and have them take away the tithe due to the priests; the result of this was that the poorer of the priests perished of starvation.[59]

---

[57]Belo, *A Materialist Reading of the Gospel of Mark,* p. 63.

[58]S. W. Baron, *A Social and Religious History of the Jews,* 2nd ed., rev. (New York: 1952 [sic]), cited by Belo, *A Materialist Reading of Mark,* p. 67. ,

[59]Theissen, *Sociology of Early Palestinian Christianity,* p. 43, quoted from Antt. 20.8.8; §181; cf. 20.9.2. §§206f.

With this understanding of the Jewish social map, mirrored in the temple system, it is understandable that struggles revolved around the temple and that many of the marginalized movements had strong negative pronouncements against the guardians of the temple system. The struggle of the Jesus movement can be assessed in terms of its vision of society and its view of the temple system.

The Temple System and the Politics of Jesus

There is good reason to suggest that Jesus and his movement had properly identified the organizing symbol of the Jewish society and its implications. Not only was the symbol identified, but it was analyzed in a proper way so that Jesus' strategy and vision manifested a comprehensive and radical critique. Jesus' activities in relation to the temple showed an understanding that any change in the Jewish social order had to be primarily a struggle against the organizing symbol, which had a strong sacred legitimation. The polemics against the temple by Jesus (Mark 11:15-19; 13:1-2) were not arbitrary but based on the understanding that because the domination by those at the top "rested principally on a deep-seated ideology, the strategy of the Jesus movement was one of ideological attack."[60]

Roots of Subversive Memory: Jesus' Attack of the Jewish
Dominant Ideology

In her work, *Natural Symbols*, Douglas pointed out that "anyone challenging authority should challenge its particular symbols and find new symbols so as to pit against one discarded form of expression another at least as coherent."[61] Arguing in a similar vein is Neusner who said that "symbol change is social change."[62] This change, of course, should not be interpreted as free from struggle because a symbol change is itself a mark that a struggle has been going on. Jesus denounced the dominant Jewish symbol in favor of a symbol, one whose origin was long repressed in the memory of the people. His criticism of the temple abuses made him an articulator of a tradition that had been repressed by the dominant ideology.

The work of biblical scholars on trajectory analysis throughout the Bible is useful for my intentions. Through trajectory analysis it is possible to see in a wide spectrum the stance of Jesus and why he cannot be classified as an articulator of the dominant Jewish social map.

Following a clue from the work of Walter Brueggemann,[63] it appears

---

[60]Pixley, "God's Kingdom in First Century Palestine," in *The Bible and Liberation*, p. 384.

[61]Mary Douglas, *Natural Symbols* (New York: Parthenon Books, 1982), p. xxii.

[62]Neusner, *Judaism in the Beginning of Christianity*, p. 39.

[63]Walter Brueggemann, "Trajectories in Old Testament Literature and the Sociology of Ancient Israel," in *The Bible and Liberation*, pp. 307-333; idem, *Prophetic Imagination* (Philadelphia: Fortress Press, 1978).

that Jesus' vehement attack against the temple system had its roots in the "liberation trajectory." This trajectory, which was in conflict with the priestly-royal line, can be perceived if we bear in mind the relationship between class and ideological production. We can trace the thread of this liberation trajectory from Moses, Abiathar, and the Mushite priesthood to the tribal confederacy and the opposition movements against the formation of the monarchy. In the opposite camp is the royal-priestly trajectory which traces its origin from the Abrahamic memory through the triumph of the monarchy over the tribal confederacy, the ideological production of priestly documents, and the formation of the priestly class in the line of Zadok to the Sadducees. That same trajectory is also discernible in the North (Israel) and South (Judah) theory, wherein the North was portrayed in line with liberation trajectory, whereas the South was seen as supportive of the royal trajectory. We can also find this trajectory in the rivalry between Mount Sinai and Mount Zion, with Mount Sinai identified with the liberation and Mount Zion with the royal trajectory. The dominance of Mount Zion as a *hieros topos* (over that of Mount Sinai)[64] signified the final triumph of the royal-temple-Zion-Sadducean ideology and the suppression of the liberation-Mosaic-Sinai-tribal-antimonarchic/priestly ideology.

Helping us connect this trajectory analysis to the New Testament are Belo and Clévenot. Belo and Clévenot's distinction of the gift system (characterized by equality, self-rule, and tribal society) vis-à-vis the system of purity (characterized by centralism, bureaucracy, sacral and royal power) complements Brueggemann's royal and liberation trajectories.[65] With this analysis I conclude that Jesus did not operate within the temple-purity framework, but that his stance was more in line with the subjugated tradition.

Rereading of Social Reality from Below and Application of the "Hermeneutics of Suspicion": Jesus and His Radical Critique

If Paul Ricoeur considers Marx, Freud, and Nietzsche as masters of the "hermeneutics of suspicion,"[66] Jesus of Nazareth can be said to be a practitioner of the hermeneutics of suspicion. He did not accept the so-called God-given reality at face value. Instead, he subjected the social map of his society to a deep and penetrating analysis. By so doing, he found out that the dominant ideas of his age were generally favorable to the interests of the ruling few. Many of the citizens did not know this, so Jesus committed himself to the task of conscientization. In many ways, Jesus

---

[64]Cohn, *The Shape of the Sacred: Four Biblical Studies,* pp. 3, 43–61.

[65]Kuno Füssel, "Materialist Readings of the Bible: Report on an Alternative Approach to Biblical Texts" in *God of the Lowly: Socio-Historical Interpretations of the Bible,* ed., Willy Schottroff (Maryknoll, NY.: Orbis Books, 1984), pp. 13–25.

[66]Paul Ricoeur, *Freud and Philosophy: An Essay on Interpretation,* trans. Denis Savage (New Haven: Yale University Press, 1970), p. 32.

tried to expose the misuse of the temple/purity system and the dominant mindset that it perpetuated. In a society in which the majority of the people had accepted their plight as fate from God, Jesus considered it his task to unmask the ideological distortion of this belief. To do so, Jesus had to challenge the religion and the god of the dominant elite through a new reading of his Jewish religious heritage.

Following the subjugated memory and tradition, Jesus placed himself in opposition to the dominant ideology. Convinced of what he saw as a distortion of Jewish religious belief, Jesus continued to unveil the true face of the religious practice of the dominant elite. Arguing from the perspective of marginalized of society and from prophetic heritage, he lambasted the religious hypocrites whose religiosity was, in fact, responsible for pushing the people to the edges of society. This is the kind of religiosity that "neglected the weightier matters of the law, justice and mercy and faith" (Matthew 23:23). For Jesus, the guardians of the temple system and the purity map did not know the real "Father," although they praised God with their lips. The extent of the ideological distortion of the dominant religious belief was revealed in Jesus' deep ideological critique: he declared that the time is coming "when whoever kills you will think he is offering service to God" (John 16:2).

On Blaming the Victims and Eyesores: Shifting the Focus

What usually escapes the perception of people is that society, to appear healthy, tends most often to put the blame on the victims. When one views reality from the top or from the standpoint of the dominant culture, the victims often get the blame. It is, however, the other way around when one views reality from the point of view of the victims and the underdogs: that those who are considered "eyesores" are actually victims of the ordering of social reality. Jesus was able to see this because he viewed reality from the epistemological privilege of the poor.

Without going into the textual controversies related to the text, John 8:1-11 details an attempt by Jesus to focus the criticism not on the victims, but on the social order and its guardians. When a woman caught in adultery was presented to him by the scribes and the Pharisees, Jesus exposed not only the hypocrisy of the so-called dignified citizens, but the bankruptcy of the purity system itself. Instead of being an instrument of redemption, the purity system pushed people to the margin. When Jesus asked the woman, "Has no one condemned you?" The woman answered, "No one, Lord." Then Jesus said, "Neither do I condemn you; go, and do not sin again" (John 8:10-11).

This does not mean that Jesus tolerated the sin of the woman, but his focus was on the purity system's failure to be an instrument of liberation. The purity system failed because it became an instrument to maintain the unjust social order and the privileges of its guardians. The shift of the focus to that of the social order rather than the victim turned the world upside down. A contemporary saying fits this point well: "You call me an 'eyesore,' a beggar, but what would you call a society that has reduced me to this state?"

By inserting himself in the margin and reading from the underside, Jesus could see the problem of his society at a systemic and structural level. For a long time, Jewish society covered this painful reality by blaming the victims. But through a hermeneutics from below, the structural basis of the social ills was exposed. Not even individual repentance would suffice.

The problem of Jesus' society was beyond cosmetic repair: A radical change was needed if there was to be social healing. This is one crucial point that distinguishes Jesus' program from that of his compatriots. It is at this point that he is more radical and more revolutionary than the Zealots, the Sicarii, the Essenes, and other movements. Jesus subverted the social order that was based on the purity map, whereas the Zealots, Essenes, and other groups struggled within the framework of the established map.

Kuno Füssel, following the ideas of Belo and Clévenot, articulated this central point in the activity of Jesus: "Jesus dies because he wishes to tear down the temple and build a distinct one from the old. This distinguishes him from the Zealots who *die for* and *in the temple.*"[67] This is made emphatic in John 2:18-22: "Destroy this temple, and in three days I will raise it up." The Gospel of Matthew also recorded this account. When Jesus had left the temple, one of his disciples came to point out the temple building. This triggered Jesus' response: "You see all these, do you not? Truly, I say to you, there will not be left here one stone upon another, that will not be thrown down" (Matthew 24:2). These sayings convey a subversion of the purity-based social order, not preservation or even renovation. Jesus ministered, lived, and died, said Elizabeth Schüssler Fiorenza, not for "purity," but for the restoration of health or "wholeness."[68]

On "Breaking" and "Tearing" the Social Map

"Breaking" or "tearing" is a necessary step for any transformative social action. Breaking is necessary if change is to happen. Change, on the other hand, is not done for its own sake because change is not good in itself. It is always related to a certain end. However, the task of transformation involves risk. Jesus took the risk, that is, the risk of breaking and tearing the Jewish social map. In the Gospel narratives, Jesus and his movement subverted the various angles of the Jewish social/purity map. The account in Mark 2:21-22 about the new wine and the old wineskin is symbolic of the breaking of the old social map. The old wineskin cannot contain the new

---

[67]Füssel, "Materialist Readings of the Bible: Report on an Alternative Approach to Biblical Texts," in *God of the Lowly: Socio-Historical Interpretations of the Bible*, p. 14. Emphasis supplied.

[68]Elizabeth Schüssler Fiorenza, *In Memory of Her* (New York: Crossroad, 1983), p. 113.

wine, or the old structure cannot contain new ideas. To force the new wine into the old wineskin would only burst it.

The tearing of the temple's curtain is also suggestive of the tearing of the Jewish social map (Mark 15:38). Jesus' total strategy, which had its beginning in those ideas considered unholy, dirty, or at the fringes and interstices of the social/purity map subverts the Jewish order. I now focus on the different aspects of the social/purity map and Jesus' tearing-down activities.

By reason of geography (geographic map), Jesus and his band of Galilean followers were already in a marginalized situation. No one expected anything good to come out of Galilee. But being identified with Galilee simply placed Jesus' transforming activity into the category of the unexpected; hence, it did not demand any fair hearing. For the power wielders, it was inconceivable that something good should come out of Galilee, Gelil ha Goyem, the district of pagans.[69] It was inconceivable that a prophet or any legitimate change agent should come from the margin. All that they expected was a prophetic voice from the center of power. If there was any initiative for change, it should come from the top and the learned, that is, from the "Who's who" of Jewish society. This point is clear in John 7:52: in the Pharisees' argument against Nicodemus (an enlightened Pharisee), they challenged him to "study the Scripture" and find out for himself that "no prophet ever comes from Galilee." In other words, the normal (which is generally based on the ruling ideas) or the common view was that no change could come from unholy places or people. To initiate change from a pagan area was actually an act of subversion. But this is precisely what Jesus did, and in no other way could he have done it, for he was concerned with radical change.

Another aspect of tearing down the social order is Jesus' ministry of healing the sick and declaring them to be clean (Mark 1:29; 2:4, 9, 11). At first glance, his ministry may not appear threatening, but for the power wielders this was subversive because what was at stake was not so much the blasphemy of Jesus in forgiving the sinners (Mark 2:5-7) or even the restoration of health to the person, but rather his undermining of their authority (power) and the temple system. Jesus' activity of forgiving the sinners was dangerous in the eyes of the guardians of the temple system because Jesus' source of authority was beyond the control of the official channel. His source of authority and power lay outside the established structure, the legitimacy of which was controlled by the hierarchy. For the power wielders of Jesus' time, any power that sprang from outside a formal power structure was dangerous to society and its use disapproved by those considered "good" citizens. By being identified with a power that had its source outside the official channels or the legitimate structure, Jesus was considered mad and even possessed by Beelzebul (Mark 3:20-27). This is often the fate of people who challenge the dominant order.

---

[69]Clévenot, *Materialist Approaches to the Bible,* p. 76.

A series of subversive activities and Jesus' constant breaking of the Jewish social map can be discerned in his violation of the sabbath law(Mark 2:23–27), violation of cultic rites related to food (Mark 7:14–23), crossing of cultural boundaries (Luke 17:11–19), overturning the tables of the money changers (Mark 11:15–19), and response to the question of the legality of paying taxes to Caesar (Mark 12:13–17).

Subversion of the sabbath rules was inescapable for Jesus. He knew that the Sabbath was designed for the good of the people (Mark 2:27), but it was used at that time as an oppressive institution. The institution was zealously guarded to protect the interests of those who benefitted from it. Jesus placed the question pointedly: "Is it lawful on the sabbath to do good or to do harm, to save life or to kill?"(Mark 3:4).

In a similar line of reasoning lies the question of food and the temple sacrifices. Matthew 12:6–7 depicts Jesus as saying, to quote from the Scripture: "I tell you, something greater than the temple is here. And if you had known what this means, 'I desire mercy, and not sacrifice.'" For Jesus to say that "there is something here greater than the temple" is to question the place that had been accorded to the temple in his beloved society. What is crucial here is not the preservation of the temple, but the promotion of life. To say that there is something greater than the temple is to put the temple under the judgment of a higher value. The temple system and the Jewish purity map are judged in terms of their contributions to the promotion of a just Jewish society.

When everything was done to preserve the temple and purity system, it is understandable that the activities of Jesus were so threatening. To say that a person is judged not on the performance of cultic purity rites but on the practice of justice is really to weaken the external power of the so-called redemptive media. Healing during the Sabbath and violation of food prohibitions were both such blatant attacks against the system that Jesus' actions were readily construed as subversive.

As one engaged in real subversion, Jesus also shook the unholy alliance of the ruling elite with the Roman imperialists. Jesus' seeming silence with regard to the Roman presence in Palestine has been used by some as an indication that Jesus was not concerned with the issue of foreign domination. Contrary to the common interpretation that Jesus was giving his approval to the payment of taxes to Caesar (Mark 12:13–17), he, in fact, used the occasion to remind the crowd of the symbolic meaning of Caesar's image. By pointing to the image of Caesar on the coin, Jesus made it clear that the coin did not belong to Israel or to its God, but to an imperialist power that had intruded into Jewish society and, hence, was to be rejected. Although there was no direct attack by Jesus against the Romans, he was very much against the Roman presence. His focus was, however, directed to the local elite who made effective use of the temple system in their collaboration with the Romans.

Decisive in his project of tearing down the Jewish social map in favor of a better tomorrow, Jesus fully identified himself with the rejects of the Jewish social order. Jesus knew that the power of change in history could be found among those who were experiencing deprivation and marginalization. He organized a group of people who were in the margins of his society's social (purity) map because he knew that these were the people who craved change. Speaking of the transformative power of the so-called social dirt, Terry Eagleton said:

> The *anawim* — the scum and refuse of society — have, like all dung, a contradictory status: the more they reveal dissolution and decay, the more politically fertile they become. If society, like the initiates whom Mary Douglas discusses, has the power to pass beyond its own boundaries and expose itself to the power of its own refuse, it can survive, but the deepest christian paradox is that it will only survive, in any case, by death. In embracing its *anawim*, a society is embracing its own death; in the act of opening itself to its absurdities it is bound to disintegrate, since it survives only by excluding these from its precariously maintained world of meaning.[70]

Those considered the dirt of society are always with us, a statement attributed to Jesus to justify their presence in society (John 12:7-8). They are and will always be with us so long as the power wielders make an idol of the social order that benefits them. They are the nagging reminders or signs of society's "failure, of the shapeless, unstructured life in its margin and crevices with which the order cannot deal without destroying itself."[71] The powers-that-be of Jesus' time did not want to be reminded of the failings of the social map that they protected. Instead, the guardians of the social map killed Jesus. But Jesus left the message that any social system (map) is judged by how it relates to its own refuse.

FUSION OF HORIZONS: JESUS AND THE CONTEMPORARY CHALLENGE IN THE PHILIPPINES

Constructing a christology that is responsive and liberating to the suffering but struggling Filipinos involves a fusion of horizons, horizons derived from the Scripture and horizons drawn from the experience and popular religiosity of the Filipino people based on a long tradition and from present expressions. From this fusion of horizons I would identify the basic tenets and main directions of a christology that is expressive of the Filipino experience and hope.

Very fertile for constructing a christology that is expressive of the

---

[70]Terry Eagleton, *The Body as Language* (London and Sydney: Sheed and Ward, 1970), pp. 70-71.

[71]Ibid., p. 67.

Filipino context is the focus on ideas such as knowing and practice (praxis), following Jesus, and an emphasis on humanity. Unlike other christologies, with their preoccupation on the divinity of Jesus — especially as a member of the Holy Trinity and all the intellectual gymnastics involved — Filipinos have shown particular interest in the humanity of Jesus. Most of the Filipino concepts attributed to Jesus, like *katoto, kasalo, kasiping, kasama, kasambahay, pakikiisa, pakikiramay,* and *malasakit,* are concepts that evolve around an idea of a person possessing the qualities of true humanhood. As has been pointed out:

> The net effect of all these words is that Christ appears as truly human, as one we can identify with. Christ is depicted not as a Son of God who throws weight around but the Son of Man who treated his disciples almost on an equal level.[72]

This is not to totally deny the presence of the divinity of Jesus in Filipino religiosity, but even the divinity is seen in the very humanity of Jesus. Jesus reveals God because God was in Jesus. To put it in the words of Paul Casperz,

> The task of Jesus' followers today is not to live in society according to a belief that Jesus of Nazareth is God. It is rather to live in society according to a faith that God is Jesus of Nazareth. They do not know God other than in Jesus of Nazareth.[73]

The focus on the humanity of Jesus goes along with the focus on following Jesus. Appropriate for a divine Jesus is to be worshipped, whereas appropriate for the human Jesus is to be followed; the emphasis is on discipleship. With this emphasis on praxis and the idea of following, it is appropriate to say that the mode or way of knowing Jesus is to follow Jesus.

There is much similarity here with the christology of Latin American liberation theology and other christologies emerging out of direct experience of the struggling poor. Generally, as Sobrino has pointed out, Western christologies have been preoccupied with "trying to show that it can be justified before the bar of reason," whereas for liberation christology and christology of struggle, what is important is its justification within the demands of a transforming praxis.[74]

Consistent with the emphasis on humanity, following, and praxis is the distinctive focus on *where* Jesus is, not so much on *who* Jesus is. Classical or orthodox christology has been preoccupied with who Jesus is, that is, the

---

[72] *People's Participation for Total Liberation,* p. 32.
[73] Paul Caspersz, "Jesus of Nazareth and Human Liberation," *Church and Social Transformation Series,* Series B4-88 (Quezon City, Philippines: Socio-Pastoral Institute, 1988), p. 12.
[74] Sobrino, *Christology at the Crossroads,* p. 348.

essence of Jesus as a member of the trinity. Virginia Fabella has taken note of this emphasis as something distinctive of the Filipino approach to christology.[75] This is also observable in the thoughts of Cariño. Speaking of the theology of struggle, Cariño noted:

> The question *where* and *how* God may be encountered and *how* Jesus may be *sought* and *followed* is confronted in the theology of struggle with the affirmation and discovery that God is indeed among those who suffer and seek freedom. . . . To be with God and *follow Jesus* is thus also to *be with the people.*[76]

To say that Jesus is a way to true humanity and as one who suffers with the people can still be abstract without posing the question "where is Jesus?" Jesus' compassion in a situation of injustice can only take the position of siding with the victims and the marginalized. To follow Jesus is to know where Jesus is. The question — where — points to another important thrust in this christology: that Jesus takes sides with the victims.

Taking sides with the victims, the outcasts, the oppressed, and the marginalized is the way to find one's humanity, as Jesus had shown. This is a major thrust of both the Scripture and the popular religiosity of the Filipinos. For taking sides and struggling with the victims, Jesus had to pay a high price, even his own life, as some Filipinos have done. Jesus' crucifixion is the highest expression not of passive suffering but of *malasakit* (vicarious suffering) and *pakikiisa* (solidarity) with the suffering people.[77] But more than this, the crucifixion and the suffering of Jesus are an outcome of struggle. He did not simply die a natural death, he was murdered, a victim of "state terrorism." Jesus' suffering, to use Leonardo Boff's words, is a "suffering born out of struggle against suffering."[78]

Finally, it is fitting to make it the last point that Jesus is the suffering and struggling people. If Caspersz could say that God is Jesus of Nazareth, in like manner we can say that Jesus is the suffering and struggling people; that if there is no other way to know God than through Jesus (among Filipino Christians), there is also no other way to know Jesus than through the suffering and struggling Filipino people. A christology that has really taken hold in the lives of people should lead to this affirmation, which the oppressed people have made, as expressed in Gaspar's perception that the

---

[75]Fabella "A Common Methodology for Diverse Christologies?", in *With Passion and Compassion: Third World Women Doing Theology,* p. 113.

[76]Cariño, "What About the Theology of Struggle," in *Religion and Society: Towards a Theology of Struggle,* p. xvii. Emphasis supplied.

[77]Cf. Fabella, "A Common Methodology for Diverse Christologies?", in *With Passion and Compassion,* p. 110.

[78]Leonardo Boff, *Passion of Christ, Passion of the World: The Facts, Their Interpretation, and Their Meaning Yesterday and Today,* trans. Robert R. Barr (Maryknoll, NY.: Orbis Books, 1987), pp. 117–128.

"collage of a people's situation of blood and tears . . . is Christ's passion in the here and now."[79] Their very own lives have found identity in the life of Jesus.

What more could we say of a people who has fully embraced the message and life of Jesus than to say that the passion of Jesus is the *pasyon ng inang bayan* (suffering of the motherland), and the resurrection of Jesus is also the resurrection of the *sambayanang Pilipino* (Filipino people).

---

[79]Gaspar, *How Long?: Prison Reflections from the Philippines,* p. 77.

6

A Search for an Ecclesiology of Struggle, Peoplehood, and Human Dwelling

In my analytical survey of the current status of the theology of struggle in Chapter II, I pointed out that ecclesiology, along with spirituality, has a marked presence in the writings of the theologians of struggle. This should not be surprising if one is familiar with a situation like that of the Philippines in which the church has a pervasive influence on the lives of the people.

Unlike the West, where it is easy to find someone who would outwardly profess to having no religion at all, or who would profess to be a Christian but with no specific church affiliation, Filipino Christians claim themselves to be members of an institutional church, even if they are "KBL" Christians, that is, even if they visit the church only for baptism *(B*inyag), wedding ceremony *(K*asal), and their own funeral rite *(L*ibing). If the theology of struggle is a theology that arises out of the people's lives, it cannot ignore the crucial importance of the church on the lives of the people; it must consider ecclesiology as an important theme in its theological construction.

It is not surprising then that the theologians of struggle have articulated their thoughts on ecclesiology; it is equally not surprising from those who, despite their strong criticism of the ecclesiastical institution, are actively involved in the life of the church and are working for its transformation. One can say that the theologians of struggle have not given up on the church, although in spite of the church the people will rise. Thus, it is proper that I pursue the theme of ecclesiology in this study and explore some creative ways of construing an ecclesiology that is responsive to the plight of the struggling Filipino people.

For a better understanding of the main tenets of the ecclesiology that I propose for the theology of struggle, I set out some lines of thought that guide this chapter.

Although some have argued that Jesus did not found a church but preached the kingdom of God (*basileia tou theou*), an interpretation that has sound basis in the Scripture, I believe it is well grounded to say that the life, passion, death, and testimony of the resurrection of Jesus provided the wellspring and inspiration for the birth of the church, the early precursor of which is the Jesus movement (see Chapter V).

When the wellspring of the church is evident in the life, death, passion, and resurrection of the one around whom the marginalized had formed a movement, we can appropriate for the church what R. J. B. Walker calls the "critical social movement," to speak of it as a "prophetico-critical religious movement" or "prophetic faith-communities."[1] I believe that this is an appropriate account, for the church that we know today emerged out of the experience of the marginalized and their response to the life and hope-giving witness of Jesus amidst their own predicament. The church, in its early inception, emerged out of the experience of social distress or from the early Christian communities' consciousness of "relative deprivation,"[2] the primary bearers of which were the marginalized. When the church forgets this "founding experience" or what Emil Fackenheim called "root experience,"[3] it surely becomes a chameleon, guided by the drive of preserving its own interest. Unfortunately, the story of the church seems to be this way.

If we consider the life, passion, death, and resurrection of the one around whom the marginalized had formed themselves and the *activity* of the Spirit in their lives as a wellspring or founding experience for the church's emergence, as well as the notion that it is a prophetico-critical religious movement, then I propose that these two insights be considered as "critical principles" with which to evaluate the life of the church today. Any construction of ecclesiology, in my understanding, should be subjected to the above-mentioned critical principles.

With this framework in mind, which shall gain more clarity as this chapter unfolds, I undertake a critique of the main paths that the church has taken, although only in a sketchy fashion, as a backdrop to the main direction in which I am heading – an ecclesiology of the theology of struggle. From this critique it will become clearer that no matter how the church claims to have a transcendental foundation, it is very much reflective of the dynamics of society, both domestically and globally. In its life, the

---

[1]See this understanding of "critical social movement" in the work of R. B. J. Walker, *One World, Many Worlds: Struggles for a Just World Peace* (London: Zen Books Limited; & Boulder, Colorado: Lynne Rienner Publishers, 1988); also Lester Ruiz, "Towards Communities of Resistance and Solidarity: Some Political and Philosophical Notes," *Tugón*, vol. 7, no. 3 (1987), pp. 4–17.

[2]See John G. Gager, *Kingdom and Community: The Social World of Early Christianity* (Englewood Cliffs, New Jersey: Prentice-Hall, 1975); see also the following works: Isenberg, "Millenarism in Greco-Roman Palestine," *Religion* 4, pp. 35–38; Kenelm Burridge, *New Heaven, New Earth: A Study of Millenarian Activities* (New York: Schocken Books, 1969); Bryan Wilson, *Religious Sects: A Sociological Study* (New York: McGraw-Hill, 1970); Hillel Schwartz, "The End of the Beginning: Millenarian Studies, 1969–1975," *Religious Studies Review*, vol. 2, no. 3 (July 1976), pp. 1–15.

[3]Emil Fackenheim, *God's Presence in History: Jewish Affirmations and Philosophical Reflections* (New York: New York University Press, 1970), p. 9.

church has both its "creative" and "restrictive" side.[4] When the church as a critical social movement stands paramount, the creative or liberating side also stands paramount; but when the dominant forces are in control, the restrictive side is also dominant.

Because the dominant ideas of the age are generally favorable to the interest of the dominant groups, the bias of this study is to retrieve the creative side, a side that has often been buried by the dominant forces of the age. To state it differently, the focus of this study is to excavate the *memoria passionis*—the dangerous and subversive memories—that out of these dangerous memories a new ecclesial paradigm may come; that out of the experience of exteriority a liberating ecclesiology can sprout.

It appears that to carry out my intention in this chapter I must employ various hermeneutical approaches. Mining the *memoria passionis*, which shape my ecclesiological construction, implies that the reigning ideas have been cast under suspicion, and those that have been buried need to be retrieved. This suggests that I have to employ not only what has been popularly called the hermeneutics of suspicion, but also the "hermeneutics of retrieval."[5] In addition, I would critique the life of the church through the hermeneutics of praxis and what I would term the "hermeneutics of theopoetic imagination." And because of the sociological and theological nature of the church, I adopt an openness to various approaches or an interdisciplinary approach in this study.[6]

I now proceed with my exploration of an ecclesiology of struggle, peoplehood, and dwelling that I believe is in consonance with the Filipino aspirations.

THE RISE OF ECCLESIOCENTRIC CHRISTIANITY

The history of the Christian church is a history that moves from the exterior to a position at the center of totality.[7] It is a history of a critical social movement inspired by the life and teachings of Jesus of Nazareth, which was slowly absorbed into the center, wherever that center may be, and which soon gained tremendous power, a power that controlled both heaven and earth, a power that moved even mighty kings and made emperors tremble. Although this did not continue unchallenged and its "house of authority" was undermined, borrowing a concept from Farley,[8]

---

[4]Theissen, *Sociology of Early Palestinian Christianity,* p. 2.

[5]Ricoeur, *Freud and Philosophy: An Essay on Interpretation,* pp. 28-32, 32-36.

[6]Cf. Julio de Santa Ana, "Conclusion," in *Separation Without Hope?: Essays on the Relation Between the Church and the Poor During the Industrial Revolution and the Western Colonial Expansion,* p. 172.

[7]See Dussel, *Ethics and the Theology of Liberation.*

[8]Edward Farley, *Ecclesial Reflection: An Anatomy of Theological Method* (Philadelphia: Fortress Press, 1982); see also his collaborative work with Peter Hodgson, "Scripture and Tradition," in *Christian Theology: An Introduction to Its Traditions and Tasks,* pp. 61-87.

this ecclesiocentrism is not completely a fossil of the past or a theological dinosaur; it is still alive. It is important then to take account of this phenomenon called *ecclesiocentrism.*

Ecclesiocentrism and Euro-Americanism: The Conquest and Creation of Third-World Peoples as its Practical Foundation

Ecclesiocentrism is a religious consciousness characterized by universalistic and totalistic thinking. This ecclesiocentric thinking, like other universalistic and totalistic conceptions, does not simply float, but is founded on the rise of some locales or peoples to center stage and the consequent peripheralization of other peoples of the world. Like the Euro-American *ego cogito*, an idea that I pursued in Chapter IV with regard to anthropology, christendom ecclesiology, to appropriate Dussel, is also the theoretical consummation of the practical oppression of the peripheries.[9] I choose not to speak of ecclesiocentrism in an academic detached fashion or in a neutral prose of so many textbooks, because this ecclesiocentrism has fed on the blood of the weak and the marginalized.

In the history of the rise of ecclesiocentrism there is also a history of the rise of one particular group, locale, race, and interest group that became the sponsor of Christianity. The rise of ecclesiocentrism is basically bound with the triumph of Rome over other centers, the triumph in general of the West (Europe and United States), and the mutual alliance of the church and powerful centers. It is an alliance of the church with the West over the East, of the North over the South. In the history of its rise, it has been identified with Euro-Americanism, capitalism, colonization and neocolonization, patriarchalism, and androcentrism.

The Rise of Christendom Ecclesiology and its Recent Modifications

The rise of christendom ecclesiology has been a long process. Christianity, before it became identified with the centers of power, was of humble beginnings. The early followers of Jesus and members of the early Christian communities were ordinary folks. Gerd Theissen, for example, described the early beginnings of Christianity as a "renewal movement" or a "Jesus movement" within Judaism, emerging between CE 30 and CE 70.[10] It was composed of people who were at the margins of power, of people who were branded atheists by the empire; it was a movement that was constantly threatened by persecution and turned into the usual scapegoat for almost all

---

[9]Dussel, *Philosophy of Liberation,* p. 5.
[10]Theissen, *Sociology of Early Palestinian Christianity,* p. 1.

crises.[11] Yet this fate changed when it was associated with the powerful or when it became the religion of the center, wherever that center might be.[12] The once-persecuted church acquired the power to make kings tremble and come with bended knees; the humble servant became a triumphant church with a strong hierarchical structure.

Ecclesiocentrism is basically a self-consciousness, a way of thinking and living, that grows out of a sense of power or of being at the center. It cannot thrive at the point of weakness or exteriority, but only among those who wield tremendous power. Espoused by the weak and those at the peripheries, as the witting and unwitting defenders of the Western-Christian-capitalist centers have charged, it is only symptomatic of the dehumanization of those at the margins.

With challenges from within and from without, this christendom-ecclesiocentric-Eurocentric ecclesiology has been terribly shaken, but it is not completely dead. Throughout its history, it has undergone some modifications, but its main elements have survived warranting the label "new" christendom.[13] Although direct instrumentation of the church by the state or the powers-that-be and vice versa has faded, new alliances have been forged based on common interests that are more subtle, be this in Roman Catholicism or Protestantism. When this ecclesiocentrism will fade, I do not know, or it may be naive to expect it to completely fade away. But with more powerful earthquakes coming to challenge the church, history is giving way to new ecclesiologies. This is treated in the later part of this chapter.

---

[11]Martin E. Marty, *A Short History of Christianity,* 2nd ed., revised and expanded (Philadelphia: Fortress Press, 1987), p. 40.

[12]The year CE 313 is considered by many as a significant date in the gradual development of ecclesiocentrism, for it was on this date that Christianity ceased to be an illegal religion. Gutiérrez is more specific in pointing out that CE 313 is the date when Christianity was tolerated (Edict of Milan), but it was only in CE 381 (Decree of Thessalonica) that Christianity became the religion of the Roman Empire. The once religio illicita had become an official religion (Gutiérrez, *A Theology of Liberation: History, Politics and Salvation,* p. 144). Some time during this period there emerged, as the famous church historian Williston Walker has pointed out, a church with a "strong episcopal organization, credal standard, and authoritative canon." See Williston Walker, *A History of the Christian Church* (New York: Charles Scribner's Sons, 1959), p. 60. It was not, however, until the Counter-Reformation and Vatican I that the zenith of an ecclesiocentric church was reached (Avery Dulles, *Models of the Church* [New York: Doubleday, 1974], pp. 31–42). From then on, noted Song, despite setbacks and persecutions, the church has been a powerful institution in the life of Western civilization (Song, *Third-Eye Theology,* p. 178).

[13]See Gutiérrez, *A Theology of Liberation,* p. 145. He takes account of the changing perspective of the church, from openness, to ecclesiocentrism, to increasing openness *(aggiornamento);* yet, even during the modern period the notion that salvific truth can only be found in the church has persisted. In fact, Metz has pointed out that the recent pope (John Paul II) is working to turn the tide toward the revival of Eurocentrism, which is another way of saying ecclesiocentrism. See, *The Emergent Church: The Future of Christianity in a Postbourgeois World,* trans. Peter Mann (New York: Crossroad, 1981), p. 93.

Theological Consciousness of Christendom Ecclesiology
and its Modifications

Christendom's theological construct of the church is basically ecclesio-centric. The church, identified with the hierarchy, is at the top and the center (*axis mundi*); it controls both heaven and earth, a power not even secular forces possess (*potestas sacra*). Its position is basically similar to my exposition of the temple in my discussion of christology (Chapter V). No one has access to the "Father" and his grace by bypassing the church. The church is the container of God's grace, and this grace only flows when its guardians — the bishops, priests, and ministers — open the valve by means of various sacraments. Instead of saying *ubi Christus ibi ecclesia* (where Christ is, there is the Church), this church affirms the adage *ubi ecclesia ibi Christus* (where the church is, there is Christ). For the laypeople to receive this grace, they must open themselves with contrite hearts and obey the teachings of the church, their mother and teacher (*mater et magistra*). Failure to do so would be reason enough for the guardians to withhold grace, thereby shutting the only avenue for salvation. Resistance can only mean anathema, excommunication, and witch hunting, a practice that has been usually carried out against the poor, most of whom are women.

While christendom Christianity strongly asserts that God is the creator of the universe and the Lord of history, such a declaration appears incongruous with its inclination to control the activity of God within the established channels of the hierarchy. Encounters with God outside the official channels are often viewed with suspicion, if not considered heretical.

If everything that is salvific is contained within the church and is under the administration of the entrusted guardians, its logical aftermath is that outside of the church there is no salvation (*extra ecclesia nulla salus*). Thus, no "one can have God as his Father, who has not the Church for his mother."[14] There is no salvific value accorded to anything outside of the church; everything needs to be converted. Other religions do not possess salvific significance whatsoever. As the sole depository of God's grace and the receptacle of God's revelation, christendom ecclesiology considers itself as the one who has the power to teach (*ecclesia docens*), the authority to sanctify, and the mandate to govern.[15] The church is always at the giving side, not at the receiving end; it is the one teaching, not the one being taught; dialogue is foreign to a christendom ecclesiology.

How is theology or the nature of theological reflection construed under christendom ecclesiology? It becomes a christendom theology, which

---

[14]Cyprian, "On the Unity of the Catholic Church," in *The Ante-Nicene Fathers,* vol. 5 (New York: Christian Literature Co., 1886–97; reprint by Eerdmans), pp. 422–23, a selection from *Readings in Christian Theology,* eds., Peter Hodgson and Robert King (Philadelphia: Fortress Press, 1985), pp. 238–239.

[15]Dulles, *Models of the Church,* p. 34.

is mainly an apology for the established dogmas of the church. The farthest that it can go is to translate or adopt the established dogmas to the contemporary times. Unless one is liberated from this ecclesiocentrism or from the house of authority of the christendom Christianity, a creative and contextual theology cannot be expected (see more in Chapter VII).[16]

Pressures, such as the rise of the modern spirit and its focus on the separation of church and state, have forced the church to open its windows from an "exclusivist" position to an "inclusivist" position.[17] Yet, even the inclusivist position, in which other religions are given salvific significance, such as baptizing the believers of other religions as "anonymous Christians" as Karl Rahner[18] does (which, I assume, the believers of other religions would quickly say: Thanks for the honor, but no thanks), could still be classified under the paradigm of new christendom because the vestiges of ecclesiocentrism are still present. Calling believers of other religions anonymous Christians seems to be a step toward tolerance, but as Hans Küng succinctly put it, it is also a "conquest by embrace."[19] It would require another step before a "pluralist" perspective could be attained.

Sociological Angle: The Christendom Church in the Philippines

To speak of theoretical consummation with practical bases is actually to say by implication that the church is both theological and sociological. L. Boff referred to these two aspects as the religious-ecclesiastical realm (institution) and the ecclesia-sacramental realm (sacrament, sign, instrument of salvation).[20] In spite of the church's claim to have a transcendental basis, a sickness of theologism, it is a social institution and, indeed, reflects in many ways the surrounding social environment. What is happening outside the church walls can be observed inside the walls of the church, for indeed the church is part of the world, although it can choose not to be.

---

[16]For a critique of the nature of theological reflection under christendom ecclesiology or house of authority, see Farley, *Ecclesial* Reflection. There is more on this issue in the next chapter.

[17]There are basically three categories with regard to Christian perception of other religions: (1) exclusivist, (2) inclusivist, (3) and pluralist. See Gavin D'Costa, *Theology and Religious Pluralism* (Oxford: Basil Blackwell, 1986). For more on the issue of religious pluralism, see Paul F. Knitter, *No Other Name?: A Critical Survey of Christian Attitudes Toward the World Religions* (Maryknoll, NY.: Orbis Books, 1985).

[18]Karl Rahner, "Christianity and the Non-Christian Religions," in *A Rahner Reader*, ed. Gerald A. McCool (New York, The Seabury Press, 1975), pp. 214–220, especially p. 219.

[19]Hans Küng, "Towards an Ecumenical Theology of Religion: Some Theses for Clarification," in *Christianity Among World Religions*, ed. Hans Küng and Jürgen Moltmann (Edinburgh: T & T Clark, Ltd., 1986), p. 120.

[20]Leonardo Boff, *Church: Charism and Power: Liberation Theology and the Institutional Church*, trans. John W. Diercksmeier (New York: Crossroad, 1985), p. 110.

If in the earlier part of this chapter I spoke of ecclesiocentrism as a theological-theoretical consummation of something practical, in this section I specifically deal with the inverse and am more specific: the practical consequences of christendom ecclesiology as experienced by the Filipino people.

The Filipinos' first encounter of christendom Christianity came through colonialist Spain and then through the Protestant North American missionaries. At the outset, it is very clear that christendom Christianity came along with colonialism, a Euro-American colonialism. In fact, I would go a little further to say that christendom Christianity was part and parcel of Western colonialism. All the mission enterprises that followed, noted Orlando Costas, accompanied the world of free enterprise, if not to say that the "missionary movement is a child of world free enterprise."[21]

This identification of Christianity and colonialism cannot be hidden—an obvious fact with the coming of Roman Catholic Christianity—because Spain was the direct sponsor, but it is a little more subtle with U.S. expansionism due to its policy of separation of church and state.[22] Nonetheless, although there was no direct use of the church by the state, the church—Roman Catholic and Protestant—contributed its fair share in the identification of Christianity with Euro-American civilization and the subjugation of the people.

The statue of Miguel López de Legaspi (Spanish conqueror of the Filipinos) in the Philippines is highly symbolic of christendom ecclesiology, clearly manifesting the alliance of the powers that be and Christianity. On one hand he holds the sword (instrument of coercion—political apparatus) and on the other the cross (ideology interpreted as instrument of deception). These two became instruments at the hands of both the state and the church. The sword was not spared when needed,[23] but it was primarily through the most lasting legacy of Spain to the Philippines—Christianity— that the Filipinos were led to submit to the "liberation" project of the conqueror. With the acceptance of this lasting legacy (except for the Muslims of the South), the conqueror had in its hand the most powerful weapon in the world to maintain its presence in the Philippines, even with

---

[21]Orlando Costas, *Christ Outside the Gate: Mission Beyond Christendom* (Maryknoll, NY.: Orbis Books, 1982), p. 63.

[22]See the analysis of Mario Bolasco on the U.S. action, which, in his opinion, really amounted to a religious policy. The United States did not directly sponsor Protestantism, like Spain with Roman Catholicism, both because of its secular character, that is, the separation of church and state, and more so because of strategic expediency. See his essay "USA and Missionary Expansion," *SPI Series, Special Issue,* Series 3, Year 5 (Quezon City, Philippines: Socio-Pastoral Institute). Mimeographed.

[23]Pedro Salgado, "Imperialism in the Church," *Faith and Ideology Series,* Series 3, Year 4 (Quezon City, Philippines: Socio-Pastoral Institute), p. 3. For further account see Valentino Sitoy, Jr., *A History of Christianity in the Philippines: The Initial Encounter,* vol. 1 (Quezon City, Philippines: New Day Publishers, 1985).

minimal military might.[24] Aware of the power that the church held, one friar boasted,

> If the king sends troops here, the Indians will return to the mountains and forests. But if I shut the church doors, I shall have them all at my feet in twenty-four hours.[25]

The christendom church also made an effective use of the sacraments and indulgences to cower the people to submission and to amass wealth.[26] Aside from royal bequests, pressure buying, and outright land grabbing, the Spanish crown and the christendom church managed to possess wealth and take hold of the most fertile lands by means of sacraments. It was noted that

> Friars were wont to whisper into the ears of their dying parishioners that a timely donation to the church would serve for a shorter tenure in purgatory.[27]

Thus, as noted by Marcelo H. del Pilar, at the height of the friars' control of the Filipinos, the friars were also in possession of "the best fields, the best haciendas."[28]

Moreover, aside from the exploitation of the people, the christendom church also implanted in the minds of Christian Filipinos a hatred against the Muslim Filipinos, which was actualized in the acts of oppression by those who happened to be Christians. Unfortunately, from then on, conflicts between the oppressive sectors of Philippine society and the Muslims of the South have been viewed as "Christian-Muslim conflicts," and the reality that they are both victims of circumstances not of their making vanishes out of sight.[29]

Christendom ecclesiology continued to operate with the coming of the United States and to the present, although it is an accepted notion that the

---

[24]See Gowing, "Christianity in the Philippines: Yesterday and Today," p. 2.

[25]Constantino, *The Philippines: A Past Revisited*, p. 77, citing "Remarks on the Philippine Islands and on their Capital Manila, 1819–1822," BR, vol. LI, p. 113 n.

[26]BCC-CO Inter-Regional Secretariat, *Basic Christian Communities: Catalysts for Liberation, Part I. Nagliliyab* (Quezon City, Philippines: Claretian Publications, 1987), p. 5.

[27]Cited in Constantino, *The Philippines: A Past Revisited,* p. 69.

[28]Marcelo H. del Pilar, cited in Pedro Salgado, "The Filipino Peasants: A Historical Perspective," *Kalinangan,* vol. 9, no. 4 (December 1989), p. 9.

[29]Eliseo R. Mercado, Jr., "The Organic Act of 1989 and the Moro People's Struggle for Self-Determination," *Sandugo,* Annual Issue (1989–1990), p. 13; also Rad D. Silva, *Two Hills of the Same Land: Truth Behind the Mindanao Problem* (Philippines: Mindanao-Sulu Critical Studies & Research Group, September 1978), p. 7; Constantino, *The Philippines: A Past Revisited,* p. 28; Ed Maranan, "Christians, Tribals, Moros: Filipinos in Search of Unity and Peace," in *Rice in the Storm: Faith in Struggle in the Philippines,* p. 95. Maranan opens the possibility that the real problem is not a Christian-Muslim conflict, but the Philippine government's neglect of the welfare of five million Muslims of the South.

church and state are separate. The Roman Catholic church, in particular, made an alliance with the new conquerors of the Filipino people (U.S.) to maintain its big landholdings.[30] It also actively took the side of the new conquerors by prohibiting priests from supporting the revolution, threatening imprisonment and exile to those priests who behaved otherwise.[31] Threatened by movements for change and social transformation both within and without, the hierarchy had given its blessings to the government to wage counterinsurgency war against the so-called dissidents and to persecute its own people, even as it condemned violence.[32] It is a persecuted church only insofar as the faithful who have opted for the people have been persecuted, but as personified by the hierarchy it is a persecuting church.

CHALLENGES TO THE CHRISTENDOM CHURCH

The christendom church did not go unchallenged. Challenges made against it include the great schism of the Eastern and Western church, which is symbolically dated 1054;[33] the Protestant Reformation of the 16th century; the rise of the modern period and all its expressions (e.g., the Enlightenment, science, secularism, the rise of the bourgeoisie, and capitalism); the challenge of the non-Christian world; the rise of nationalist movements; and the eruption of the poor, the majority of whom are women. Of all these challenges, I consider the rise of nationalist movements and the eruption of the poor and of women as the final stage toward the birth of a new ecclesial paradigm, challenging the church to open its windows (*aggiornamento*).

Protestant Reformation: Reformation "From Within"
Christianity and the Western Culture

After the great schism of the East and the West, which undermined the totalization of the church under the leadership of Rome, the Protestant Reformation followed. The Protestant Reformation represented a challenge to a church that controlled heaven and earth, opening the floodgates of

[30]Mario Bolasco and Rolando Yu, *Church-State Relations* (Manila: St. Scholastica's College, 1981), pp. 61–62.

[31]See Victoria Narciso-Apuan et al., *Witness and Hope Amid Struggle: Towards a Theology of Struggle and Spirituality of Struggle,* Book II (Manila: Forum for Interdisciplinary Endeavors and Studies, 1991), p. 56.

[32]"Sin Leads Mini-Inquisition Against Progressive Clergy," in *Philippine Report,* vol. 4, no. 8 (August 1987), p. 3. It appears here that violence, for the church hierarchy, refers only to revolutionary violence, whereas it remains silent to "systemic violence." See Pedro Salgado, "The System is Violent," in *Philippine Society: Reflections on Contemporary Issues,* Kalinangan Book Series 1 (Quezon City, Philippines: Institute of Religion and Culture, Phils., 1990), pp. 19–26.

[33]Marty, *A Short History of Christianity,* p. 108.

heaven so that grace may flow for all those who need it without the direct control of the church hierarchy. For a people who, for a long time, had been under the control of a church with all the prerogative to teach, to govern, and to sanctify, liberation from this church was long overdue. The rise of Protestantism helped to shatter ecclesiocentrism by focusing on the individual's access to God, something that was previously controlled by the church. Viewed from this perspective, we can see that the Reformation was an expression and a demand of the time.[34]

Yet the Protestant Reformation, in spite of its challenge to christendom ecclesiology, had its own limitations, blindness, and forgetfulness. Like other movements, it was a child of its own time and context. It challenged christendom Christianity and undermined its power, but it too carried the christendom, triumphalist, crusading mentality and converted the Bible into a Protestant pope. Just like the church from which it emerged, whenever opportunities arose, Protestants were driven to put up a Christian civilization, which in the long run made Protestantism a *Kulturprotestantismus*,[35] losing its critical principle. Protestantism was a quarrel "within" the same house — Christianity — and "from within" Western culture. In fact, the Reformation can be interpreted as a religious side to the modern-Enlightenment-secularist-bourgeois challenge to christendom. Protestantism needs to live up to its motto: *ecclesia reformata et semper reformanda.*

The Modern-Enlightenment-Secularist-Bourgeois Challenge: Its Limitations and Forgetfulness

The rise of the modern period would be better understood if viewed in relation to the feudal medieval christendom. From the point of view of the

---

[34]While the Reformation is also an expression of the rising bourgeoisie, we should not simply equate Protestantism with individualism or a burgerliche religion, as if to say that the feudal-medieval church did not need reformation. Gutiérrez seemed to imply the equation of Protestantism and individualism, even to suggest that "individualism" is the essence of Protestantism, by citing G. W. F. Hegel. See his essay, "Two Theological Perspectives: Liberation Theology and Progressivist Theology," in *The Emergent Gospel: Theology from the Underside of History*, p. 230. Metz also suggested that individualism emerges "as it did with the Reformation." See *The Emergent Church: The Future of Christianity in a Postbourgeois World*, p. 89. This, in my judgment, is not quite accurate, for individualism cannot be onesidedly advanced as the offspring of the Reformation. In fact, it can even be argued conversely that the growth of individualism contributed to the emergence of the Reformation. I think it is better to see these factors (individualism, Reformation, Enlightenment, French Revolution) as mutually reinforcing each other.

[35]See Neill Q. Hamilton, *Recovery of the Protestant Adventure* (New York: The Seabury Press, 1981), for a critique of American "culture Protestantism." Also see Chapter IV of this book on my critique of American "manifest destiny," because it illuminates the notion of culture Protestantism. In that chapter I show the four basic distortions of manifest destiny: (1) the equation of Christianity with American culture, (2) the chosen people as the superior race, (3) the moral superiority of the chosen people, and (4) market-capitalism as Western civilization. See also Alisdair I.C. Heron, *A Century of Protestant Theology* (Philadelphia: The Westminster Press, 1980), p. 75.

Enlightenment, christendom Christianity was a bastion and citadel of narrow-mindedness, a powerful institution that was a hindrance to the progress of the modern world because of its control in almost all aspects of life, even in matters considered as scientific truths. Scientific discoveries and theories that ran counter to the long-held beliefs of the church were considered heretical and thus worthy of an anathema (Nicholas of Cusa, Copernicus, Bruno).[36] The feudal and hierarchical structure was also contrary to the spirit of the emerging bourgeoisie.

There was no other way for the modern period to emerge without shattering the stronghold of the christendom. In fact, secularism could be interpreted as a move of the modern world to withdraw from the church's totalizing control and to maintain its autonomy. With its secularist move, the sphere of religion under the modern period was narrowed, oftentimes limited to the private, although from time to time it was drawn to support and justify some courses of action taken.

More than relegating religion to the private sphere, Western scientific secularism has moved in the direction of secular atheism, which has appeared with two faces: (1) secular-liberal atheism and (2) Marxist atheism. Although Marxist atheism has always been understood as dangerous to religion, it is my view that secular-liberal atheism is more of an enemy to religion than Marxist atheism. Secular-liberal atheism undermines religion itself because it is construed as a mere projection (Feuerbach and Freud). Marx, on the other hand, did not question religion as such but only in relation to a criticism of society. This means that religion is not the *source,* but a *product* of an alienating condition which in turn creates alienated consciousness.[37] I agree with Jan Milic Lochman's interpretation that Marx's criticism of religion "is meaningful only in the setting of social criticism."[38]

The Nationalist-Anticolonialist Challenge to the Church

Due to the unholy alliance of the church and colonizing powers, Christianity, as a consequence, became an object of attack; it was viewed, or is still viewed in some countries, as a capitalist vessel. Nationalist consciousness is critical of the church, even viewing missions, as pointed out by T. O. Beidelman, as representing the most naive and ethnocentric facet of colonialism.[39] "The dubious alliance of Christianity with colonialism," —

---

[36]Marty, *A Short History of Christianity,* p. 243.

[37]See Baum, *Religion and Alienation: A Theological Reading of Sociology,* pp. 7–40. Also a similar point in Welch, *Protestant Thought in the Nineteenth Century,* p. 214. Welch, in my judgment, brought out a correct interpretation of Marx regarding religion when he pointed out that for Marx the real enemy was the perverted social order, of which religion was a consequence (p. 214).

[38]Jan Milic Lochman, *Encountering Marx: Bonds and Barriers Between Christians and Marxists,* trans. Edwid H. Robertson (Philadelphia: Fortress Press, 1977), p. 83.

[39]T. O. Beidelman, *Colonial Evangelism* (Bloomington: Indiana University Press, 1982), p. 6.

a fact that is unnecessary to deny or qualify in the postcolonial era—noted S. J. Samartha, "did not make it easy for persons of other faiths to have a genuine understanding of the message of Christ, because more often than not colonial Christianity obscured the luminous face of Jesus Christ."[40]

The church and its mission have suffered much from the day that colonized peoples realized its alliance with colonial powers. Nationalist movements in China, North Korea, Vietnam, Burma, and elsewhere, took the form of anti-Christianity, which usually meant the expulsion of Christian missionaries, declaring them *persona non grata*, and confiscation of church properties.[41]

Nationalist challenge to the christendom church was strong in the Philippines, but it did not follow the same course as in other parts of Asia in which nationalist struggle took an anti-Christianity stance. Yet, the Filipinos did not take the imposition of the christendom church passively. About every 25 years throughout the Spanish period, as pointed out by Peter Gowing, the Filipinos raised the banner of revolt for religious as well as economic and political reasons.[42] Filipino nationalist challenge started as early as the nativistic revolts and continued during the struggle for *Filipinization* of the church and the 1896 revolution against Spain,[43] to the coming of the North Americans, to the present. Because the church shared the same interests with the colonizers (clearly luminous during the Spanish colonial times), it became a focus of nationalist challenge, even as the Filipinos were already christianized. The Philippine Independent Church (PIC) is a living expression of this Filipino nationalist challenge to the christendom church. Due to its nationalist orientation, not surprisingly, the United States helped to undermine its existence by favoring and establishing a strategic alliance with the Roman Catholic Church.[44]

Although the christendom church has been able to maintain its influential presence in the Philippines, it cannot fully sanitize itself anymore from the inroads of nationalist consciousness. Nationalist and progressive members of the church sector and laypeople have been pressing the church, Catholic and Protestants alike, to take a more nationalist orientation.

The Irruption of the Non-Christian World

Together with the irruption of nationalist movements one also finds the irruption of the non-Christian world, which enables us to say along with

---

[40]S. J. Samartha, *Courage for Dialogue: Ecumenical Issues in Inter-religious Relationships* (Maryknoll, NY.: Orbis Books, 1981), p. 20.

[41]Walbert Buhlmann, *The Coming of the Third Church* (England: St. Paul Publications, 1974), p. 47.

[42]Gowing, "Christianity in the Philippines: Yesterday and Today," p. 3.

[43]*Filipinization* here is understood, as pointed out by Richard Deats, in the sense of the Filipino struggle for ecclesiastical independence and Filipino leadership. See his work, *Nationalism and Christianity in the Philippines* (Dallas: Southern Methodist University Press, 1967), p. 6.

[44]Bolasco, "USA and Missionary Expansion," *SPI Series, Special Issue,* p. 13.

Pieris that "the irruption of the Third World is also the irruption of the non-Christian world" (except in Latin America and the Philippines).[45] This is certainly the case of Asia, the home of many living religions.

The non-Christian world had long resisted the crusading, christianizing, and civilizing mentality of the Christian West. Peoples of other faiths have realized that their religion, unlike the way religion is viewed by many Westerners, is essentially a way of life, a way of being a people, and that to abdicate their religious faith is tantamount to their death as a people. For this reason the peoples of other faiths have offered strong resistance in order to maintain their way of life, as in the case of Muslim Filipinos.

After years of missionary effort, the major living religions of Asia have survived, whereas the missionary enterprise has been able to gain new grounds only in places like Africa, Latin America, and the Philippines [except the Muslim areas of Mindanao], where other major living religions are absent.[46] This is certainly the case in the southern Philippines (particularly Sulu and Lanao districts), as pointed out by T. Valentino Sitoy, Jr., where Islam has been well established and the inhabitants have imbibed a consciousness as a "distinct religio-cultural community."[47]

Along with other challenges to the christendom church, the challenge of other living religions to the Christian way of living has contributed much to the opening of church windows to the world. And the wind seems to be in favor now of a dialogic way of relating to people of other living faiths.

The Poor, Feminist, and the Challenge of Persons of Color to the Church: Classism, Sexism, and Racism

One important challenge that has confronted the church in our times is the irruption of the poor, the racial outcasts, and women, an irruption that cuts across the ghettos of Western affluent cities and the slum areas and barrios of Asia, Africa, Latin America, and other places. The irruption of the poor, in particular, is an irruption that cuts across gender and race, although feminist movements have pointed out that most of the poor are women.[48]

---

[45]Aloysius Pieris, "The Place of Non-Christian Religions and Cultures in the Evolution of Third World Theology," in *Irruption of the Third World: Challenge to Theology,* p. 113.

[46]Although there is strong indication that Africa will soon become a powerful Christian voice, Pieris has a different perception of Asia. For him the circumstances indicate that Asia "will always remain a non-Christian continent." See his work, *Asian Theology of Liberation* (Maryknoll, NY.: Orbis Books, 1988), especially p. 74.

[47]Sitoy, *A History of Christianity in the Philippines: The Initial Encounter,* p. 32.

[48]Elizabeth Schüssler Fiorenza, *Bread Not Stone: The Challenge of Feminist Biblical Interpretation* (Boston: Beacon Press, 1984), p. 44. Fiorenza has strongly argued against those who label the feminist theological endeavor as peripheral in comparison to the liberation of the poor by saying that the majority of the poor are women. She contends that, "If liberation

If the previous challenges to the church were confined within the Western and Christian tradition, perhaps even inspired by the emerging bourgeoisie (Protestantism), this challenge is, I believe, more radical and indeed very threatening to the church. Hodgson has accurately pointed out that "it is more radically 'from below' than the first [pointing to Protestant Reformation], which really occurred more 'from within' Western culture than from below and outside it."[49]

Christian and non-Christian poor, peoples of color, and women, after centuries under domination, have now awakened from their long slumber and are struggling to remove the shackles of oppression. Because the christendom church has been traditionally allied with the wealthy and the powerful, the challenge of these marginalized groups is equally a challenge not only to the state authorities, but to the church as well. The intensity of this challenge has become like a thunder that the church, especially in Latin America and the Philippines, cannot pretend not to hear anymore, nor hide behind the facade of neutrality, nor dillydally with regard to a response. In this situation the church is challenged to respond: either to take side with or opt for the poor, the peoples of color, and women, which is an option for change, or to be on the side of the status quo, which is actually an abortion of the future.

The Response of the Church to the Challenges

Wave after wave of challenges have made their impact on the church, each one sending shock waves that have made the church respond, either by hardening its defenses or by adaptation, reformation, and new openness.

The initial response of the Roman Catholic Church to the Protestant Reformation was to harden its defenses (Counter-Reformation). On the other hand, the Protestant groups also hardened their position, resulting in violent encounters. All these violent encounters were transported to the remote barrios of third-world countries.

While the response of the Roman Catholic Church, especially at the advent of modernity, was strong resistance to every form of liberalism and modernism, most clear perhaps in the *Syllabus of Errors*,[50] the so-called

---

theologians make the 'option for the oppressed' the key to their theological endeavors, then they must articulate that 'the oppressed' are women" (p. 44).

[49]Peter Hodgson, *Revisioning the Church: Ecclesial Freedom in the New Paradigm* (Philadelphia: Fortress Press, 1988), p. 76. See a similar point in Metz, *The Emergent Church: The Future of Christianity in a Postbourgeois World,* pp. 48-66. Metz sees the "grassroots reformation," something that has found expression in grassroots Christian communities, as the second and true reformation from below. This grassroots reformation has a reformational (not reformist) effect on the churches in the affluent countries, although Protestants and Catholics have different routes to take: (1) Protestants—invoking grace in the senses, and (2) Roman Catholics—invoking grace in freedom.

[50]Marty, *A Short History of Christianity,* pp. 247-250. The *Syllabus of Errors of 1864* is a

mainline Protestants easily felt at home with liberalism, although some within this Protestant group turned to neo-orthodoxy after being disillusioned with liberalism and modernity.[51]

Beginning with Pope Leo XIII, the Roman Catholic Church made a more "adaptive" or "diplomatic" approach to liberalism. It also shifted from a concentration in the Papal States to a stock market portfolio.[52] Theologically, it also shifted from Augustinianism to an emphasis on the thoughts of Aquinas.[53]

A momentous event in the life of the Roman Catholic church that opened its windows to new ideas was Vatican II. What had been stirring in the parishes and Christian communities finally found articulation in the Council: the christendom church giving way to a more mystical and communal understanding of a church (communitas fidelium).[54] From this Council there sprung new encyclicals which became sources of inspiration for greater involvement in society among Filipino Catholics.

Like its Latin American counterpart (CELAM) and its stance: "preferential option for the poor," the Asian bishops also made a historic statement during its meeting in Manila (November 1970) when it affirmed that the church in Asia must be the "Church of the Poor."[55] Although the church, especially the heirarchy, has not been consistent in living up to the full implications of this declaration, it can be considered a significant step.

On the other hand, the Protestant churches, particularly the mainline Protestant churches and the National Council of Churches in the Philippines (NCCP), have grown in their awareness and commitment to the task of social transformation. NCCP's critical social stance all the more heightened during the Marcos years when it had to stand against blatant violation of the people's right to life, although not without opposition from member churches, for example, the United Methodist Bishops. Along with the NCCP, the Council of Bishops of the United Church of Christ in the

---

clear example of the Roman Catholic Church's condemnation of modern sentiments. See also Juan Luis Segundo, *Theology of the Church: A Response to Cardinal Ratzinger and a Warning to the Whole Church,* trans. John W. Diercksmeier (New York: Winston Press, 1985), p. 5, regarding his critique of the fallibility of the church magisterium and the Supreme Pontiff, as exemplified in the *Syllabus of Errors.*

[51]See Heron, *A Century of Protestant Theology,* pp. 74–98. For the neo-orthodox or "dialectical" (not the dialectics of Hegel, but Kierkegaard – understood as a contrast between God and human) theologians (e.g., Karl Barth, Rudulf Bultmann, Emil Brunner, and others), the liberal theologians were falling into the pitfall of *Kulturprotestantismus* and an idolatrous dead end; thus, they fought to reverse the tide of liberalism and its theological starting point.

[52]Joe Holland and Peter Henriott, *Social Analysis: Linking Faith and Justice,* rev. & enlarged (Maryknoll, NY.: Orbis Books, 1983, in collaboration with Center of Concern, Washington, D.C.), p. 75.

[53]Ibid; See also Gutiérrez, *A Theology of Liberation,* p. 35.

[54]Míguez Bonino, *Doing Theology in a Revolutionary Situation,* p. 157.

[55]Julio Xavier Labayen, "The Church of the Poor," in *Rice in the Storm: Faith in Struggle in the Philippines,* p. 31.

Philippines (UCCP) has been more open in its criticism of the status quo and its statements addressed to the radix of the Filipino situation. As its statement goes:

> For as long as peasants remain landless,
> For as long as laborers do not receive just wages,
> For as long as we are politically and economically dominated by foreign nations,
> For as long as we channel more money to the military than to basic social services,
> For as long as the cause of social unrest remains untouched,
> There will be no peace.

Alongside the increasing openness of the church to the plight of the suffering majority, however, is the mushrooming of the forces of closure — the national security regimes and their alliance with influential church officials. In concrete practice it appeared that, although the social encyclicals of the church were moving in a progressive direction, the church became polarized, with the hierarchy wanting to hold the tide of social transformation, whereas at the womb of this old church there emerged a new way of being a church, an *ecclesiogenesis*.[56]

In spite of continuing repression, it appears that the *signum temporum* is in the direction of the emergence of a new church under a new ecclesial paradigm. The praxis of Christians in the struggle bears witness to this emerging ecclesial consciousness, which is also a vision. To this search for a new ecclesial paradigm I now turn my attention.

TOWARD A NEW ECCLESIAL PARADIGM

The various challenges have paved the way for the advent of a new ecclesial paradigm or a new way of being a church. Reactionary forces have taken various steps to bring to a halt its advance, but this new ecclesial paradigm is gaining ground. Slowly the creative and liberating side of the church has been expanding, and so has the consciousness that the church does not exist for itself (*pro se ipsa*) but for the life of the world (*pro mundi vita*). At least the people no longer acknowledge that there is only one way of being a church, that is, the hierarchy's way.

The countercurrents in the church are trying to prove by action, not by high-sounding philosophical arguments, that Marx is wrong to speak of religion or the whole of Christianity as an "opium of the people," although

---

[56]Leonardo Boff, *Ecclesiogenesis: The Base Communities Reinvent the Church,* trans. Robert R. Barr (Maryknoll, NY.: Orbis Books, 1986).

he was right and still is right when speaking about the religion of the dominant class.

However, we cannot fully rely on challenges from the outside for this new ecclesial paradigm to grow. The search, which is also a struggle for a new ecclesial paradigm, must continue both in its practical and theoretical aspects. It is in the direction of this emerging ecclesial paradigm that this study pursues some new ways of construing the church, so that a new church, especially for the Filipino people, may fully bloom — a church of the people and a church that is nationalist and democratic.

Clearing the Space for the Birth of the New Church

The birth of the new ecclesial paradigm requires clearing the space for it to grow or sprout, just like any plant. There are already cracks in the institutional church, cracks from which one can start the clearing in order that the seeds of the new ecclesial paradigm may greet the sunshine and grow. The captivity of the church has not been absolute because there are still people inside the institution who, out of their experience of exteriority, have done something to help the new ecclesial paradigm grow. This task involves struggling and concientizing work in the church, letting it understand where it stands, decentering ecclesiocentrism, being a prophet-in-residence, retrieving the other side of the church, that is, the memory of suffering, and calling it to repentance and conversion.

Asking the Question: Where is the Church?

Part of the struggle to restore the church to its right senses is to raise the question: Where is the church? If you recall, the question *where* has been consistently asked in the previous chapters. In speaking about church renewal, Cariño gives clarity to the point I am asserting. "In approaching this task of ecclesiastical renewal," he said:

> it applies a historical and popular hermeneutic of the church's history: *where* has the church been, *where* is it now, *where* are the Christians, *where* should they be? It looks at the *past*. . . . It looks at the *present* and the *future*.[57]

By focusing on *where,* I call on the church to take account of its life, how this life has been lived, where and with whom the church has been identified. To properly evaluate where the church is and to visualize where it is moving, it is helpful to take an historical look such as I have done in the course of this chapter.

Asking where the church is is a hermeneutical demand, if the church is to

---

[57]Cariño, "The Theology of Struggle as Contextual Theology: Some Discordant Notes," *Tugón*, p. 215. Emphasis supplied.

be renewed. When I say hermeneutical demand, I suggest not simply taking the chronological "whereabouts" of the church, but its "political whereabouts"; to ask the "hermeneutical where" is to engage in political hermeneutics. To ask where the church is is not to ask the church to make a stand, as if it were not already standing somewhere, but to ask it to take account of its social location or its option. To ask the church to make a stand without understanding that it is already standing somewhere is to forget that there is really no neutral church; it is not politically neutral even in its silence. A lie is not simply the opposite of falsehood, for even silence is a lie in a situation when truth needs to be spoken.[58]

Bishop Erme Camba, General Secretary of the United Church of Christ in the Philippines, has proposed a fourfold schema of church responses that I think is useful in identifying the whereabouts of the church and the direction of the theology of struggle's view with regard to ecclesiology.[59] The first response is what Camba called "collaboration." This stance has two manners of expression: (1) full collaboration with the powers-that-be in the maintenance of the existing social structure, and (2) "critical collaboration," which has been suspected of being more collaboration than critical. Cardinal Sin is noted for this stance. Camba identified the second stance as "noninvolvement," which can also be subdivided into three parts: (1) the "spiritualist," (2) the "escapist," and (3) the "wait and see." The third stance is classified as the "reformist type" and in turn is subdivided into four subtypes: (1) social gospel-charity, (2) social gospel-human rights, (3) social gospel-political type, and (4) critical distancing. The last or fourth type is the "politically involved" church or Christians. Churches in the Philippines have responded to the situation in various ways and one classification may not be enough to categorize all these stances. Of these four types presented, theologians of struggle have chosen the fourth. More of this will become clearer as I continue to unfold the character of a new ecclesiology.

The Church as a Site of Struggle Within a Wider Struggle

For the new church to emerge, it must itself be a site of struggle, with a view toward the ongoing wider struggle. The church is an arena where a specific form of struggle has to be waged alongside the overall struggle of the Filipino people. Not only the world outside the walls of the church but, as the *Damascus Document* put it, "The Church itself has become a site of struggle."[60]

Theologically and sociologically, the struggle is a necessity: theologically, it is the church's calling to be a sign and instrument of liberation;

---

[58]See Comblin, *The Church and National Security State,* p. 15.

[59]Bishop Erme Camba, "Spectrum of Church Response to the Peoples Struggle for Change," *Kalinangan,* vol. 5, no. 3 (October 1985), pp. 11–12, 33.

[60]*The Road to Damascus: Kairos and Conversion* (Copyrighted for Philippine Edition by Socio-Pastoral Institute, 1989), p. 9.

sociologically, a struggle in the church (ecclesiastical) is necessary if it is to become fully, and without any reservations, an instrument of liberation. Waging a struggle in the church is strategically beneficial to the wider struggle, for the oppression of the Filipino people is not only socioeconomic, but also ecclesiastical and theological. Christians who have struggled inside the church are contributing something to the wider struggle for liberation. On the other hand, the church experiences itself a renewal and transformation. A renewed church cannot exist apart from a renewed society, whereas a renewed church also contributes to the renewal and transformation of society.

Decentering Ecclesiocentrism

Decentering ecclesiocentrism is an act of subversion, of throwing the center off balance. Decentering requires various approaches. Because the center claims to possess the original message, one approach is to question even the quest for originality and to see the center's truth claim as simply a "regime of truth," that is, that power is constitutive of truth, in Foucaultian fashion.[61] Decentering can also take the form of advancing the idea of "paradigm shifts,"[62] or it may take the form of a deconstructive critique of Western logocentrism, of which christendom ecclesiology is a concrete example.[63] It may also take the form of looking at reality from the underside of history and subjecting the dominant center to an ideological critique, a critique of various forms of totalization and universalization, approaches that have been taken by liberation and feminist theologies. These various approaches can contribute to the task of decentering ecclesiocentrism and in creating more caesuras in the Western church's control of third-world churches, a *condition sine qua non* for the birth of the new ecclesial paradigm. However, a decentering critique is incomplete if not accompanied by concrete political struggle and empowerment of the marginalized.

Retrieving the Memoria Passionis: Remembering the Dismembered, Uncovering the Subversive Memories, and Searching for Alternative Histories vis-à-vis The History

A people may be oppressed for centuries, but if this people has not forgotten its history of suffering, this is indicative that its oppression is not

---

[61]Foucault, "Nietzsche, Genealogy, and History," in *Foucault Reader,* pp. 76–100; idem, "Truth and Power," in *Power/Knowledge: Selected Interviews and Other Writings,* 1972–77.

[62]See Thomas S. Kuhn, *The Structure of Scientific Revolutions* (Chicago: University of Chicago Press, 1962).

[63]Mark C. Taylor, *Erring: A Postmodern A-theology* (Chicago: University of Chicago Press, 1984); idem, *Deconstructing Theology* (New York: Crossroad, and Chico, California: Scholars Press, 1982); John D. Caputo, *Radical Hermeneutics: Repetition, Deconstruction, and the Hermeneutic Project* (Bloomington and Indianapolis: Indiana University Press, 1987).

yet absolute, that the people still retain the notion that things are not right. It might be that this memory, no matter how flickering, is the only space left where humanity is still experienced and is a starting point for transformative action, hence, it is fittingly called "dangerous memory."[64]

A triumphalist-clerico-fascist-ecclesiocentric church is a church that has forgotten its *memoria passionis* or is trying to suppress it. From the point of view of the power wielders, the people's remembrance of their *memoria passionis* is a threat, something that has to be stopped quickly, because of its subversive potential. In order to prevent the people from retrieving their memory of suffering, the ruling elite propagates the understanding that the people's plight is natural or bombards them with cultural tranquilizers so that they may forget their suffering.

Nourishing this *memoria passionis* would seem to appear as something contrary to the Christian teachings, especially with regard to forgiveness and reconciliation. It has been commonly expressed that "to forgive is to forget" and to reconcile. Forgiveness is, I believe, endangered by simply associating it with forgetting, for the violation done against the victims is more likely to be repeated. Much better would be to say that to forgive is to "remember" the "dismembered" vis-a-vis *the* history of progress as interpreted by the powerful.[65] The birthing of a new ecclesial paradigm, I believe, is only possible when the *memoria passionis* of the church is retrieved.

Calling the Church to Repentance and Conversion:
A New Reformation

To call the christendom church to offer a humble *mea culpa*, that is, to repent, would seem to be most unthinkable.[66] But this is precisely what is needed before we can expect a church to be in solidarity with the people, much more so if we have to speak of the church of the people or the church of the poor. A church can only repent if it realizes that it has deviated from its calling and has participated in the domination of the people. And more than the term *realization* can convey, repentance (*metanoia*) also means "turning away," that is, turning away "from" its alliances with the forces of death so that it may be free "for" the victims and their struggle for the liberation of all.

Although the church has been held hostage by christendom mentality, its

---

[64]Metz, *Faith in History and Society: Toward a Practical Fundamental Theology,* p. 171.

[65]Walker, *One World, Many Worlds: Struggle for a Just World Peace,* pp. 21–26; cf. Foucault, "Nietzsche, Genealogy, History," in *Foucault Reader,* pp. 76–100. This deals with Foucault's understanding of history, his critique of traditional history, and his genealogical method that employs two approaches: (1) *Herkunft* (descent), and (2) *Entstehung* (emergence).

[66]See Maria Clara Lucchetti Bingemer, "Third World Theologies: Conversion to Others," in *Theologies of the Third World: Convergences and Differences,* Concilium, eds. Leonardo Boff and Virgil Elizondo (Edinburgh: T. & T. Clark Ltd, 1988), p. 120.

liberative and creative side is still alive. It is from this liberative and creative side, a side that has remained stored in the lives of the poor and in their memory of suffering, that God's spirit calls the church to repentance. It would be naive to expect the call to repentance to originate from the comfortable, but it can only be expected from the wounded side of the church. The poor, being the most wounded, play a very important role as the leaven in the renewal of the church, for they fully represent the wounded side of the church; they are the reminders that everything is not all right. "The Church's extraordinary power of regeneration," said Pierre Bigo, "wells up from an inexhaustible source, the world of 'the poor.' "[67]

Repentance and conversion for a church that has long been identified with the powers-that-be means repentance and conversion for the poor. This requires what the famous passage in Philippians 2 conveys: (1) humility, (2) service, and (3) solidarity with the marginalized.[68] The conversion of the church is necessary so that it may become a church in solidarity with the poor.

A New Way of Knowing and Being a Church: Characteristics of a Church Under the New Ecclesial Paradigm

The epiphany of a new ecclesial paradigm is already discernible; it is discernible at the margins, peripheries, nooks and crannies, and cracks of the institutional church. It would be hard to fully articulate and hold it captive with precise systematic categories because much still remains to be clarified by concrete practice. Yet, the people's experience of pathos and their fragmentary foretaste of a new community enable us to construct the images of this new ecclesial paradigm. I now explore the images, figures, and characteristics of this new ecclesial paradigm.

The Church as a Prophetico-Critical Movement: Prophetic "Detachment" Born out of Solidarity with Exteriority to Protest Ecclesiocentric Totalization

In the introduction to this chapter I expressed some suggestions regarding a church construed as a prophetico-critical movement. I consider this as a proper description of a new ecclesial paradigm because, like other critical social movements, the church grew out of the crucible of persecution and exteriority. From this experience of exteriority springs its precious pearl of prophecy. The church, understood as a prophetico-critical movement,

---

[67]Pierre Bigo, *The Church and Third World Revolution,* trans. Jeanne Marie Lyons (Maryknoll, NY.: Orbis Books, 1977), p. 124. The importance of the poor in the renewal of the church has been an enduring emphasis of liberation theology.

[68]See Albert H. van den Heuvel, *The Humiliation of the Church* (London: SCM Press, 1966), p. 53.

serves as a reminder that the highways of the so-called "progress" in the modern world is littered with victims, that the modern world is a world full of fractures.[69]

I have chosen this aspect to be the first category because this notion seems to set in a proper light our search for a new ecclesial paradigm, in the sense that it is useful for the church to come to a realization of who it is, where it is, and where it should be going (identity). To speak of the church as a critico-prophetical movement is to remind it of its root experiences, so that it may come to terms with its origin and destiny (identity); it is to anchor the church, as in the case of any critical social movement, in its *memoria passionis*; hence, it is called to exercise a prophetico-critical function. The true identity of the church is to be a prophetico-critical movement, and to deviate from this identity is to lose its sense of direction, to miss the target (*hamartia*), to enter into a Babylonian captivity.

Prophetic criticism, prophetic vision, and prophetic solidarity: the task of social transformation.   Essential to any prophetico-critical movement is the exercise of prophetic criticism, prophetic vision, and prophetic solidarity. These practices find correspondence in Dussel's construal of the base Christian communities as "communo-utopian praxis" and as "prophetico-community praxis of liberation."[70] A prophetico-critical movement, of which the base Christian community is an excellent expression, is capable of prophetic-criticism by virtue of its identification with exteriority. "They provide the 'whence,'" said Dussel, "of the ethico-prophetic critique of the prevailing morality of domination."[71] Prophetic criticism does not spring from well-secured social institutions. Well-secured institutions have their mouths full so that, like dogs, they do not bark. Only from the experience of woundedness springs the fruit of prophetic denunciation of the *what is*.

But the *what is* is not only denounced because of the people's experience of suffering, the *what is* is also denounced because the people have gained prophetic vision in and through their suffering, because the *what is* negates the much better tomorrow. And along with the prophetic denunciation of the *what is* is the annunciation of a new vision.

This prophetic denunciation and annunciation is not done in detachment — detachment from the totalizing center, yes. But prophetic detachment is made possible in solidarity with exteriority, not in order to add to the victimized population, but in order to struggle with the victims for transformation.

---

[69]Walker, *One World, Many Worlds: Struggles for a Just World Peace*, p. 26. Social movements are in fact a very good guide to some of the major lines of fracture in the modern world (p. 26).

[70]Enrique Dussel, *Ethics and Community*, trans. Robert Barr (Maryknoll, NY.: Orbis Books, 1988), pp. 84–85.

[71]Ibid., p. 85.

The church and the posture of prophetic atheism: The challenge of idolatry. The early Christian communities were not so much engrossed with the problem of atheism as with idolatry. In fact, they were the ones who were charged as atheists. With the advent of secularism brought about by the rise of the modern period and the kind of geopolitics that the church entered into, that is, its alliance with the capitalist West against the so-called communists, the church shifted its focus of attack to that of atheism. The church defended itself against secular atheism, but it has been the fear of communist atheism that has preoccupied the energies of a church that has identified its interest with the capitalist West. Because the enemy is communism and communism is construed as atheistic, the church has to focus its theological armaments on atheism. What a theological agendum it is that is dictated by the church's unholy alliance with the capitalists!

What I consider to be a real threat is not atheism but idolatry. Atheism does not feed on the blood of the innocents; it is the idols of death that demand sacrifice. Idolatry is not absent even in countries that claim to be secular. National security ideology is such an idol: in defense of its name millions of people are sacrificed. Pablo Richard grasped this point succinctly in saying that "in an oppressed world, the fundamental enemy of the gospel is not atheism, but idolatry."[72] In the face of the idols of death, atheism is a demand; atheism is an evangelical witness; atheism is faithfulness to the gospel. In the words of Ernst Bloch, "Only an atheist can be a good Christian."[73]

The Church as a Witness to Suffering, Hope, and Struggle: Retrieving the Dangerous Memories for the Struggle of the Present in Creating a New Future

The church as a witness to suffering. A triumphant church is not a witness to suffering but instead a witness to comfort and privilege. In fact, it tries to bury the people's memory of suffering or anaesthetize the people with regard to their suffering.

When the church's consciousness is that of a prophetico-critical movement, it truly becomes a witness to suffering; its very existence is a witness (*martyria*) to suffering. As a prophetico-social movement it stands in solidarity with those who have given their lives in previous generations, as well as with those who are yet to be born, in the form of prophetic witnesses to the present. It suffers because its plight and destiny is one with the

---

[72]Pablo Richard, *Our Struggle is Against the Idols,* Reprinted by Community Formation Center, Ozamiz City, Philippines (1984).

[73]Ernst Bloch, cited in José Míguez Bonino, *Room to Be People: An Interpretation of the Message of the Bible in Today's World,* trans. Vickie Leach (Philadelphia: Fortress Press, 1979), pp. 9–25. Also Antonio Pérez-Esclarín, *Atheism and Liberation* (Maryknoll, NY.: Orbis Books, 1978), especially pp. 194–197.

suffering people, and it suffers in resistance to suffering. The persecution of the faithful individuals and communities in our times — Fr. Rudy Romano, Fr. Tulio Favalli, Atty. Alfonso Surigao, Rev. Amando Añosa, Rev. Vizminda Gran, and others, to name but a few — is a testimony to this. The moving words of Vizminda Gran (Pastor, United Church of Christ in the Philippines, murdered on May 1, 1989), is a treasure worth quoting:

> It would be good to die seeing the dawn and brightness of the morning. But if my life is needed in the night to usher in the morning, then, I have nothing else to give, because I am poor, but this life of mine.[74]

Church as a collective witness to hope: resurrection as insurrection and hope.   Suffering does not necessarily lead to hope; it may lead to fatalism, despair, and hedonistic play. The church, as a prophetico-critical movement, is a witness to suffering that has blossomed in hope, and conversely it has also become a hope that bears witness in suffering. At the heart of religion, and in particular, the church as a prophetico-critical movement, gushes out the dream and hope of a better future.[75] It is a dream and hope driven by *memoria passionis*, but confirmed through the eyes of faith in the *memoria resurrectionis* of Jesus.

When people seem to be driven into the abyss of despair, the church must remain a bulwark of living hope; it must be a witness to a collective hope. "For if despair is a collective evil," said Segundo Galilea, "nourished by the shadows and frustrations of human society until it enslaves the heart of humankind, hope must have a collective witness. . . . That collective witness is the church."[76]

Church as a witness to struggle.   Not only is this church a witness to suffering and hope, but it is also a witness to struggle. In remembering the memory of suffering, it struggles; in its attempt to take account of the hope that is in itself, it struggles; in solidarity with the past, it carries on the struggle; in anticipation of the future, it struggles. Thus we can call this church under the new ecclesial paradigm a struggling church.

When a church retrieves the memory of suffering, it does so not because it loves to dwell on this painful past, but because this long memory of suffering is an indication of the church's solidarity with the cause of those who suffer and die, even without seeing the dawn. To retrieve this memory represents the church's refusal to consign to oblivion and vanity the struggles and hopes of those who have given their lives before us. To

---

[74]*Kalinangan,* vol. 12, no. 1 (1992), p. 27, citing *Magnificat* (Published by the Association of Women in Theology or AWIT, vol. 3, no. 2, October 1989).

[75]Cf. Aloysius Pieris, "Faith-Communities and Communalism," *East Asian Pastoral Review,* vol. 26, nos. 324 (1989), p. 300.

[76]Segundo Galilea, *Spirituality of Hope* (Maryknoll, NY.: Orbis Books, 1988), p. 91.

retrieve is to carry forward the aspirations of previous generations through the struggle of the present generation. It is not the entertaining of a dead past, or even an "empathy" or an "identification" with their struggles, but the continuation of our struggle now that is an act of solidarity with the dead and those who are yet to be born.[77]

I recall the reaction of a North American friend of mine when I shared with him the barbarity of U.S. soldiers during the Philippine-American war—a war that the United States wants to forget. His immediate reaction was: "What do you want me to do, apologize?" Forget about that idea of apologizing, I thought to myself, as if these barbarities against the Filipinos were something of the past. What is needed is to continue the struggle. This is how we should express our love and solidarity with those who have gone even before us, and this is how we should express our love for those who are yet to come, much more so, to think along with the ecologists, that "we no longer inherit the earth from our parents; we borrow it from our children."[78]

The Church as a Site and Gestalt of Freedom: The Mission of Creating "Democratic Spaces" and People Empowerment

Under the new ecclesial paradigm, I see the church as a gestalt and site of freedom with a mission to create democratic spaces beyond its own religious communities. Through its witness to the wider community and its active involvement in organizing base Christian communities and people's organizations, the church contributes to the regaining of the people's freedom, to their empowerment, and to the expansion of democratic space.

Throughout its history, the church as a figure and site of freedom has always been present, even in christendom ecclesiology. When the church is fully conscious of its origin and destiny as a prophetico-critical movement, the site of freedom becomes wider and the gestalt of freedom more visible. On the other hand, when institutionalism has triumphed, this site of freedom narrows. Whenever the memory of suffering, the experience of marginality, and the resolve to struggle are present, freedom is present. In the act of struggle, freedom is present and human dignity is experienced. From the struggle of those who have chosen to be prophets-in-residence and from the communities that have been formed out of their struggle for the struggle, the church as a site of freedom is discernible.

When the whole institution takes a serious prophetic stand, we can say that it has become a very luminous gestalt of freedom. In the Philippines, some churches and national church bodies have become visible sites and

---

[77]See Elizabeth Schüssler Fiorenza, "Remembering the Past in Creating the Future: Historical-Critical Scholarship and Feminist Biblical Interpretations," in *Feminist Perspectives on Biblical Scholarship*, p. 63.

[78]Walker, *One World, Many Worlds: Struggles for a Just World Peace*, p. 101.

gestalts of freedom. The National Council of Churches in the Philippines, recalled La Verne Mercado, became a "compound" or a "sanctuary" of people who were taking refuge from the repressive measures of the dictator Marcos.[79] To become a "sanctuary" (Hebrew—*Nutz*), commented Capulong, is an essential calling of the church.[80] When repressive regimes have declared every place as "no man's land," the church must be ready to stand as a haven for the victims, a place where the weak are empowered. Filipinos should not find it difficult to think of the church as a haven because it resonates very deeply with their cherished custom of hospitality. This is the kind of hospitality that rural people are familiar with, in which even the last fatted chicken had to be slaughtered for the visitors.

New Ecumenism Under the New Ecclesial Paradigm

Ecumenism is construed differently under the new ecclesial paradigm. In order to understand this lucidly, it would be of help to trace in brief the changes that have accompanied the churches' understanding of ecumenism. La Verne Mercado made the following observation:

> Ecumenism in the Philippines has developed to a certain degree from ecumenism as an inter-confessional activity to ecumenism as a dimension of Christian life, from inter-church cooperation to inter-faith relationships, from church concern to *service to the world*, an ecumenism that goes beyond ecclesial frontiers into the larger struggle for peace, justice and unity of the whole human society.[81]

It should not be difficult to notice that in this new ecumenism the interaction is not primarily among churches but rather between the church and the world. The churches relate ecumenically in relation to a common and shared world, more particularly to the world of the victims or what is often referred to as the "bleeding points" of history. It is an ecumenism rooted in the awareness of a common plight and unity in the struggle—a "revolutionary ecumenism" as del la Torre would put it;[82] it is an ecumenism that spreads like fire especially at the grassroots level (grassroots ecumenism); it is, I believe, an ecumenism with a stronger bond of unity among the people.[83] Although doctrinal differences are not denied, the common realization of unity in the struggle has enabled the people of

---

[79]Mercado, "Towards a New Ecumenical Vision," *Tugón*, p. 193.

[80]Noriel Capulong, "Sanctuaries as Communities of Justice and Peace," *Tugón*, vol. 8, no. 3 (1988), p. 289.

[81]Mercado, "Towards a New Ecumenical Vision," *Tugón*, pp. 190–191. Emphasis supplied.

[82]de la Torre, *Touching Ground, Taking Root*, p. 84.

[83]Sammie P. Formilleza, "People's Theology: Faith-Life Reflections of Grassroots Filipino Christians," *Simbayan*, vol. 8, nos. 2 and 3 (1989), p. 17; also Carlos Ocampo, "Taking the Struggle to the Churches," *Simbayan*, vol. 5, no. 1 (February 24, 1986), p. 4.

various faiths and ideologies to transcend and respect differences for the common weal.

The Church as a "Deliberating" Community: Explorations on Liberative Ways of Living

This notion of a church as a "deliberating" community is my appropriation of what has been used to characterize the critical social movements, particularly in the work of Ruiz.[84] Ruiz advanced the understanding that "deliberation" is not simply a tool, but is constitutive of the very existence of communities of resistance and solidarity, a notion that I would like to appropriate for a church under the new ecclesial paradigm. When we speak of deliberation as constitutive, it means that deliberation should characterize the very life of the church itself; its life is deliberative. Deliberation is not only a dialogical approach of communication, but is the very description of the life of the church itself. Its ways of understanding, of communicating, of relating, and of dwelling are deliberative.

In the christendom church the hierarchy, through the pope, bishops, and priests, is the axis of power: Power emanates from the top and trickles to the bottom. The hierarchy has everything to give, but the laity have nothing to give at all, except to receive. In a deliberating community, the organization is structured in a democratic and participatory manner in which everyone is empowered and contributes meaningfully for the benefit of the community. Hierarchical ways of relating are subjected to criticism, and humane ways of relating are explored.

The Church as a Witness to One World, Many Worlds: Struggles for Self-Determination

History is de facto replete with cases in which the church has been intolerant of other worlds, even if de jure it claims to be "catholic." Can we speak of the church as a witness to one world with many worlds? Honestly, it is difficult to conceive of the church in this way because it is hard to draw something from experience. But, I still insist in speaking of the church as a witness to one world with many worlds, not so much because this is the dominant observable reality, but because it is a demand that the church should be a witness to, a world with many worlds if this world in which we live is to have a future. "The pursuit of just world peace and new forms of solidarity," contended Walker, "must be rooted in an equal respect for the claims of both diversity and unity. *One World must also be Many Worlds.*"[85]

---

[84]Lester Ruiz, "Towards Communities of Resistance and Solidarity: Some Political and Philosophical Notes," *Tugón,* vol. 7, no. 3 (1987), pp. 4–14.

[85]Walker, *One World, Many Worlds: Struggles for a Just World Peace,* p. 5. Emphasis supplied. I owe the title of this subtopic to Walker.

A church whose sense of self-understanding is that of a prophetico-critical movement should not find the call of one world with many worlds as something remote from its experience. But such a call is a problem for the christendom church because it has always raised its own particularity into a totality, which is not the case with a prophetico-critical movement. The church as a prophetico-critical movement is conscious of its particularity because of its experience of location in exteriority; this church does not make claims for all people by virtue of being the center or the *telos* of history. Struggling for its own identity and resisting the absorption of its difference from any totalizing center, it knows the world as many worlds. It can accompany the journey of communities that are struggling for self-determination and resist making the state's interest the supreme criterion of unity.

Yet the church as prophetico-critical movement also realizes that although there are many worlds there is indeed one world. The one world is a shared world, and what is considered to be of "common" interest is not defined by the most powerful; rather, the common is the space carved out by the interaction of differences through communicative praxis and deliberation.[86]

The New Ecclesial Paradigm as a Witness and a Sign of a New Way of Being a People (Peoplehood) and Human Dwelling

An act of witness is at the same time a seed of a new tomorrow. The new ecclesial practice, especially as expressed in struggling faith communities, is both a witness and a sign of a new way of peoplehood and human dwelling.

The new ecclesial practice as a witness to a new humanity and peoplehood.   The church under the new ecclesial paradigm is indicative of an experience of a new humanity and peoplehood. In fact, we can speak of the emerging church as a new humanity and peoplehood. We have in the birth of a new church a witness to a new humanity arising—neither static nor complete, but a humanity in a journey and in travail.

In the previous chapter on christology, I spoke of Jesus as a paradigm of what it means to be truly human, at least for Christians, not simply human in the common existential-ontological sense, but human in the face of the disfigured and marginalized people. Because the faithful Christian communities are the followers of Jesus, the humanity that was so luminous in Jesus can be discerned in the life and practice of these faith communities. "The new Christian community," claimed Comblin, "represents the new person,

---

[86]Ruiz, "Towards Communities of Resistance and Solidarity: Some Political and Philosophical Notes," *Tugón,* p. 12.

as opposed to all social individualism and totalitarianism, be it ecclesial, civil, or military."[87]

The new ecclesial paradigm as a seed and a sign of a new way of thinking and dwelling. Walker's words for critical social movements fit properly for the church conceived as a prophetico-critical movement. This church appears weak, vulnerable, and cannot be expected to make an impressive transformation of society, but in its negation of the negativities and its vision and longing for *alternative possibilities*, it becomes important for thinking about the future. Its significance, for Walker, does not lie in an overt power that can make impressive changes, but rather in the fact that it carries the *seeds* of a new understanding of what it means to live in a secure world (a new understanding of security), a new understanding of what it means to dwell humanly, and a new understanding of what it means to speak of a community.[88] Moving further, we should expand our notion of a church, as suggested by Sallie McFague in her book *The Body of God: An Ecological Theology*, to speak of it as a "sign of the new creation" — characterized by a new understanding of humanity's place in the scheme of things, and the interrelationship and interdependence of all bodies (human and nature), while underscoring their differences.[89]

Church sacraments, particularly baptism and the eucharist, give a glimpse of the nature of this human dwelling. The eucharist conveys the notion that a true community involves the practice of sharing "one bread" and living as "one body" and as "one people." This is in consonance with an age-old Filipino practice known as *bayanihan* (mutual sharing and cooperation) and the notion of *utang na loob*, understood as "debt of human solidarity" owed to all.[90] In a true community individuals see their lives as a debt of human solidarity, and they express their sense of indebtedness in the spirit of *bayanihan*. It is in this sense that our notion of *bayani[han]* or hero is radically altered, for in the practice of *bayanihan* not only one becomes a *bayani* or hero, but the whole community.[91] Baptism, on the other hand, seals one's membership into a caring and supportive wider family or community. The *padrino system*, understood positively within the context of baptism, is a practice that points to the need for widening the family.

L. Boff, speaking about the base ecclesial communities, asserted a

---

[87]Comblin, *Retrieving the Human*, p. 11.

[88]Walker, *One World, Many Worlds: Struggles for a Just World Peace*, p. 5. Also see Lester Ruiz, *Practices of Freedom and Interpretation: The University, Counterhegemony, and Moral Responsibility in the World Community* (1989), pp. 8-10. Mimeographed.

[89]See Sallie McFague, *The Body of God: An Ecological Theology* (Minneapolis: Fortress Press, 1993), particularly pp. 197-212.

[90]See Barbara E. Bowe, *Reading Paul Through the Filipino Eyes*. Mimeographed.

[91]See Sr. Myrna Francia, "When Demons are Cast Away," in *Kalinangan*, vol. 10, no. 3 (September 1990), p. 34.

similar point to the one I am making when he saw these communities as holding a prophecy or a promise that is slowly being realized in history:[92] It is a prophecy that the old is passing away and the new has come and is to come. Although "it is crucified, it is persecuted, it exists in suffering and struggle, but it exists."[93]

Although the reality of the new church is primarily a promise, and at most a foretaste, this is an important contribution of the emerging faith communities. The church, understood as a promise, conveys a notion of truth; it is a truth not simply founded on the "what is," but on that which is "not yet." Truth solely construed as "what is" has no defenses against absolutist claims, even the claim of the institutional church. When the church is viewed as a promise, it refuses to be completely identified with the dominant structures and its critical posture is maintained. Ideology, understood in the negative sense, always seeks to provide a comprehensive God's eye view of reality; whereas religion, as lived by the prophetico-critical-faith communities, as noted by Pieris, always seeks to block any messianic claim to offer an absolute blueprint of the future.[94]

What I call the new church is only discernible in its fragile form, but it is slowly in the process of being born. It is arising from the bleeding points of history, not from the lofty places of the mighty and the privileged. Deep discernment, which is a gift of the Holy Spirit, is needed to have the leaven of this new church work. We can either put ourselves in a position that slows down its coming or put ourselves at the service of this new emerging church.

---

[92]Boff, *Ecclesiogenesis,* p. 33.

[93]Comblin, *Retrieving the Human,* p. 29. See a similar point by Dussel in *Ethics and Community,* pp. 78–87.

[94]Pieris, "Faith-Communities and Communalism," *East Asian Pastoral Review,* pp. 300–301.

7

In Search of a Theological Method

Issues proper to theological method are usually raised at the very beginning of a theological construction. This is done to set at the start the author's understanding of the nature of theological reflection and its tasks, basic hermeneutical premises,[1] sources, norms/criteria, and how to get on with the process of theologizing (methodology).

In my case, however, instead of putting the issues related to method at the beginning of this study, I decided to put them in the last chapter, not out of fear that my method will be construed as a "dragon at the gate" that would scare off potential readers, as in the case of Francis Fiorenza's mind-twisting and highly sophisticated methodological finesse,[2] but to convey my own pilgrimage in this search of a method.

To carry out the intent of this chapter on theological method, I take a cursory look at the present status of theological reflection, appropriating the notions "house of authority" and "fragmentation of theology" (Farley) as a framework in this critique.[3] After this cursory critique, I explore the kind of theological reflection that has emerged after the collapse of the house of authority, specifically advancing the case of the theology of struggle as a theology outside the house of authority, or as an emerging theological paradigm.[4] And extending the insights of Farley—something

---

[1]I use the word *hermeneutical* in the senses identified by Mark K. Taylor in his work, *Remembering Esperanza: A Cultural-Political Theology for North American Praxis* (Maryknoll, NY.: Orbis Books, 1990), pp. 46–75.

[2]Francis Schüssler Fiorenza, *Foundational Theology: Jesus and the Church* (New York: Crossroad, 1984), pp. xiv, 249–321.

[3]Farley, *Ecclesial Reflection: An Anatomy of Theological Method.* For further treatment of the topic, see Farley and Hodgson, "Scripture and Tradition," in *Christian Theology: An Introduction to Its Traditions and Tasks,* pp. 61–87; see also *Theologia: The Fragmentation and Unity of Theological Education* (Philadelphia: Fortress Press, 1983).

[4]The theology of struggle, like the whole genre of liberation theology, is, in my understanding, a new theological paradigm. What theologians have argued for liberation theology can be equally applied to the theology of struggle. See Chopp, *The Praxis of Suffering: An Interpretation of Liberation and Political Theologies,* especially pp. 134–148. Chopp argued that liberation theologies constitute a paradigm shift in terms of context, content, experience, and interpretation of Christianity. See also Sölle, *Thinking About God: An Introduction to Theology,* pp. 32–41. For a different interpretation, cf. Tracy, *Blessed Rage for Order: The*

that my Third-World eye could not miss but that Western theologians may likely fail to see — I view this house of authority as the dominant theologies of the West. This is the house of authority that claims to be the *norma normans* of theological reflections from which Third World peoples want to be liberated.

From my critique of theological constructions which, for long, have claimed to be the *norma normans*, I proceed to the main exposition of how theological reflection is done in the theology of struggle and how the major issues of sources, norms/criteria, and community of accountability are to be interpreted. Lastly, I expound my proposal for hermeneutical premises and the methodological-hermeneutical spiral that should guide the theology of struggle.

CRITIQUE OF THEOLOGY UNDER THE HOUSE OF AUTHORITY: ITS COLLAPSE AND FRAGMENTATION

Theology Under the Orthodox House of Authority: A Critique

It is not difficult to understand the notion "house of authority," for we can easily derive that from our experience. Suffice it to say, for my purposes here, the general mode of theologizing under the classical orthodoxy revolved around the notion of "authority." This does not mean that all theological reflections after the collapse of the house of authority do not have the notion of authority anymore, but under the classical criteriology, as Farley put it, "what settled the [theological] disputes and grounded the judgments were not so much evidence-gathering inquiries as appeals to some entity, place, or person which was regarded as authoritative."[5] Thus when we ask, What made you say that? or What is your basis for saying so?, the likely answer is that of the old refrain, "For the Bible tells me so" (Protestants), or because the Pope or the dogma of the church says so (Roman Catholics).

Why do the *vehicles* of ecclesial process — tradition, biblical canon, and the institutional church — become authoritative? Although the process is long, as analysed by Farley, it finally leads to the *identification* of the earthen vessels with divine revelation or from the belief that there is "identity of content between what is divinely willed [revealed] and what is humanly asserted."[6] One need only think of how pastors are introduced before they preach or how they begin their sermons. The Sunday liturgist

---

New Pluralism in Theology. Political and liberation theologies, for Tracy, can be classified under neo-orthodoxy in terms of "subject referent" and "object referent" (p. 30).

[5] Farley, *Ecclesial Reflection: An Anatomy of Theological Method,* p. 27.

[6] Ibid., p. 38.

will usually say, "Now lets hear the Word of God from The Reverend so and so. . . . " Here, the interpretive character of all preaching of the Word of God is not brought to the open. Thus, although sermons are now challenged by critical members, they still dangerously convey an identification of preaching with the Word of God.

How does theologizing proceed from this house of authority? It can only be as citation, explication, translation, and at best adaptation of church dogmas, church encyclicals, pronouncements of the church magisterium, and the Bible, which constitute the eternal and infallible *principia*.[7] What can one do with an infallible given other than cite, comment, explicate, and translate it in the most "faithful" manner according to the original formulation? This mode of theologizing has been completely oblivious of the fact that these so-called eternal theological deposits were also sedimented interpretations. Under the house of authority it is completely inconceivable to think of other modes of theologizing except that of citation, explication, translation, and adaptation. A contextual theology cannot be expected under the house of authority; this is only possible after its collapse.

The Collapse of the Classical House of Authority and the Rise of Another House of Authority

The rise of the modern period brought with it the collapse of the orthodox house of authority. While historically we can say that the house of authority had already collapsed, theology, in spite of its advances, has not been out completely from the house of authority. The modern missionary enterprise, even at its most progressive point, still operated in the theological mode of translation or adaptation.

Not even with the rise of the Western liberal mode of theologizing can we comfortably say that it has been liberated from the theological mode of the orthodox house of authority, because it too has been oblivious of its own context.[8] McAfee Brown treated this issue sharply when he noted the following remark of a Latin American theologian during a theological conference of North and South American theologians: "Why is it that when you talk about *our* position you always describe it as 'Latin American theology,' but when you talk about *your* position you always describe it as 'theology'?" This is not a simple matter of forgetting, but is deeply

---

[7]Farley, *Theologia: The Fragmentation and Unity of Theological Education*, p. 41.

[8]See Sölle, *Thinking About God: An Introduction to Theology*, p. 33. Sölle contends that liberal theology, especially in relation to its use of the Bible, still looks for "timeless norms and statements in the Bible. Despite its insistence on the historicity of scripture it does not go far enough in historical-critical terms, because it leaves out issues of social history" (p. 33).

grounded in the understanding that Western theology is "normative," whereas other theologies are "derivative."[9]

Because liberal theology is oblivious of its context, it too has assumed the role of *norma normans*—the house of authority for others. While Farley has called our attention to tradition, biblical canon, and the institutional church as the main pillars of the house of authority, from my third-world perspective I would say that aside from these three pillars, Western theological formulations have long served as the house of authority for third-world theological formulations. I have to carry forward what Farley has not pursued in his critique of the orthodox house of authority and say that Western theologies have become for us the house of authority. These theologies have not only stifled our theological creativity, for we ended up as theological *compradors*, but have also become instruments of Western control and domination. In fact, this is the primary angle that I emphasize in speaking about the house of authority.

Fragmentation of Theology After the Collapse of the House of Authority

Modernity's advent, while it brought with it the much-needed collapse of the house of authority, also gave birth to the fragmentation of various disciplines, and theology was no exemption. I am not suggesting that specialized studies need to be abhorred, but am only emphasizing the message that in the fragmentation of theology its notion as *habitus* of the human soul has been dislodged in favor of theology understood as "practical know-how" for ministerial work.[10] This is especially acute in liberal academic Protestant theological education, although Roman Catholic education is not exempt, even with its program of seminary formation.

This loss of a sense of theology as *habitus* in exchange for "practical know-how" is lamentable, a malaise in our understanding of theology. It is like the malaise of a person who can see an individual tree in the forest but has no view of the whole forest, a view that is obviously vital to derive meaning and render a radical critique. Practical know-how theology has produced "experts" in certain fields, but they often render lifeless interpretations of traditions that are waiting to be sold in the theological market to the practical theologians and ministers who, in turn, have to sell their appropriated interpretations to the lay consumers.

The loss of *habitus* is unfortunate: theology has lost the notion of praxis, something that the current liberation theologies have emphasized. The position of theology among the academic disciplines, although always

---

[9]Robert McAfee Brown, *Theology in a New Key: Responding to Liberation Themes* (Philadelphia: The Westminster Press, 1978), p. 77.

[10]Farley, *Theologia: The Fragmentation and Unity of Theological Education*, pp. 29–48.

threatened and marginal, has contributed to the promotion of the deceptive understanding that it is objective and not itself propelled by some "interests"—be it "cognitive" in the Habermasian sense,[11] or "class" in Marxist thought. What is often concealed is that the so-called objective knowledge of the specialist, as Farley has pointed out, creates a "tunnel vision" that fails to understand the way specialty knowledge becomes servile to the wider societal struggles.[12]

The theology of struggle, as I understand it, like other theologies within the genre of liberation theology, attempts to restore the idea of theology as *habitus*, although not in the sense of *inward* soul saving, but *habitus* turned *outward* as wisdom praxis, as suggested by Hodgson, that is, active involvement in the transformation of the world.[13] I believe that the theology of struggle can fulfill this move to restore *habitus* as integral liberation because its spirituality is part and parcel of its method (more explanation later).

FAREWELL TO THE HOUSE OF AUTHORITY, FAREWELL TO INNOCENT THEOLOGY: A DISENCHANTMENT OF THE WESTERN DISENCHANTMENT OF ITS OWN DISENCHANTMENT

Thanks to the collapse of the classical house of authority, which the rise of the modern period has brought about, and to the Enlightenment, a watershed of Western contribution to the rest of humanity, long-entrenched mystifications were demystified, the new human being was released from the clutches of oppressive authorities, and scientific knowledge was unleashed. Its quintessential form is expressed in the motto *Aude sapere*, that is, "dare to know," have a critical mind, subjecting everything to critical inquiry. Enlightenment (*Aufklärung*), as Immanuel Kant put it, is an *Ausgang*, an "exit" from the stifling house of authority.[14]

Once the classical house of authority had collapsed with the triumph of the Enlightenment spirit and rationality, the modern spirit soared high, fully confident that, with Prometheus unbound, nothing could stand in the way of progress. Theology, following the tune of the times and confident in human rationality, also became primarily a reflective inquiry. Its logical

---

[11]Jürgen Habermas, *Knowledge and Human Interests,* trans. Jeremy J. Shapiro (Boston: Beacon Press, 1971).

[12]Edward Farley, *The Fragility of Knowledge: Theological Education in the Church and the University* (Philadelphia: Fortress Press, 1988), pp. 14–15.

[13]See Peter Hodgson, *Constructive Christian Theology Class Pak* (Fall 1992), pp. 10–11. Mimeographed.

[14]Michel Foucault, "What is Enlightenment?" in *Foucault Reader,* pp. 32–50.

aftermath was the rise of "academic theology," the prioritization of the "cognitive crisis,"[15] or the crisis of the intelligibility of religious faith in a secular world, and its primary loyalty became that of the "academic community," or whatever "community of inquiry," while not totally negating the other "publics."[16]

Yet, it did not last long: The symbol of Prometheus was soon displaced by Dionysius, for the much celebrated progress had become a juggernaut to everything that stood in the way, even its own creator. The promised material progress only left many in grinding poverty and in massive suffering, whereas the few wallowed in opulence. This caused a series of disenchantments that appeared in varied, even adversarial, expressions, such as the neo-orthodox theologies' backlash against liberalism, the rise of critical theories proclaiming the end of innocent critique, the criticism of "instrumental rationality,"[17] Foucault's genealogical critique of modernity's madness,[18] the critique of Western logocentrism or metaphysics of presence,[19] Hans-Georg Gadamer's move to the retrieval of tradition and a refocus on prejudice,[20] and Martin Heidegger's notion of the role of preunderstanding.[21] Theology, like other disciplines, was severely affected by this disenchantment, as expressed in neo-orthodoxy, political theologies, and revisionist moves.

There is reason to celebrate the Western disenchantment with its own disenchantment. But this disenchantment, from the point of view of

---

[15]See the critique of Welch, *Communities of Resistance and Solidarity,* pp. 1–14. Welch identified two fundamental crises of Christian theology, namely, (1) cognitive (conceptual), and (2) moral. Most liberal and revisionist theologies have focused on the first dimension of the crisis (although not negating the second crisis), whereas feminist and liberation theologies concentrate on the second. If the cognitive crisis predominates, the usual issues and questions that are emphasized are: the nature of language about God, the truth claim of theology, the possibility of belief, and so forth.

[16]Tracy, *Blessed Rage for Order: The New Pluralism in Theology,* pp. 6–7. Although traditionally the primary public of the Christian theologian is the church community, Tracy advanced the interpretation that in the modern period the fundamental loyalty of the theologian has been to that of whatever "community of inquiry" she or he belongs. For a more detailed treatment, see his work *The Analogical Imagination: Christian Theology and the Culture of Pluralism* (New York: The Crossroad Publishing Company, 1981), pp. 3–46.

[17]Habermas, *Knowledge and Human Interest;* Max Horkheimer and Theodore W. Adorno, *Dialectic of Enlightenment* (New York: Seabury Press, 1972); also see Paul Lakeland, *Theology and Critical Theory: The Discourse of the Church* (Nashville, Tennessee: Abingdon Press, 1990), pp. 30–36.

[18]Foucault, *Madness and Civilization: A History of Insanity in the Age of Reason;* idem, *Discipline and Punish: The Birth of the Prison,* trans. Alan Sheridan (New York: Vintage Books, 1979).

[19]See Chapter VI, n. 63.

[20]Hans-Georg Gadamer, *Truth and Method* (New York: The Seabury Press, 1975).

[21]Martin Heidegger, *Being and Time,* trans John Macquarrie & Edward Robinson (London: SCM Press Ltd, 1962).

third-world peoples, needs to be disenchanted. I say this for the reason that in spite of the growing acceptance of the hermeneutical (interpretive and constructive nature) character of theology, there is still that tendency in Western theologies to be preoccupied with ontological and transcendental approaches that often leave out issues of social history.[22] The rise of third-world theologies is an expression of this disenchantment with the disenchantment of the West with its own disenchantment (the *third disenchantment* — Third World).

Yet, third-world theologians have something to learn, both negatively and positively, from Western disenchantment with its own history.[23] Western disenchantment with its own disenchantment will help them to identify better their location and to sharpen their theological positions, even as they consider their respective context as the primary matrix or *locus theologicus*, if they see their theological constructions against that background. This, I suggest, is specifically true of the emerging theology of struggle in the Philippines.

THE THEOLOGY OF STRUGGLE AS A NEW WAY
OF DOING THEOLOGY

No one starts a theological construction *de novo*; we are born in a community, both domestic and global, that has shaped our thoughts, and from these materials we start. Whether we like it or not, we have to engage with various interpretations, for they affect either our liberation or continuing enslavement. This means that we can learn and appropriate from the experiences and insights of others, both negatively and positively. In addition, although we have different contexts, we share many things in common, even a common destiny, even though we live in constant denial of this reality. Likewise, the theology of struggle, although it seeks to respond faithfully to its primary context and questions that arise from it, cannot really maintain a closed-door policy or shut out any engagement with other thoughts.

**Theology of Struggle's Notion of Theology:
Discerning the Priorities and Directions Through the Scylla
and Charybdis of Theological Navigation**

In undertaking this theological voyage, I have picked up some experiences and insights of others which, in my judgment, can serve as lighthouses

---

[22]See Sölle, *Thinking About God: An Introduction to Theology,* p. 33.

[23]See Dermot Lane, *Foundations for Social Theology: Praxis, Process and Salvation* (New York/Ramsey: Paulist Press, 1984), pp. 56–82. Lane suggested that a fruitful relation with critical theory is needed. Although this theory has some weaknesses, its basic critique, like its critique of instrumental rationality, of an interest-laden quest for knowledge or critique of pure knowledge, of the pervasiveness of the mechanistic paradigm in industrial societies, and others, is something that would help enrich praxis-oriented theologies.

as I continue to navigate. Some of the lighthouses will be drawn from my critique of the house of authority and its collapse, both in its classic and modern expressions, and from the Western disenchantment with its own disenchantment. Along with the lighthouses garnered from the Western disenchantment with its own disenchantment (although others may see more) — either as negative warnings or positive insights — I also consider among the lighthouses such phenomena as the rise of liberation theologies, the struggle of third-world peoples, and the Asian background of the Philippines. These lighthouses, as I emphasize again, are juxtaposed with the primary matrix of my theological reflection — the Philippine context and the Filipino people's experience of suffering, hope, and struggle — as detailed in Chapter I. Now I identify some of the lighthouses and the main directions.

The first main thrust (with no connotation of priority) that my theological construction of the theology of struggle take is contextualization. Although the Western world had set the stage for the collapse of the house of authority, and in the course of time has generated *correctives* [24] — which are steps leading to contextualization — neither contextualization nor liberation from the house of authority has been achieved fully, because the dominant Western theological works are still oblivious of their contextual nature.

It is only lately, under the strong impetus of the rise of third-world countries from the ravages of colonialism — a development that has greatly helped pave the way for pluralism[25] — that a contextual mode of doing theology has really gained ground; thus, it is much freer from the house of authority than what had been accomplished in Western liberal and neo-orthodox theologizing, yet without totally abandoning being a Christian theology.[26] The thrust on contextualization, something that has been vigorously spearheaded by third-world theologies and that the dominant Western theologies have not accepted without a fight, constitutes one of the main directions in which the theology of struggle is moving.

---

[24]Farley, *The Fragility of Knowledge,* p. 26.

[25]See David J. Krieger, *The New Universalism: Foundations for a Global Theology,* Faith Meets Faith Series (Maryknoll, NY.: Orbis Books, 1991), p. 10. Krieger advanced the interpretation that one of the reasons for the emergence of pluralism was the "rise and fall of colonialism." The rise of colonialism made contact possible, but the fall of colonialism is, in my judgment, the final blow to the "exclusivist" mindset of the Christian West, which also made possible the emergence of contextual theology. Hence, I would like to emphasize the connection between pluralism and contextualization. There is no contextualization of theology outside a pluralist understanding of the world.

[26]Some feminists have seen the necessity of abandoning Christian theology. See, for example, Mary Daly, *Beyond God the Father: Toward a Philosophy of Women's Liberation* (Boston: Beacon Press, 1973); see also "The Essential Challenge: Does Theology Speak to Women's Experience?" in *Women's Spirit Rising: A Feminist Reader in Religion,* eds. Carol Christ and Judith Plaskow (San Francisco: Harper & Row, 1979), pp. 19–24; Carr, *Transforming Grace: Christian Tradition and Women's Experience,* pp. 9, 95–99.

Due to the colonial and neo-colonial character of theological education in third-world countries, although theological irruptions have been going on, third-world theologies have shared the fate of Western theologies. I refer in particular to the fragmentation of theological education brought-about by Western-secular modernity, wherein theology as *habitus* has been lost, at least in liberal-Protestant seminaries of client third-world countries. The *habitus* aspect of theological education has perhaps been reincarnated in such courses as spirituality and discipleship, but in many cases theology as *habitus* is left for the individual theological student—a private life struggle demanded by the secular world.[27]

Third-world theological constructions and the theology of struggle in particular need to retrieve and revise this notion of theology as *habitus* (understood as soul saving) in terms of theology as *habitus* of transformative praxis. Liberation theology has spearheaded a notion of theology that moves in this direction with its emphasis on praxis. It is along this second main contour that I navigate my theological construction.

Consistent with the fragmentation and the loss of *habitus* is, in my opinion, the privileging in most Western theological reflections of academia as the proper locus to do theology.[28] Other "publics" of theology are of course considered, but the issues raised, the concerns pursued, the perceived primary tasks of theology, the idiom and language, the theological method, the partners in dialogue, the interlocutor, and the audience indicate that academe is the privileged locale to theologize. Rather than privileging academe, the theology of struggle privileges the community of the suffering and struggling people, particularly the "nonpersons."[29] This is the third main direction that my theological construction takes.

Another positive move of Western theological reflections, after the

---

[27]David Lochhead, *The Dialogical Imperative: A Christian Reflection on Interfaith Encounter, Faith Meets Faith Series* (Maryknoll, NY.: Orbis Books, 1988), p. 2. Yet the secularist garb is deceptive, because religion, argued Lochhead, "keeps on intruding where they are not supposed to be" (p. 2).

[28]See the criticism of Comblin in his book, *The Church and the National Security State*, pp. 1–9.

[29]The theology of struggle is more specific and unequivocal, along with other liberation theologies, in locating its perspective from the experience of the nonpersons (not the nonbelievers); the poor are the interlocutors. See McAfee Brown, *Theology in a New Key: Responding to Liberation Themes*, pp. 60–64. It could be argued that my privileging of suffering and struggling community is not something foreign to theologies that arose out of and have been inspired by the Western disenchantment with its own disenchantment, such as the European political theologies like those of Metz and Moltmann. Yet the construal of suffering of political theologies, in my perception, is more directed to the suffering human subject in general and to the bourgeois person in particular, to the problem of affluence and the disastrous effect of scientific-instrumental rationality, and the possible conversion of the Western bourgeoisies to the struggle of the more oppressed, especially of third-world peoples. See Metz, *Faith in History and Society: Toward a Practical Fundamental Theology;* idem, *The Emergent Church: The Future of Christianity in a Postbourgeois World;* see also Moltmann, *The Crucified God.*

collapse of the house of authority and its disenchantment with its own disenchantment is the realization of the linguisticality of one's existence and the emphasis on preunderstanding and prejudice. These are important insights and realizations that may enrich third-world theological constructions. Rather than simply following a nominalist understanding of language, as if language were only a medium of communication, a notion of language as that which structures our understanding is a vital point that should aid third-world theologians in their attempts to arrive at their own contextual theologies. My theological construction (fourth lighthouse) incorporates the insights of hermeneutics, but moves further to a sociopolitical analysis.[30]

Lastly, ideological critique, hermeneutics of suspicion, and hermeneutics of retrieval, all of which have arisen after the collapse of the classical house of authority and the Western disenchantment with its own disenchantment, are important insights. In the hands and praxis of the struggling victims, however, they take a different form and purpose. These hermeneutical insights are not inherently liberating, but in the hands of the struggling communities, suspicion is suspicion of dominant ideologies, and retrieval is retrieval of dangerous memories. In this study, I incorporate the insights of these hermeneutical theories, and put them in the hands of the struggling people.

The Nature and Task of Theology Reinstated

Culling from the various issues and points raised, I identify the nature of the theology of struggle as: (1) a reflexive/reflective activity of Filipino communities who are involved in the struggle; (2) a struggle that is discerned in light of the Christian faith, through the vehicle of traditions or Scripture, which are interpreted appropriately; (3) informed by the contemporary situation (both domestic and global) through the agency of various analytical and critical theories; (4) the interpretations and analysis of which are carried out through Filipino idioms; and (5) for the continuation of the liberating struggle of the Filipino people (praxis).[31]

From this definition, the theology of struggle is clear on its stand that it is basically a reflexive/reflective activity within a particular faith commitment, indeed, a *fides quarens intellectum*, or a *habitus* turned outward as transformative praxis. Even if this reflexive/reflective activity would someday turn into a sedimented form (text on theology) and become one

---

[30]Liberation theology has already moved in this direction, a path that Taylor has also suggested for hermeneutics to follow, that is, incorporate sociocultural analysis. See *Remembering Esperanza*, p. 58

[31]Cf. Carlos H. Abesamis, "Faith and Life Reflections from the Grassroots in the Philippines," in *Asia's Struggle for Full Humanity*, ed. Virginia Fabella (Maryknoll, NY.: Orbis Books, 1980), p. 128.

subject matter in academia called theology, to be studied even by those who do not share a similar faith commitment, it is still a product of a faith community. It is only within the context of faith commitment that to do theology or to theologize is possible. Others can study this theology, like studying the history of ideas, but it is not an engagement in theological reflection.[32]

As basically a reflective act within a faith commitment, the theology of struggle has as its objective the enhancing and sharpening of the struggle. It is not so much about God-talk or God-language as it is about "God-walk"[33] or God-praxis or theopraxis in the struggle. The theology of struggle seeks to convey an understanding of theology in which the context—that of the suffering and struggle of the people—is the primary *locus theologicus*, which is interpreted through the agency of various critical theories and discerned through the eye of faith. The theology of struggle is a contextual theology, taking "Filipinoness" (inculturation) in light of its larger background—Asian—within the purview of societal transformation (liberation thrust).[34]

Moreover, the theology of struggle sees theological reflection more as a community activity, with some individuals having a native charisma of articulation and writing, whereas others have acquired skills through years of studies. But they all derive their inspirations from the spirit of the community, and they all serve the community. Like the waves of the ocean, the theologians, lay and trained, although "they happen to be more conspicuous parts of the ocean but themselves are part of the ocean, and of the same substance with it. The ocean will bring forth its waves as the people its [theologians]."[35]

Sources, Norms/Criteria, Community of Accountability

Theological construction involves the use of materials or sources, follows some norms or criteria, and must clarify its community of accountability. Constructing a theology is not possible without sources, for theological ideas, to paraphrase Mao, do not simply fall from the sky, but build on some materials here on earth.[36] It also follows some norms or criteria,

---

[32]See Abesamis, "Doing Theological Reflection in a Philippine Context," in *The Emergent Gospel*, pp. 112–123; cf. Paul Tillich, *Systematic Theology*, vol. 1 (Chicago: The University of Chicago Press, 1951), pp. 3–68; cf. Pamela Dickey Young, *Feminist Theology/Christian Theology: In Search of Method* (Minneapolis: Fortress Press, 1990), p. 58.

[33]Frederick Herzog, *God-Walk: Liberation Shaping Dogmatics* (Maryknoll, NY.: Orbis Books, 1988).

[34]Dingayan, "The Temple, the Beggar, and the Tourist: Some Biblico-Theological Reflection," *Kalinangan*, p. 10.

[35]Avila, *Peasant Theology: Reflections by Filipino Peasants on their Process of Social Revolution*, p. 70.

[36]Mao Tse-Tung, cited in Georges Casalis, *Correct Ideas Don't Fall from the Skies: Elements*

although in many cases they are not clearly stipulated, yet the norm always shapes the choice and the interpretation of materials. And because theology emerges from a community experience and has consequences for the community, it must clarify to what community it is accountable.

Theology of Struggle's Sources for Theological Construction

Constructing a theology involves interpretation and appropriation of various sources. For the theology of struggle, I have identified at least five sources, namely: (1) the Filipino people's experience, (2) the context or situation, (3) sociopolitical-cultural analysis and expressions, (4) traditions and dogmas, and (5) the Scripture.

The Filipino people's experience and cultural expressions. Experience, when considered as a source for theological construction, should not be construed as *brutus factum*; it is an interpretation of an interpretation. In fact, there is no place to start outside of interpretation *sub specie aeternitatis* (from the standpoint of eternity). Because experience is an interpretation that can also serve as a grid for interpretation, Tillich considered it instead as a medium, although I agree with Hodgson that it can be both a medium and a source.[37] At this juncture I consider it as a source, but in my hermeneutical proposals later on I view it as a medium.

Specifically, because experience is always an interpretation, I have opted to see the experience of the Filipino people through the eyes of the suffering and struggling people. This is the kind of experience that I consider to be an important source for constructing the theology of struggle. Others would of course see the general experience of the Filipino people differently.

Although it can be assumed that the majority of these suffering and struggling Filipinos are women, I would rather make explicit the importance of women's experience as a source. It would not be accurate to speak of the theology of struggle without giving due credit to what Gaspar called the "nurturing impact of a feminist perspective."[38] The theology of struggle is a faith reflection of those involved in the struggle, a sizeable number of whom are women; thus, the theology of struggle cannot but be explicit in considering women's experience as a source for theological construction.

Unlike some countries where the emergence of feminist concerns came as something separate and later on united with other movements for a

---

for an Inductive Theology, trans. Sister Jeanne Marie Lyons and Michael John (Maryknoll, NY.: Orbis Books, 1984). The complete version of this paraphrase is: "Where do correct ideas come from? Do they fall from the skies? No. Are they innate in the mind? No. They come from social practice and from it alone." (Mao Tse-Tung, 1963).

[37]Hodgson, *Constructive Christian Theology Class Pak,* p. 17. Mimeographed.

[38]Gaspar, "Doing Theology (in a Situation) of Struggle," in *BCCO-Notes,* pp. 35–38.

common struggle, the women's struggle in the Philippines has always been viewed as part of the whole united effort for national liberation. Being part of the whole united struggle, this means that feminist theological reflections have taken place under the umbrella of the theology of struggle. Women may put a different label on their theological reflections some time in the future, but struggling women in the Philippines have, up to this time, viewed their struggle as part of the overall Filipino struggle.

We must also remember the rich Filipino cultural expressions. The theology of struggle considers popular culture and religiosity as an important source for theological construction. Of the three categories commonly used to describe the attitudes of people toward popular religiosity in the Philippines—(1) preservation of traditional culture and religiosity, even in some cases romanticizing it; (2) rejection, a minority one; and (3) critical appropriation of popular religiosity—theologians of struggle generally fall in the third category.[39] The theologians of struggle acknowledge the revolutionary potential of popular religiosity. The social ethicist Ruiz, for example, sees in popular or folk religiosity, such as the *pasyon* and others, a "non-bourgeois expression of a people's dwelling towards its liberation which does not reject the deeply religious dimension of criticism."[40] A scientific orientation to revolutionary change, especially one that involves some form of class or social analysis, may consider the popular expressions inchoate but, for Bolasco, to recognize the revolutionary potential of the popular culture or folk religiosity does not necessarily contradict the class approach.[41]

Moreover, the theologians of struggle have also shown keen interest in symbols, art, drama, and poems as sources. They believe, along with Ponce Bennagen, that "as more and more people actively participate in the production and use of symbols, they will also transform themselves as individuals and as communities."[42]

The importance given to symbols as a source for theological construction is also true of art. Art, for the theologians of struggle and others who are committed to the struggle, functions to evoke the senses of the people, awakens them to their true dignity, and helps them to see other ways of thinking and dwelling.

Context or situation. Context or situation can be viewed as the broad ambit that includes experience as a subset, as Hodgson did; or the context

---

[39]"A Philippine Search for a Liberating Spirituality," *Kalinangan,* vol. 10, no. 1 (March 1990), p. 24.

[40]Ruiz, "Towards a Theology of Politics: Meditations on Religion, Politics, and Social Transformation," *Tugón,* p. 42.

[41]Mario Bolasco, "Notes on Theologies of Liberation as Politics," in *Liberation Theology and the Vatican Document: A Philippine Perspective,* p. 107. Cf. LDF Fajardo, "Myth, Illusion and History," *Justice and Peace Review,* vol. 1, no. 2 (1986), p. 8.

[42]Ponce Bennagen, "Symbols by the People and for the People," *Kalinangan,* vol. 8, no. 3 (September 1988), p. 6.

and situation could be differentiated, making the context the broader dimension and situation as something specific, as in the case of Farley.[43] Here, I interpret context and situation in one sense, and I make experience a distinct category, a more specific consciousness of a situation encountered. Context covers a broad field — political, economic, and cultural, in both domestic and global aspects — but it is the particular situation that serves as the springboard for theological formulation.

The context, as understood in the theology of struggle, is analyzed and interpreted through native wisdom and social-analytical tools that are deemed useful, not through "transcendental phenomenology" or some eidetic maneuver, because it is not particularly concerned with identifying the perduring structures and the ontological existentials, although these are not totally negated. This context, socially analyzed, shapes the questions raised, the themes, and the manner in which theological construction is carried out.

Sociopolitical-cultural-critical theories and analysis.   This aspect could be covered under context or situation, but I decided to give it distinction to make sure that its relevance is not missed. There are various sociopolitical-cultural-critical theories that may aid in the theological construction. A decision regarding which of them are useful should heavily depend on, in my judgment, the nature of the subject investigated, although preference for one critical and explanatory theory over another may be dictated by the ideological presuppositions of the theories considered and the goal of the theologian, such as liberation theology's preference for dialectical sociology over that of functionalism, or its use of dependency theory over that of developmentalist analysis.[44]

In order to avoid any misunderstanding regarding how the sociopolitical-cultural-critical theories should become a source of theological construction, I think a caveat is in order. When I say that sociopolitical-cultural-critical theories should be a source for theological construction, I mean that the source should be construed as "constitutive" of theological reflection, as argued by C. Boff, and not in the sense of "application."[45] In the same vein, Míguez Bonino clarified this point when he argued that social analysis be treated as constitutive for theological reflection because "theology has no other way of 'knowing' the realm of the political except through such analysis; theology has no direct access to the political subject matter."[46]

---

[43]Farley, *Good and Evil: Interpreting a Human Condition,* pp. 16–17. Cf. Hodgson, *Constructive Christian Theology Class Pak,* p. 17.

[44]Míguez Bonino, *Toward A Christian Political Ethics,* pp. 44–47; For the use of dependency theory in liberation theology, the classic case is the work of Gutiérrez, *A Liberation Theology,* specifically, pp. 49–57.

[45]Boff, *Theology and Praxis: Epistemological Foundations.*

[46]Míguez Bonino, *Toward a Christian Political Ethics,* p. 45.

Traditions and dogmas.   The faith that we have is also a *fides ex auditu*, a faith we have heard from others, a faith we have received from previous generations. But how these traditions and dogmas get interpreted greatly matters in terms of whether they would pull us down or become guiding stars as we face the future. Archbishop Thomas Roberts's aphorism, "Tradition is the living faith of the dead, traditionalism is the dead faith of the living,"[47] succinctly points out both the danger and the value of tradition. The same could also be said of dogmas.

Traditions and dogmas are prison houses when they are construed as eternal truths to be applied for all times and places. This construal of traditions does not help in the struggle for liberation, nor specifically for the purpose of authentic theological construction. A contextual theology is absolutely impossible when traditions and dogmas become reified. But when they are understood as products of their own times, as models of theological articulations (McFague),[48] as local theologies (Robert Schreiter),[49] as a moment in the interpretation process – not a closure (Severino Croatto),[50] or as sedimented interpretations (Farley/Hodgson),[51] they serve as important sources for theological constructions. This is much more so if the traditions retrieved are in the form of dangerous and subversive memories. It is in this sense that I employ traditions as an important source.

Bible/Scripture as a source: The place of Scripture.   Theological construction, if it wants to be called Christian theology, must consider the Bible or Scripture as indispensable; it is a classic text for Christian theology. However, its usefulness for a liberating theological construction is also dependent on how it is construed as a source. I suggest that the Bible or Scripture, as an important source for theological construction and in particular for the theology of struggle, should be viewed relative to life, and more specifically to the life of the community. Life takes first place! As Carlos Mesters put it:

> The people's main interest is not to interpret the Bible, but to *interpret life with the help of the Bible.* They try to be faithful, not primarily to the meaning the text has in itself (the historical and literal meaning), but to the meaning they discover in the text for their lives.[52]

Life is not for the Bible, but the Bible is for life; it should promote life, be at the service of life, and not the other way around. Faithfulness to the

---

[47]Archbishop Thomas Roberts, cited in Lakeland, *Critical Theory and the Church*, p. 143.
[48]McFague, *Models of God: Theology for an Ecological, Nuclear Age*, p. 43.
[49]Robert Schreiter, *Constructing Local Theologies* (Maryknoll, NY.: Orbis Books, 1985).
[50]Croatto, "Biblical Hermeneutics in the Theologies of Liberation," in *Irruption of the Third World: Challenge to Theology*, pp. 152-153.
[51]Farley and Hodgson, "Scripture and Tradition," in *Christian Theology: An Introduction to Its Traditions and Tasks*, pp. 61-87.
[52]Carlos Mesters, *Defenseless Flower: A New Reading of the Bible*, trans. Francis McDonagh (Maryknoll, NY.: Orbis Books, 1989), p. 9. Emphasis supplied.

Bible does not mean fitting one's life to biblical times; nor is it measured by claims to originality or by a meticulous process of repetition, but by the pursuit of a life-generating meaning that is reproduced as our context engages in a dialectical interplay with that of the text. The Bible and Christianity as a whole "contains something of truth not because of its origins, but because it liberates people now from specific forms of oppression."[53]

With an understanding of the significant place of the Bible—crucial but relative to life—we can now understand the nature of its authority and inspiration. Authority is not based on inerrancy and plenary inspiration but on the Bible's *function* for the community.[54]

The placement of the Bible with regard to life, when properly pursued, actually avoids Itumeleng Mosala's warning of absolutizing the Bible and making it an instrument of domination.[55] Richard is aware of this danger, for he makes this point emphatically: "If we absolutize the Bible as if it were a direct and material word of God, our history will be imprisoned by the text and eventually wiped out," and there could not be a "worse domination than that imposed in the name of 'sacred' text."[56] To absolutize the Bible is actually to imprison history in the text and freeze the activity of God in the Bible. This has to be opposed because the Word of God is more than the Bible and the activity of God is outside the Bible (although also through the Bible).[57] If this is the case, my understanding of the place of the Bible in theology opens the possibility of acknowledging the salvific value of other faiths and also the possibility of using the Bible in a "dialogical imagination" approach with other non-Christian classic texts.[58]

Norms and Criteria of the Theology of Struggle

Norms operate even in theological constructions that do not clearly explicate their norms. They serve as criteria in the selection of sources, in what is given focus and importance, and in the interpretations rendered.

---

[53]Welch, *Communities of Resistance and Solidarity*, p. 53.

[54]Christine E. Gudorf, "Liberation Theology's Use of Scripture: A Response to First World Critics," *Interpretation: A Journal of Bible and Theology*, vol. 41, no. 1 (January 1987), p. 8. Gudorf considers the authority of the Bible, particularly in liberation theology, as based on the function that it plays for the life of the community; also see David Kelsey, *The Uses of the Scripture in Recent Theology* (Philadelphia: Fortress Press, 1975).

[55]Itumeleng Mosala, "The Use of the Bible in Black Theology," *Voices in the Third World*, vol. 10, no. 2, (June 1987) pp. 90–109.

[56]Pablo Richard, "The Bible as Historical Memory of the Poor," *Theology in the Third World*, Series 2, Year 4 (Quezon City, Philippines: Socio-Pastoral Institute), p. 7. Mimeographed.

[57]See Karl Rahner, "Scripture as the Church's Book," in *Foundations of Christian Faith: An Introduction to the Idea of Christianity*, trans. William V. Dych (New York: The Seabury Press, 1978), p. 370.

[58]See Kwok Pui-Lan, "Discovering the Bible in the Non-Biblical World," in *Lift Every Voice: Constructing Christian Theologies from the Underside*, eds. Susan Brooks Thistlethwaite and Mary Potter Engel (San Francisco: Harper and Row, 1990), p. 275.

They also affect the choice of sociopolitical-cultural-critical theories. I think it is more intellectually honest to make the norms of one's theological construction clear, rather than pretend that there are no guiding norms, except what is given by the text and the context.

Identifying and locating these norms has been a thorny and controversial concern, even in one genre of theological reflection — feminist theological constructions.[59] This was not so much the case in the early period of Christianity, the *regula fidei* or *articuli fidei* were the accepted norms, and much more so during the Middle Ages. Today there is no easy resolution of this issue because various considerations interact here, especially given the collapse of the classical authority (Bible, traditions, and magisterium) and the authority of the Western church.

In my judgment, the once safe havens of theological norms are already highly questionable, whether as to their cognitive validity or practical consequences. The Scripture, traditions, and ecclesiastical magisterium are not perceived anymore as ersatz or substitute divine presence by a world that has come of age; thus, no longer are they unquestionable and infallible norms. I would not say that the Bible as a whole is the norm, for such a position would bypass the years of labor by historical-critical and literary critics, which have enabled us to understand that the Bible itself is replete with conflicting thoughts. Neither would I locate the norm exclusively in the world behind the text, or in front of the text, or in the present praxis, or in the future.[60]

Because I primarily perceive theological reflection as *habitus*, more properly understood as liberation in its integral and wholistic sense, the norm that guides my method, the choice of materials, the interpretation and appropriation, and that arbitrates any meaningful and truthful claim is that which contributes to liberation/redemption.[61] Subjecting theological claims to the bar of reason is not totally rejected, but is made relative to what is liberational. Liberation is the norm, which can be: in the Bible; in the traditions; in the present liberating praxis of critical social movements; in the *han*, to use an important concept of Minjung theology; or in the agony, longings, and imaginations of the oppressed. Even indigeneity (Filipinoness) does not stand by itself without being viewed in relation to the criterion of liberation. Luna Dingayan conveyed this position quite clearly:

> I do believe that the kind of theology we need in Asia today is not just a
> theology that can make use of Asian resources, but more importantly a

---

[59]See, e.g., Young's analysis of various positions on the issue, particularly that of Ruether, Fiorenza, and Letty Russell, in *Feminist Theology/Christian Theology: In Search of Method,* pp. 23–48.

[60]See Letty M. Russell, *Authority in Feminist Theology: Household of Freedom* (Philadelphia: The Westminster Press, 1987), in which she argues that feminist theology cannot fully establish its norm from the past or the present, but in the future, in the not yet (pp. 18–21).

[61]de la Torre, *Touching Ground, Taking Root,* p. 180.

theology that could redirect these Asian resources in a way that could best serve the people of Asia.[62]

Specifically, I view the liberation of the Filipino people as the norm of the theology of struggle. Everything that contributes to the continuing struggle for liberation of the Filipino people supports the norm, whereas everything that contributes to the dehumanization of the Filipino people is contrary to the norm. In a little more detailed fashion, although not exhaustively (see Chapter IV), this liberation means the right to self-determination, the restoration of their self-identity as a people and greater rootedness into their culture (indigenization), socioenconomic and political well-being, and the formation of an ecological sensibility.

Theologies that do not acknowledge the norm I raised here fail to be truly liberational. I make this bold assertion not without the expectation that other theologies might come to my attack — even companion theologies of liberation — denouncing my claim as another exclusive-particular-turned-absolute universal, similar to the criticism that liberation and Black theology have earned.[63] It should be understood, however, that a claim like this has to be expressed in ultimate categories because what is at stake is decisive for the survival of that particular community itself. And, indeed, I do not consider other theologies as liberational if they deny this claim, a claim necessary for the Filipino people's identity and survival. Yet "particularity and exclusivity do not need to go hand in hand," as Young aptly pointed out.[64] To say it in a more positive vein, although the liberation of the Filipino people is the specific concern of the theology of struggle, this liberation, however, should always be construed in relation to the liberation of others, including nature. The Israelite-Palestinian conflict illuminates this point. I say this with pain and shame that for so long I frequently used the exodus model of liberation (the Israelites' release from Egyptian slavery and conquest of Palestine) without sensitivity that, from the experience of the Palestinians, what I have construed as "liberating" has been synonymous with conquest and subjugation of a people.[65]

---

[62]Dingayan, "The Temple, The Beggar and The Tourist: Some Biblico-Theological Reflections," *Kalinangan,* p. 10.

[63]See Frank Chikane, "EATWOT and Third World Theologies: An Evaluation of the Past and Present," in *Third World Theologies: Commonalities and Divergences,* ed. K. C. Abraham (Maryknoll, NY.: Orbis Books, 1990), p. 151. When Black theology, for example, asserts "blackness" as the norm, it is not a universalistic assertion that is associated with totalization. It is a particular-decisive norm, but it has to be asserted in absolute and universal fashion because, if this is not acknowledged and respected by all, it is to do violence to the very survival of the Black people. See, for example, James Cone, "God is Black," in *Lift Every Voice: Constructing Christian Theologies from the Underside,* pp. 81-94. This is not intended, however, to deny the temptation that one form of liberation theology may assume that it is the liberation theology.

[64]Young, *Feminist Theology/Christian Theology,* p. 79.

[65]See Naim Stifan Ateek, *Justice, and Only Justice: A Palestinian Theology of Liberation* (Maryknoll, NY.: Orbis Books, 1989). Cf. Marc Ellis, *Toward a Jewish Theology of*

The Community of Accountability

Rather than privileging the academy or the university, the theology of struggle parts ways with common Western theological constructions, for the theology of struggle is certain of its primary public, that is, of its primary community of accountability — the suffering and struggling Filipino people in general, and the ecclesial communities in particular. In Chapter II, I pointed out that the theologians of the struggle have not given up on the church but struggle within the church as prophets-in-residence. Theological schools or seminaries in the Philippines are operated by churches or are at least church-related institutions, and they are not religious departments within a secular university whose primary accountability is to the academic institution. I think Maria Clara Lucchetti Bingemer is right to speak of third-world theologies, among which the theology of struggle can be classified, as primarily *"ecclesial* theologies."[66]

When the suffering community is the primary community of accountability, the direction of theological reflection is also different. Instead of focusing on untangling conceptual contradictions, synthesizing conceptual contraries and polarities, diads, dilemmas or trilemmas, or identifying cognitive lacunas, hiatuses, and caesuras in the interest of the academic community or community of inquiry, the theology of struggle is concerned with concrete sociopolitical contradictions that its primary public has been undergoing. Not that it is anti-intellectual, but its interest in cognitive issues is primarily for the praxis of the "community of suffering."

When the community of suffering people is the primary community of accountability, theologians perceive their role and relate to each other differently. What Samuel Rayan described for third-world theologians is observably true among theologians of struggle when they meet.[67] They do not form an academic club or an exclusive association of theologians primarily for the purpose of presenting research, publication, and professional advancement (important as they are), but they see each other as sisters and brothers — companions in the struggle — and their deliberations are directed toward the advancement of the people's cause.

What I consider as the community of accountability should be differentiated from the term *audience.*[68] Community of accountability, as I use it

---

Liberation (Maryknoll, NY.: Orbis Books, 1987). Although Ellis writes from a Jewish perspective, he equally calls the Jewish people to stop its crimes against other peoples (Palestinians, Nicaraguans, Black South Africans, etc.) and reminds them of their own history of suffering. This memory of suffering is betrayed, argues Ellis, when, in the name of Jewish political empowerment, other communities become victims.

[66]Maria Clara Lucchetti Bingemer, "Third World Theologies: Conversion to Others," in *Theologies of the Third World: Convergences and Differences,* Concilium, eds. Leonardo Boff and Virgil Elizondo (Edinburgh: T. & T. Clark Ltd, 1988), p. 118.

[67]Samuel Rayan, "Third World Theology: Where Do We Go From Here?", in *Theologies of the Third World: Convergences and Differences,* p. 138.

[68]*Audience* for Schreiter means the community of accountability. See *Constructing Local Theologies,* pp. 36–37.

in this theological construction, is the primary community to which one is committed, a community in which a particular theology claims to speak and serve. In the case of the theology of struggle, this community of accountability is the suffering and struggling Filipino people. The audience can be any other group or community of readers and respondents in which a theologian seeks to communicate or engage in a dialogue. This work, for example, has its primary community of accountability in the struggling Filipino people and has as its primary audience (not exclusively) academically trained laypeople and theologians, not only in the Philippines, but also in other parts of the world. Otherwise, if my target audience or readers had been the peasants and farmers in the Philippines, I would have written this work differently.

Hermeneutical Presuppositions and Method

Theological construction is a hermeneutical activity through and through. I do not mean to say that everything consists of interpretations, as if to say that everything were just a matter of interpretation, or that I do not take seriously the "nondiscursive" world, or that there is nothing beyond the text (*il n'y a pas de hors-texte*) which, according to the literary critic Frank Lentricchia, is pure and simple *fin-de-siècle* formalism.[69] What I want to convey is that there is no point of departure that is not an interpreted space; thus, there is no foundation free from interpretations for a theologian to ground her or his interpretation. In this sense we can grant that it is interpretation all the way down, like the proverbial turtles upon turtles all the way down.

Interpretations, however, like all interpretations, are inextricably bound to concrete practices (nondiscursive); thus, they represent a contested activity that involves either life or death of a people.[70] We live by our interpretations, according to our constructed worlds, and, if so, then we also let others die by our interpretations.[71] Interpretations kill!

Thus, hermeneutics in the sense that I am using it here is not only that moment when one acquires a tool and interprets a text or context, but it covers that which is constitutive of the very being's way of living and apprehending the world, of the being's possibility of understanding, interpreting, deciding, and judging. It deals with dimensions that shape the person's social consciousness, that affect his or her reading and interpretation of realities, as well as the more specific activity of interpreting text and context.

Before proceeding to the methodology that I propose for the theology of struggle, I establish first some hermeneutical premises.

---

[69]Frank Lentricchia, *After the New Criticism* (Chicago: The University of Chicago Press, 1980), p. 310. Other terms that Lentricchia uses for *formalism* are: "aestheticism," "isolationism," and "new hedonism."

[70]See, e.g., Dussel, *Philosophy of Liberation*, p. 5.

[71]See McFague, *Models of God*, p. 28.

*Hermeneutical Premises: Farewell to Methodological
Manicheanism and Paving the Path for a Theological Method*

Theology, in its wedlock with modernity, has produced children in the
form of theologians who have forgotten that they have bodies that bleed
and experience hunger, who have thought that they are pure souls or minds
hovering above the earth with electronic cameras, who have thought of the
complete separation between mind (*res cogitans*) and facts (*res extensa*).
From these children came an approach to theology that is characterized by
William Lloyd Newell as "methodological Manicheanism,"[72] a methodology that has forgotten its own location.

After experiencing disenchantments, the citizens of the modern period
have filed a divorce with modernity's positivism, although others have
fallen into the opposite camp of solipsism, relativism, cynicism, and
pietism. From Edmund Husserl's move to take account of the subject's
"life-world," Heidegger's notion of "being-in-the-world" and the linguisticality of human understanding, Marxian ideology critique, sociology of
knowledge, and, until the rise of hermeneutics and the North American
"new historicism,"[73] the direction has been toward a greater realization that
we understand as we do because we "exist" as we do (understood existentially and phenomenologically) and, conversely, we exist as we do because
we interpret as we do.

To put it differently, there is no clean space—*tabula rasa*—from which
to start; we do not need it, for understanding or interpretation is only
possible because we are not *tabula rasa* subjects. The life-world (intention-
ality, intersubjectivity, temporality, and embodiment) that is constitutive of
our very being provides the prereflective horizon from which experiences,
events, and things are given meaning.[74] In fact, the prereflective aspect of
our existence or preunderstanding constitutes the horizon in which realities
get interpreted. What Gadamer calls prejudice also serves a similar
purpose.[75] Prejudice (*prejudicium* or *Vorbegriffe*) in the Gadamerian sense
is the *conditio sine qua non* of knowing. One's prejudice, understood as a
priori, according to Newell, "is the ontological and epistemological possibility of seeing and knowing at all."[76]

Whereas these theoretical proposals point in the proper direction, they
have remained at the ontological and epistemological level. All human

---

[72]William Lloyd Newell, *Truth Is Our Mask: An Essay on Theological Method* (Landham:
University Press of America, 1990), p. ix.

[73]See Edmund Husserl, *The Crisis of European Sciences and Transcendental Phenomenology*, trans. David Carr (Evanston: Northwestern University Press, 1970); Heidegger, *Being
and Time;* William Dean, *History Making History: The New Historicism in American
Religious Thought* (Albany, N.Y.: State University of New York Press, 1988).

[74]See Ogletree, *Hospitality to the Stranger: Dimensions of Moral Understanding*, p. 106.

[75]Gadamer, *Truth and Method*, pp. 235–274; also see Newell, *Truth is Our Mask*, pp. 27–49.

[76]Newell, *Truth Our Mask*, p. vii.

beings have preunderstandings, prejudice, and an a priori vision that shape how realities get interpreted, but ontological analyses do not take into consideration the sociopolitical components; they do not consider the concrete specifics in which prejudice, for example, takes shape in social classes and power blocks that dominate others in defense of some interests; they do not take into account that although all peoples have prejudices, the prejudice of third-world peoples can be necessary for their survival, while the prejudice of the powerful is imperialistic. By remaining at the ontological level, "history" gets "abbreviated" into "historicity."[77] It almost touches the ground, but the move has been aborted and left hanging in limbo.

Cornel West's critique of Richard Rorty's *Philosophy and the Mirror of Nature* aptly strengthens the point I am claiming:

> To tell a tale about the historical character of philosophy while eschewing the political content, role and function of philosophy in various historical periods is to promote an *ahistorical approach in the name of history*. To deconstruct the privileged notions of objectivity, universality and transcendentality without acknowledging and accenting the oppressive deeds done under the aegis of these notions is to write a *thin* (i.e., intellectual and homogenous) history; that is, a history which fervently attacks epistemological privilege but remains relatively silent about political, racial and sexual privilege.[78]

An "ahistorical approach in the name of history" is a fitting line to characterize the move to historicality that does not touch the ground in which one gets dirty, hungry, and killed.

West's powerful critique finds a similar antecedent in Marx and Engels' criticism of Ludwig Feuerbach.[79] As with these modern ahistorical approaches in the name of history, Feuerbach vigorously challenged speculative thoughts and identified his stand:

> I differ *toto coelo* from those philosophers who pluck out their eyes that they may see better; for **my** thought I require the senses, especially sight; I found ideas on materials which can be appropriated only through the activity of the senses.[80]

Although Marx and Engels acknowledged the contribution of Feuerbach, they saw that the Feuerbachian-turn-to-the-self or to the realm of the senses still did not completely touch the ground. For Engels, specifically, he could only say in referring to Feuerbach that "the lower half of him is

---

[77]Metz, *Faith in History and Society: Toward a Practical Fundamental Theology*, p. 131.

[78]West, review of *Philosophy and the Mirror of Nature*, p. 184. Emphasis supplied.

[79]Frederick Engels, *Ludwig Feuerbach and the Outcome of Classical German Philosophy* (London: Lawrence and Wishart Ltd., 1947), p. 6.

[80]Ludwig Feuerbach, *The Essence of Christianity* (New York: Harper and Row, 1957), p. xxxiv.

materialist; the upper half is idealist."[81] Or, in Marx's term, Feuerbach is a "contemplative materialist" who speaks of sensuousness but not "sensuousness as practical activity."[82] Mr. Firebrook (Feuerbach) remained a bourgeois materialist and stopped short in general psychology and anthropology without grounding his actors/actresses in history, in the same way that many hermeneutical theories stop short in ontology and historicity or in the linguisticality of understanding and interpretation.

What I am suggesting is that we need to proceed into a sociopolitical-cultural analysis, for here we can see how one's location, preunderstandings, and prejudices really shape the way we constitute the human dwelling, both locally and globally. Mark K. Taylor has pointed in the direction of giving due account to the cultural and political side while preserving the relevant insights of hermeneutical theories. Taylor has correctly pointed out that Gadamer, for example, "does not explore 'the who' of discourse in a way that introduces into hermeneutics the rich details of social location, which are to my [Taylor's] mind so essential to the complexities of interpretation." [83]

What Taylor has suggested, other liberation theologians have long insisted and struggled for, although in a different vein. Liberation-oriented biblical exegesis and political hermeneutics have pointed out the need for existential questions to give way to political questions. Let me now summarize the points and implications of these basic hermeneutical presuppositions.

First, understanding and interpretation are rooted in the human being's historicality, that is, they are understood not only ontologically but socioculturally (economics, politics, and culture). The sociology of knowledge has enabled us to understand that ideas do not simply float, but are linked to communities' experience, social status, contradictions, and struggles, although not to be understood in a rigid-determinist way; it is not to be understood in a one-way direction, but is to be construed as a sort of "harmonic reinforcement" between social experience and ideology.[84]

---

[81]Engels, *Ludwig Feuerbach and the Outcome of Classical German Philosophy,* p. 49.

[82]Ernst Bloch, *On Marx* (New York: Herder and Herder, 1971), pp. 54, 56, citing Marx.

[83]Taylor, *Remembering Esperanza,* p. 58. Emphasis supplied.

[84]Jacques Maquet, *The Sociology of Knowledge: Its Structure and its Relation to the Philosophy of Knowledge,* trans. John F. Locke, First printing by Greenwood, 1973 (Boston: Beacon Press, 1951), p. 32; also Schreiter, *Constructing Local Theologies,* pp. 78-79; cf. Pieris, *Asian Theology of Liberation,* pp. 27-29. See also Cornel West, *Prophecy Deliverance!: An Afro-American Revolutionary Christianity* (Philadelphia: The Westminster Press, 1982), pp. 95-147, for an appropriate critique of what he calls vulgar and muscular Marxism. For an understanding of social harmonic reinforcement between a certain thought (high christology in John's Gospel) and concrete communal experience, see the work of Jerome Neyrey, *An Ideology of Revolt: John's Christology in Social Science Perspective* (Philadelphia: Fortress Press, 1988), pp. 116-117.

Theology, being a product of the community, is not an exception; if we speak of the sociology of knowledge, we can also speak of the sociology of theology. This means that, following Segundo, "no one links up with the absolute truth except in an effort to give truth and meaning to one's own life."[85] What is projected to heaven is reflective of what has been going on in the earth, or, as pointed out by Peter Berger in his work *Sacred Canopy*, "everything 'here below' has its analogue 'up above.' "[86]

Second, premised on the first point, a reading of texts and social contexts is not simply a reading of what is there, but is always from the very beginning an interpretation; there was no point in time when there was no interpretation, no *tabula rasa*. Because interpretation is constitutive of one's social being, it is highly questionable to speak of an interpreter-as-virtuoso who is completely able to detach the *brutus factum* from one's self as if he or she were a passive object, as if the categories used by the interpreter were not themselves part of this world or culturally laden, or as if language did not shape our experience and interpretation. The reality is that "all data are theory-laden," to use the oft-quoted lines of N. R. Hanson.[87] In fact, the reading of a text or context reveals not only what is read, but perhaps even more, as David Lochhead has pointed out, that "what is understood affects not only the reality which is understood but the perspective from which it is understood."[88]

Third, readings or interpretations that are oblivious of their locations, or that claim to be neutral, objective, timeless, and universal, should be viewed with suspicion and subjected to ideological critique. For, in spite of their grandiloquent appearance and formal clarity, they often conceal the ideological intentions at work; they conceal that what is oftentimes called truth is constitutive of power; hence, there is a need for a hermeneutics of suspicion and ideological critique.

Fourth, the dominant ideas of the age are generally the ideas of the triumphant and the powerful. The ideas, memories, and experiences of history's losers and victims are often muted and buried, for the remembrance and recovery of these memories and experiences are empowering to the victims and threatening to the power wielders.

Fifth, anyone who has committed oneself to the people's struggle must employ a hermeneutics from the underside, a subversive hermeneutics that overturns reigning conceptions in order to get into the buried memories. Thus there is need, along with the hermeneutics of suspicion and ideological

---

[85]Segundo, *Liberation of Theology*, pp. 80, 107.

[86]Peter Berger, *The Sacred Canopy: Elements of a Sociological Theory of Religion* (New York: Doubleday, 1967), p. 34. See a similar point by Walter Rauschenbusch, *A Theology for Social Gospel* (New York: Macmillan, 1917), pp. 167–187.

[87]N. R. Hanson, *Patterns of Discovery* (Cambridge: Cambridge University Press, 1958).

[88]David Lochhead, "The Liberation of the Bible," in *The Bible and Liberation: Political and Cultural Hermeneutics,* p. 79.

critique, for a hermeneutics of retrieval, not simply a retrieval of memories and traditions in general, but of the dangerous and subversive memories in particular.

Sixth, a hermeneutics for struggle and liberation, following a different starting point, does not have to adopt a God's eye view. A hermeneutics for struggle and liberation is not so much concerned with getting rid of one's presuppositions, as in identifying what they are and in taking account of one's location in favor of the marginalized.

Finally, interpretation is a struggle—it is a struggle for the right to interpret, a struggle of interpretation, and an interpretation of the struggle. Theology, being an interpretive activity, is one of such struggles. The theology of struggle seeks to be a companion in the struggle of the people, interpreting theologically the context of struggle as it itself is waging a theological struggle.

Method: A Way of Doing the Theology of Struggle

A person who has dedicated himself or herself to social transformation must be equipped with a method—a way of living, knowing, seeing, analyzing, interpreting, and critically appropriating events, facts, and texts. I think it is primarily a question of how a person sees that influences the content. Segundo draws us to this emphasis when he said:

> It is the fact that the one and only thing that can maintain the liberative character of any theology is not its content but its methodology. It is the latter that guarantees the continuing bite of theology whatever terminology may be used and however much the existing system tries to reabsorb it into itself.[89]

When I say that a method is a way of living, knowing, seeing, analyzing, interpreting, and critically appropriating texts and contexts, it should be clear that I do not think of method simply as a technical or "know-how" knowledge to be mechanically applied, but as a "way" (Greek — *methodos*)[90] of living, doing, and interpreting; it is "something that we are and by which we are continually transformed."[91] The method of the theology of struggle is itself the act of doing theology in a specific context; its method is also its

---

[89]Segundo, *Liberation of Theology,* p. 40. The importance that Segundo gives to methodology finds expression in the "hermeneutical circle" that he has developed. There are four decisive factors in Segundo's circle. The first factor refers to a kind of experiencing reality that brings one to ideological suspicion; second, the ideological suspicion is applied to the whole superstructure and in particular to theology; third, a suspicion is directed at the prevailing interpretations, particularly that of the Bible; finally, a new hermeneutic comes into being, that is, a new way of interpreting (p. 9). The focus should be on "being liberative" rather than "talking about liberation."

[90]Krieger, *The New Universalism: Foundations for a Global Theology,* p. 10.

[91]Chopp, *The Praxis of Suffering,* p. 141.

spirituality. The *goal* of life in the theology of struggle is also the *art* of living it; this is how method as *techne* should be understood.[92]

A method is not simply a set of principles, a *depositum fidei*, frameworks, and techniques to be applied at specific contexts and revised when not workable; a method, as understood in the theology of struggle, is inextricably bound with the act of struggling, interpreting, and theologizing. If we start with making sure that the principles to be followed are already precise, it is more likely that we will end in a paralysis of analysis, a people with a high blood pressure of creeds but an anemia of deeds. McAfee Brown has picked up the catch involved here: "If we so choose, we can always postpone the jump from thought to action."[93] We can always reason that we are not yet clear about the issues, that we still need to attend some more seminars, or read more books before we can jump into action. And because there are always uncertainties, it is more likely that we will postpone the decision to act, as if to postpone the decision is not itself a decision, or as if not to act is itself not acting.

The theology of struggle's method is embedded in its spirituality: It is not a set of separate principles and techniques to be applied; the very act of doing is itself the unfolding of the method; its very method is life itself as lived, in which acting and interpreting find their unity, so that it makes sense to affirm with Hispanic women theologians that "reflection" is "inherently action."[94] In the very act of reflection there is action, in the very act of transformation there is reflection. One need not wait for principles to come from somewhere; they come along as people continue to struggle; acting goes along with the process of waking up (conscientization).

I now identify the steps of the methodology that I am proposing for the theology of struggle. Again the steps should not be understood mechanically but for purposes of presentation. In actual practice we do not really follow the steps rigidly, they are only for pedagogical purposes. It is like learning the basics of karate with all the numbered steps involved. But in the defense of one's life, one need not exactly have to follow the steps from number one and so on in their order. One has to act automatically, not even conscious of the steps involved. So it is with the method of the theology of struggle, because the method is itself the doing of theology by those who are already committed to the struggle of the people.

Of first consideration in doing the theology of struggle is to identify one's location or "insertion," as Joe Holland and Peter Henriott would put it, and

---

[92]See Pieris, " Towards an Asian Theology of Liberation: Some Religio-Cultural Guidelines," in *Asia's Struggle for Full Humanity*, p. 91.

[93]Robert McAfee Brown, *Unexpected News: Reading the Bible with Third World Eyes* (Philadelphia: Westminster Press, 1984), p. 22.

[94]Ada Maria Isasi-Diaz and Yolanda Tarango, *Hispanic Women: Prophetic Voice in the Church* (San Francisco: Harper & Row, 1988), p. 90.

experience conversion to the people.[95] Questions must be raised, for example: Where and with whom are we locating ourselves as we start the process of theological reflection? From whose experience and perspective are we viewing and interpreting social realities? Specifically, if theology claims to be of and for the victims, it must interpret social realities from their perspective.

The awareness of one's location, the perspectival character of one's interpretation, and the association of the reigning ideas with the powerful should lead a hermeneut to constantly engage in hermeneutics of suspicion and ideological critique as part of any deliberate interpretive task. I emphasize the word *deliberate* because the hermeneutics of suspicion is already present in the process of conscientization, but this should be made explicit in a deliberate interpretive activity (theological reflection). The hermeneutics of suspicion must be applied both to the text and the social context. This constitutes the second step in the hermeneutic process.

Third, another step in the hermeneutical process is engagement in social analysis of the context and exegetical explication of texts. This is an attempt to diagnose the social body with all the needed critical theories and an attempt to explain the texts with the use of various exegetical and explanatory theories.

On the part of the social body, social analysis is a means by which the context of the contemporary interpreter is analyzed. On the other hand, if social analysis is a means of analyzing the contemporary context, various exegetical and explanatory tools handle the texts: the world behind the text,[96] and the world projected by the text in front of itself.[97] I view the

---

[95]Holland and Henriott, *Social Analysis: Linking Faith and Justice,* p. 9.

[96]Social world criticism and literary approaches appear to be the trend, and the historical-critical approach has been proven to have cracks. See Fernando F. Segovia, "Towards a New Direction in Johannine Scholarship: The Fourth Gospel from a Literary Perspective," *Semeia* 53 (1991), p. 1. Christopher Rowland and Mark Corner have also pointed out that the historical-critical method has been rigid in its judgment of the past, but in no way has it made the text a judgment upon us today. See *Liberating Exegesis: The Challenge of Liberation Theology to Biblical Studies* (Louisville, Kentucky: Westminster/John Knox Press, 1989), p. 37.

[97]Literary approaches can provide a corrective to those methods that focus on the meaning and context behind the text, because it provides a way of interpreting in which the message is perceived in front of the text, or an interpretation in which the text projects a world that we may dwell in poetically. Yet, although they claim to project a message in front of the text, many literary critiques tend to remain in the maze of linguistic protocols and structures; they fail to critique the reader and his or her world that shapes the reading, or see the literature as in some ways rooted in the social conditions of the people. Howard Clark Kee, a New Testament scholar, has expressed his displeasure with those literary and linguistic approaches that limit their range of inquiry to the grammar, syntax, and interlingual functions. For him, sociolinguistics offers a better approach because it ties the language to the social context. See his work, *Knowing the Truth: A Sociological Approach to New Testament Interpretation* (Minneapolis: Fortress Press, 1989), pp. 55-60. One approach, which for Clark Kee neglects the context (and even the text), is the structuralist method (p. 61). Literary approaches could

various exegetical-critical approaches—historical, social world criticism,[98] and literary criticism—as having their proper place in the exegetical-explication process; knowing their strengths and weaknesses is important.

Fourth, the hermeneutics of retrieval constitutes a further step in the process. Retrieval of buried memories, traditions, and interpretations can now be executed in a proper light, in view of the hermeneutics of suspicion and ideology critique. Apart from the hermeneutics of suspicion and ideology critique, hermeneutics of retrieval would just be a continuous enslavement to the tradition—a dead weight of the past.

Fifth, there is the act of theological discernment, fusion of horizons, and imaginative projection. This fifth stage is the synthesizing stage: The various data, the exegetical results, and the analytical insights have to be discerned in the light of faith. C. Boff would put this stage as the theological reflection proper, or that which makes the "theologicity" of theology.[99] What makes theology a theology is not the material object, but the manner or the *modus operandi* in which it develops its material object. The proper theological products come in when, to use Gutiérrez's definition of theology, we arrive at a critical reflection on praxis in the light of God's word.[100] It is the eye of faith that transposes the material objects into theological products.

Involved at this stage is the attempt to fuse various horizons—people's traditions and contemporary situation (diachronically) and various horizons within the contemporary situation (synchronically).[101] This fusion of horizons should not be understood as a reconciliation of contradictions between the past and the present or between competing claims in the present, but as a fusion of horizons derived from the experience and

---

be saved from the captivity of any form of formalism, as if text is all that matters (another form of escape from history—ahistoricism), if it is also informed by the insights of social world criticism, more specifically the sociology of knowledge. See the analysis of William Dean on the criticism of Frank Lentricchia to the Yale Derrideans in his book, *History Making History: The New Historicism in American Religious Thought*, p. 9. To remain at the formalistic level is another form of ahistoricism, because it fails to see the context of the reader and the contextual nature of the text. See Lentricchia, *After the New Criticism*.

[98]Understanding the text or literature as an expression of the historico-material condition is an approach that liberation hermeneutics puts foremost, making it so appropriate for ideological critique. A few biblical writings that emphasize the importance of the historico-material condition and the ideological undergirdings of literary productions are: Füssel, "Materialist Readings of the Bible: Report on an Alternative Approach to Biblical Texts," in *God of the Lowly: Socio-Historical Interpretations of the Bible;* Norman K. Gottwald, *Tribes of Yahweh* (Maryknoll, NY.: Orbis Books, 1979); also idem, *The Bible and Liberation: Political and Social Hermeneutics;* Bello, *A Materialist Reading of the Gospel of Mark;* Clévenot, *Materialist Approaches to the Bible.*

[99]Boff, *Theology and Praxis: Epistemological Foundations,* pp. 132-154.

[100]Gutiérrez, *A Theology of Liberation,* p. 9.

[101]Cf. Gadamer's notion of "fusion of horizons" in *Truth and Method,* p. 273. Fusion should not be understood, argues Gadamer, by covering up the tension between the text or the past and the present but, in fact, by letting this come out to the open (p. 273).

perspective of the suffering and struggling victims—a fusion with dangerous memories (diachronically) and a fusion of horizons with contemporary companions in the struggle (synchronically), like feminists, Blacks, Latin Americans, and struggling peoples at the heartland of First World countries.

Alongside the activity of discernment and fusion of horizons is the act of imaginative construction. To do theological construction is as an act of imagination; it is an imaginative activity. This is something that is in the nature of theology but has for a long time been muted by the dominance of theologies that made philosophy its *theologia ancilla* and by positivistic theologies—fundamentalist and liberal—that have been driven to prove the correspondence of their truth claim with some form of realities.[102]

Not only is imagination innate to theology in general, it is truly innate for a theology that is expressive of the sighs, hopes, and longings of a subjugated people. If the dangerous memories need to be narrated, the new future needs to be imagined because it is not given in the "what is" of the present. Theology's truth claims and relevance cannot be fully established by appeals to the "what is," but perhaps more by its power to evoke the imagination toward a new way of dwelling.

Ruiz has picked up the direction of theology, I am asserting, when he speaks of theology's location at the "interface of the political and the sacred," which means that "it is both a bridge and a metaphor between that which 'is' and that which 'is not.' "[103] Theology has the character of metaphor and poetics: It is in a sense metaphoric (*meta-pherein*) because it enables one to see through the pathos of the people not only the "what is" but "what might be,"[104] that is, of the new possibilities that cannot be simply derived from the logic of the present. It has the character of poetics because it projects a world that people might inhabit not simply according to the logic set by the "what is" but also "poetically." This demands, in Hodgson's paraphrase of Heidegger, that "one must learn not only to think and read poetically but also must build and dwell poetically."[105]

Pursuing further the poetic and metaphorical character of theology, I would say that to "dwell" and "build" poetically" is, of necessity, to "dwell politically"—from poetics to political praxis and vice versa. What can be said of poetry is, in a sense, true of theology and of the theology of struggle in particular. To appropriate what Alves said about "politics" and "poetry,"

---

[102]For a critique of the correspondence theory of truth, especially in relation to theology, see, for example, Fiorenza, *Foundational Theology: Jesus and the Church,* pp. 271–276.

[103]Ruiz, "Towards a Theology of Politics: Meditations on Religion, Politics, and Social Transformation," *Tugón,* p. 32.

[104]See Sallie McFague, *Speaking in Parables: A Study in Metaphor and Theology* (Philadelphia: Fortress Press, 1975), p. 57.

[105]Hodgson paraphrasing Heidegger from his essays "Building Dwelling Thinking" and " . . . Poetically Man Dwells . . . " in *Poetry, Language, Thought,* trans. Albert Hofstadter (New York: Harper & Row, 1971). See Hodgson, *God in History: Shapes of Freedom,* p. 92.

I would say that "politics" without theology (poetry) "will cease to be the art of making the future present, and will become the science of the administration of the existing order."[106] Finally, we are back to the hermeneutical circle by moving again to the stage of insertion/praxis, but now as a renewed and enriched insertion. This is not, however, a return to the beginning praxis, but to an enriched, transformative praxis. The theology of struggle has accepted the challenge of Marx's eleventh thesis to Feuerbach: "The philosophers have only *interpreted* the world in various ways, the point however is to *change it.*"[107]

WHEN WRITING ENDS: COMMENCEMENT OF ACTION

How tempting it is to stay at this level of reflection, but I have to stop if action is to commence, although reflection should never end just because action is to commence. Although this reflection can be construed as a form of praxis, as others have done, I believe that this has to end, and there is no substitute to be concretely immersed in the life of the people from whom this theology claims to derive its inspiration and for whom it is intended to serve. If the well-known Enlightenment motto stopped with *Aude sapere*, the theology of struggle, along with other liberation-oriented theologies, moves further and says, *Aude emancipare!*[108] Dare to struggle for your liberation!

---

[106]Rubem A. Alves, *The Poet, The Warrior, The Prophet* (Philadelphia: Trinity Press International, 1990), p. 112.

[107]Karl Marx, *Theses on Feuerbach,* in Frederick Engles, *Ludwig Feuerbach and the Outcome of Classical German Philosophy* (London: Lawrence and Wishart Ltd., 1974), p. 78.

[108]See Lane, *Foundations for a Social Theology: Praxis, Process and Salvation,* p. 71. Lane speaks of the focus on "praxis" as the other side of the Enlightenment — e.g., Marxism. See also a similar point in Sobrino, *Christology at the Crossroads: A Latin American Approach,* pp. 34–35, 348; Farley, *The Fragility of Knowledge,* pp. 3–16.

Index